THE LIBRARY LIST

Complete Contact Info for All U.S. Public Libraries

The easy way to get your book in
hundreds of libraries!
Including tips from librarians on
how & why they buy books!

Publisher's Note

As owner of a small publishing company, I started this list to help organize contacts for informing libraries about our books. Looking libraries up on the internet is rather time consuming when it comes to searching out emails and addresses on various websites and clicking back and forth, state by state. Thanks to my secretary, Sandra Grabman, all of this information is now in one place.

And even better: Sandra tracked down helpful libraries to ask them how they select books and for any tips they could give that could help the struggling publisher in these sad economic times. The advice is just as valuable as the contacts themselves. Also, when possible, we've listed any special collections the library maintains, for those of you with regional titles.

Please feel free to email me at benohmart@yahoo.com to report any outdated or wrong information. We want to keep this book in print and current, so please keep us informed!

Thanks for reading, and here's hoping you sell a lot of books!

Ben Ohmart
February 2010
Compiled by Sandra Grabman

The Library List
© 2010. BearManor Media. All rights reserved.

Published in the United States of America by:
Bear Manor Media
PO Box 71426
Albany, Georgia 31708
www.bearmanormedia.com

ISBN 1-59393-255-3

Book and cover design by Darlene Swanson of Van-garde Imagery, Inc. • www.van-garde.com

Advice from Selected Librarians

Ann Arbor District Library
343 South 5th Avenue
Ann Arbor, MI 48104
(734) 327-4263
smithjp@aadl.org
http://www.aadl.org/

Due to the volume of our orders, we primarily use review journals like LJ, Kirkus, Publishers' Weekly, NYT Book Review, etc. We also use publishers' catalogs for subjects that may not be reviewed (e.g., home plans, deck building, that sort of thing). We consider patron suggestions as we cannot cover everything! The Library collections are broad and intended to serve all patrons well, although we do not focus on extremely academic subjects. We do add paperbacks, both trade and mass market.

In order to reach a broad market for publications, I would encourage authors/publishers to try to get the book in a review journal. That's where you'll get the exposure.

Ardmore Public Library
320 E Street NW
Ardmore, OK 73401
(580) 223-8290
(580) 221-3240 Fax
LHaggerty@ardmorelibrary.org
http://www.ardmorepublic.lib.ok.us/

We do stock paperbacks and we do not necessarily look for a Library Journal review.

Our collection development policy begins on page 7 of our policy manual (http://www.ardmorelibrary.org/about/Ardmore_Public_Library_Policy_Manual_2009.pdf) and covers in detail how we select for and maintain our collection.

Baltimore County Public Library
320 York Road
Towson, MD 21204
(410) 887-6137
lwisotzk@bcpl.net
http://www.bcplonline.org/

As a public library our mission is to purchase titles for our collections which will be of interest to the greatest number of residents of

Baltimore County. We do use LJ as a resource for reviews along with about a dozen other resources. We focus on purchasing popular interest titles; titles that will appeal to infants through seniors. The media plays a big role in our selection since what people read about in current magazines, or see discussed on talk shows or other TV shows will impact the number of requests we get from our customer base. One of the goals of our library is to provide materials for the school age child to help with learning as well as for the adult to help with life-long learning. However, we do not focus on a specific genre. The collection is built to reflect a wide range of tastes/interests therefore a very wide range of topics from a wide range of publishers.

We order the majority of our titles from major vendors. If titles are suggested by our customers but are not supplied by these vendors we would need to really consider the added costs that might ensue.

We do consider titles published by local authors, that is residents of Baltimore County.

Brooklyn Public Library
Grand Army Plaza
Brooklyn, NY 11238
(718) 230-2100
AskALibrarian@oclc.org
http://www.brooklynpubliclibrary.org/

Authors and publishers may submit review copies and/or promotional information relating to books (or materials in other formats) that they wish to be considered for purchase by Brooklyn Public Library (BPL). These materials must meet the criteria as stated here.

Materials Selection Policy:
Each type of material will be considered in terms of its own kind of excellence and for whom it is intended. There is no single standard that can be applied in all cases. Somematerials may be judged primarily in terms of artistic merit, scholarship or their value as human documents; others are selected to satisfy the recreational and entertainment needs of the community.

Review copies and promotional information may be sent to:
Office of Materials Selection
Brooklyn Public Library
10 Grand Army Plaza
Brooklyn, NY 11238
(Note: Because of the volume of submissions, BPL cannot return review copies.)

Please include the following information:

- Format of material (print, media, etc.), bibliographic citation, ISBN, intended age level/audience (i.e., juvenile, young adult or adult), price and publication date

- Information about the author

- Copies of relevant reviews (preferred review sources include Booklist, Library Journal, School Library Journal, Horn Book, The Bulletin of the Center for Children's Books, Publishers Weekly, Kirkus Reviews and VOYA)

- Ordering availability. BPL prefers to purchase through established library book vendors (e.g., Baker & Taylor). It is not the library's current practice to order from Amazon.com or other online book vendors. If the title is only available directly from the author, it may take several months for BPL to complete the purchasing process. Please keep in mind:

- The BPL librarians who select materials consider and order thousands of titles each year. For this reason, the library does not notify individual authors or publishers of the order decisions made about each of the many titles it is asked to consider for purchase.

- Records for titles that are selected can be viewed in the BPL catalog (http://catalog.brooklynpubliclibrary.org) within six months of receipt of the material.

Burlington County Library System
5 Pioneer Boulevard
Westampton, NJ 08060
(609) 267-9660
(609) 267-4091
gsweet@bcls.lib.nj.us
http://www.bcls.lib.nj.us/

We usually purchase based on reviews and Library Journal is one of the journals we use to select. We also purchase based on customer requests and recommendations. The library buys a wide variety of genres and yes, we do have paperbacks. Actually, we have lots of them. If you have an author/book you would like us to consider you can always email me and I will be glad to pass the info along to our selectors.

Cedar Falls Public Library

524 Main Street
Cedar Falls, IA 50613
(319) 273-8643
(319) 273-8648 Fax
cedarfallslibrary@gmail.com
http://www.cedar-falls.lib.ia.us/

The best way would be for you to let us know where it has been reviewed. We don't just go by Library Journal, but we do generally order materials that have been reviewed by periodicals like that. We do make exceptions for local materials.

Connecticut State Library

231 Capitol Avenue
Hartford, CT 06106
1-866-886-4478
(860) 757-6503 Fax
BJLinck@sclib.org
http://www.cslib.org/

We generally find new books to consider by looking for reviews of new books in journals related to the three main departments of the Connecticut State Library--history & genealogy, law, and government information.

Cortez Public Library

202 North Park
Cortez, CO 81321
(970) 565-8117
jhowland@cityofcortez.com
http://www.cityofcortez.com/
  government/public_library

Book don't have to be reviewed first in the Library Journal before we'll purchase it. Paperbacks are included in our collection. We sometimes deal with publishers directly, but it is easier to get the books through a jobber.

Crowell Public Library

San Marino Public Library
1890 Huntington Drive
San Marino, CA 91108
(626) 300-0775
(626) 300-0121 Fax
adallavalle@CityofSanMarino.org
http://sanmarinopl.org/

We are a small library, serving a local city of 13,500. We are 50% Asian, 50% Caucasian, and most residents are college graduates with upper level incomes. We have a limited budget. We buy according to reviews (but not just Library Journal), best seller lists, patron requests, and the needs/wants of our community.

Crystal Lake Public Library
126 Paddock Street
Crystal Lake, IL 60014
(815) 526-5102
(815) 459-9581 Fax
kmartens@crystallakelibrary.org
http://www.crystallakelibrary.org/

We use multiple sources for selection of materials including library review journals, publisher information, fliers, requests from our patrons. Yes, we also include paperbacks if appropriate.

Custer County Library
447 Crook Street
Custer, SD 57730
(605) 673-4803
(605) 673-2385 Fax
cuslib@gwtc.net
http://www.custerlibrary.com/

We do accept paperback books. I do use Library Journal for reviews and book selection, but other reputable sources are also considered (Nebr. Press, SD Hist. Soc., Mountain Press, Pub....for local presses) as well as reviewing best-sellers lists, book distributors lists, suggestions from patrons, etc... About any source that brings current and "of-interest" books to our reading community.

Denton Public Library
3020 North Locust Street
Denton, TX 76209
(940) 349-8752
Library@cityofdenton.com
http://www.cityofdenton.com/
    pages/library.cfm

Our collection development and branch librarians check reviews in a number of professional library journals as well as in various newspapers and magazines. We do carry paperbacks, in the case of materials not available in hard-back. We are a public library, so select based on the interests of our customers.

Falmouth Public Library
300 Main Street
Falmouth, MA 02540
1-888-439-8850
(508) 457-2559 Fax
info@falmouthpubliclibrary.org
falmouthpubliclibrary.org

The selectors for the books in our library's collection generally order books that have been well reviewed in a number of publications such as Library Journal, Kirkus, Publisher's Weekly, Booklist, and School Library Journal.

We also order titles that are named on the best seller lists of publications such as the New York Times.

Glendale Public Library
5959 W. Brown Street
Glendale, AZ 85302
(623) 930-3531
eLibrarian@GLENDALEAZ.com
http://www.glendaleaz.com/library/

The collection development
librarians select books from library
review sources that fit our collection development policies. We
accept suggestions and donations
from the public and then review
them to determine if they should
be purchased or added to the
collection.

Hall County Library
127 Main Street, NW
Gainesville, GA 30501
(770) 532-3311
amixson@hallcountylibrary.org
http://www.hallcountylibrary.org/

We acquire material in all three
ways. When book budgets are
lean we tend to stick with reviews,
proven publishers or recommendations in articles or from other
librarians.

Henrico County Public Library
1001 North Laburnum Avenue
Richmond, VA 23223
(804) 652-3200
(804) 222-5566 Fax
ER@henrico.lib.va.us
http://www.henricolibrary.org/

Our staff rely on reviews of material in standard resources, Booklist,
Publisher's Weekly, Library Journal,
Kirkus and so on. The selection
process is supported by selection
criteria listed in the collection
development plan. Paperbacks are
included in the collection.

Lake Region Public Library
423 Seventh Street NE
Devils Lake, ND 58301
(701) 662-2220
(701) 662-2281 Fax
lakeregion.pl@sendit.nodak.edu
http://www.ci.devils-lake.nd.us/
    departments/library.html

Anything we purchase does
not have to be reviewed in any
journal. It's basically up to me (and
heavily influenced by best seller
lists, etc.). We buy from our local
bookstore, B Dalton (in Grand
Forks), various book jobbers
(Edward R Hamilton, et al.), but
almost never from patrons/visitors
walking in and offering something for sale. We don't buy from
Amazon.com or bn.com, either,
but are working to get ourselves a
business/institutional credit card,

so that may change. I sometimes (not often) buy stuff when information is sent to us thru the mail.

Margaret Herrick Library
333 S. La Cienega Boulevard
Beverly Hills, CA 90211
(310) 247-3020
soka@oscars.org
http://www.oscars.org/library/index.
  html

We get some of our books from Larry Edmunds Bookshop, who has been good about keeping us abreast of BearManor Media titles-in fact, we've got two of your books on our shelves!

Yes, I like to read reviews for the books before ordering, and yes, we do collect paperbacks!

Montana State Library
P. O. Box 201800
Helena, MT 59620
(406) 444-3115
jkammerer@mt.gov
http://msl.state.mt.us/

According to our collection development policy, the Montana State Library acquires and manages the following materials in all formats:

Montana state publications
Natural resource information about Montana
Professional library development material

Northfield Public Library
210 Washington Street
Northfield, MN 55057
(507) 645-6606
lynne.young@ci.northfield.mn.us
http://www.ci.northfield.mn.us/
  library/

We purchase paperbacks, but a review certainly helps to get us to purchase it. Mostly, we try to buy for what we think will be useful to our community. We have a relatively small materials budget and a VERY small library, so we're careful with what buy.

Palm Beach County Library System
3650 Summit Boulevard
West Palm Beach, FL 33406
(561) 233-2600
pbclref@pbclibrary.org
http://www.pbclibrary.org/

We use review sources such as LJ, PW, Booklist, etc. We purchase based on author or subject performance for each branch: what has been popular in the past. We also purchase for current demand. We tend to avoid buying mass market paperbacks unless they are from popular authors who also publish in hardcover. But we buy trade paperbacks because of size and better binding.

Post Falls Public Library
821 N. Spokane Street
Post Falls, ID 83854
(208) 773-1506
jreiss@cin.kcl.org
http://postfallslibrary.kcl.org/

We have a collection development document. About 90% of materials are from reviewed sources (Booklist, Library Journal, New York Times, etc.) About 8% is purchased for patron requests. About 2% is purchased through other means, such as salespeople.

Roswell Public Library
301 North Pennsylvania Avenue
Roswell, NM 88201
(575) 622-7101
rplref@roswellpubliclibrary.org
http://www.roswellpubliclibrary.org/

Books are chosen based on reviews in several sources, including Library Journal; the information in publishers' catalogs; and the selecting librarians' knowledge of our community and its reading needs and tastes. Recommendations from our library patrons are also appreciated and will be considered. We do order paperback books, although the budget line for mass market paperbacks is rather small because we receive so many in donations. We welcome information about new books and prefer to receive it in the mail. It will be routed to the librarians who order for the relevant collections.

San Antonio Public Library
600 Soledad
San Antonio, TX 78205
(210) 207-2500
Margo.Guzman@sanantonio.gov
http://www.mysapl.org/

We purchase popular materials on a wide variety of subjects from our print vendor, Baker & Taylor. We look for materials that have been favorably reviewed in Library Journal, Publishers Weekly, and Booklist. We do carry paperbacks.

Sarasota County Library System
1660 Ringling Boulevard
Sarasota, FL 34236
(941) 861-5468
scortright@scgov.net
http://www.sclibs.net

The main vendor used in purchasing books is Baker & Taylor, mainly because it is easiest on the finance department. We are not opposed to direct orders, though. Yes, we do purchase hardbacks and paperbacks. Because we are a public library we have a wide range of subjects on our shelves. Some of our libraries have specialization areas such as genealogy and books in different languages. Many sources are used in addition to library journals when considering purchases. I have had authors (mostly, local) drop off their book for review with hopes of making a sale. Catalogs from many publishers are sent. The budget has been a major factor of late as to what is purchased. Everyone has been affected by the economy so I am sure you understand that.

We do have a collection development policy which is available for viewing through the library website.

Scranton Public Library
Lackawanna County Library System
Albright Memorial Library
500 Vine Street
Scranton, PA 18509
(570) 348-3000
(570) 348-3020 Fax
betty@albright.org
http://www.lclshome.org/albright/

A very high percentage of what we add to our shelves is patron-driven, but being a public library we try to have a bit of everything that reflects our community's wants and needs. We include paperbacks. We use many journals and resources to help us in our selection.

Texarkana Public Library
600 West 3rd Street
Texarkana, TX 75501
(903) 794-2149
(903) 794-2139 Fax
txarkpublib@txar-publib.org
http://www.txar-publib.org/

We look at reviews from a variety of library tools including Library Journal and School Library Journal. We may also be searching in a specific subject area because sometimes donations specify a particular subject area. Patrons also submit "Request for Purchase" forms, which we consider. We do have a small collection of paperbacks.

Thomaston Public Library
60 Main Street
Thomaston, ME 04861
(207) 354-2453
TPL@thomaston.lib.me.us
http://www.thomaston.lib.me.us/

Our accession policy is not exactly set in stone. Purchases are made at the discretion of the director, and recommendations are submitted by all staff members, who each have their own methods for selecting titles.

If you'd like us to consider purchasing a title feel free to send us promotional material by email or by the post office. As a general rule we do not accept mass market paperbacks, reference books, obscure or rare books, or VHS tapes.

Topeka & Shawnee County Public Library

1515 Southwest 10th Avenue
Topeka, KS 66604
(785) 580-4400
thartman@tscpl.org
http://www.tscpl.org/

We consider several factors when looking at what materials we will add to the library's collection. These include:

- Reviews (we do use Library Journal)
- Cost
- Subject coverage (do we have a lot of materials on this topic already?)
- Will it hold up to the rigors of circulation?
- Local interest
- Who the author is and if we have purchased other books by them were they very popular
- Is the topic something that is currently popular
- Has it been mentioned on the news / talk shows.

Those are just a few of the things we consider. You can find out more about how we select materials by looking at our collection development policy. We do purchase paperbacks for the collection. We don't necessarily focus on one particular genre, but we do try to purchase in areas that are popular.

Westbury Public Library

445 Jefferson Street
Westbury, NY 11590
(516) 333-0176
(516) 333-1752 Fax
contactus@westburylibrary.org
http://www.westburylibrary.org/

We generally select our books from book reviews in sources such as Library Journal, Kirkus, Publisher's Weekly, etc. Occasionally we accept donations from authors, but these are approved by a librarian or the director. Our paperback collection is made up mainly of popular fiction titles, which we already have in the collection and a standing order of romance fiction. Titles which we want to get updated on a regular basis, such as travel books and certain reference books, are on a standing order with our book supplier.

The Library List

Note:

When there are several branches of the same library, this list will show only the one that appears to be the main library.

All libraries listed have general collections. Those that also have a special collection or a newspaper archive that seems more extensive than most have a notation about it at the end of that library's listing.

Most have genealogy resources, so they're not specified in this list.

State libraries that appear to have only government-related collections are not listed.

ALABAMA

Adelia M. Russell Library
318 Church Street
Alexander City, AL 35010
(256) 329-6796
(256) 329-6797 Fax
alexcity@amrlibrary.net
http://www.alexandercityonline.
   com/library.htm

Atmore Public Library
700 East Church Street
Atmore, AL 36502
(251) 368-5234
http://www.atmorelibrary.com/

Auburn Public Library
749 East Thach Avenue
Auburn, AL 36830
(334) 501-3190
weblibrary@auburnalabama.org
http://www.auburnalabama.org/
   library/

Autauga Prattville
Public Libraries
254 Doster Street
Prattville, AL 36067
(334) 365-3396
(334) 365-3397 Fax
jearnest@appl.info
http://appl.info/
Local history

B. B. Comer Memorial Library
314 N. Broadway
Sylacauga, AL 35150
(256) 249-0641
bbclibrary@sylacauga.net
http://www.sylacauga.net/library/

Baldwin County Library
Cooperative
P. O. Box 399
Robertsdale, AL 36567
(251) 970-4010 or 937-0204
bclcdirector@gulftel.com
http://www.gulftel.com/bclc/

Bay Minette Public Library
205 W. Second Street
Bay Minette, AL 36507
(251) 580-1648
(251) 937-0339 Fax
jbailey@ci.bay-minette.al.us
http://www.cityofbayminette.org/
   PAGEVIEW.aspx?ID=3

Bessemer Public Library
400 Nineteenth Street N.
Bessemer, AL 35020
(205) 428-7882
(205) 428-7885 Fax
osmith@bham.lib.al.us
http://bessemer.lib.al.us/
Local history

Birmingham Public Library
2100 Park Place
Birmingham, AL 35203
(205) 226-3600
E-mail thru website
http://www.bplonline.org/
Local information & history

Cheaha Regional Library
935 Colleman Street
Heflin, AL 36264
(256) 463-7125 Phone/Fax
cheahareglibrary@centurytel.net
http://cheaharegionallibrary.org/

Cullman County Library System
200 Clark Street NE
Cullman AL 35055
(256) 734-1068
(256) 734-6902 Reference fax line
http://www.ccpls.com/
US, state & county history
The Beyer-Karter Collection
The Herfurth Collection
The Johnson Photographic Collections
Family files

Decatur Public Library
103 Faye Drive
Decatur, AL 35603
(256) 584-0230
sandymccandless@prodigy.net
http://www.decatur.lib.al.us/

Demopolis Public Library
211 E. Washington Street
Demopolis, AL 36732
(334) 289-1595
(334) 289-8260 Fax
demopolis.public.library@
   demopolisal.gov
http://www.demopolislibrary.info/
Local history

Enterprise Public Library
101 E. Grubbs Street
Enterprise, AL 36330
(334) 347-2636
(334) 393-6477 Fax
http://www.enterpriselibrary.org/

Eufaula Carnegie Library
217 N. Eufaula Avenue
Eufaula, AL 36027
(334) 687-2337
(334) 687-8143 Fax
http://www.ecl.lib.al.us/

Fairfield Public Library
Gary Avenue
Fairfield, AL 35064
(205) 783-6007
lperry@bham.lib.al.us
http://fairfield.lib.al.us/

Florence-Lauderdale Public Library
350 N. Wood Avenue
Florence, AL 35630
(256) 764-6564
(256) 764-6629 Fax
E-mail thru website
http://flpl.lib.al.us/
Local history

Gadsden Public Library
254 College Street
Gadsden, AL 35901
(256) 549-4699
E-mail thru website
http://www.gadsdenlibrary.org/

Gardendale-Martha Moore Public Library
995 Mount Olive Road
Gardendale, Al. 35071
(205) 631-6639
(205) 631-0146 Fax
csmith@bham.lib.al.us
http://gardendale.lib.al.us/

Harrison Regional Library System
Shelby County Public Libraries
50 Lester Street
Columbiana, AL 35051
(205) 669-3910
(205) 669-3940 Fax
broberts@pelhamonline.com
http://www.shelbycounty-al.org/

Hoover Public Library
200 Municipal Drive
Hoover, Al 35216
(205) 444-7800
E-mail thru website
http://www.hooverlibrary.org/

Hueytown Public Library
1372 Hueytown Road
Hueytown, AL 35023
(205) 491-1443
hueytown@bham.lib.al.us
http://www.hueytown.org/htnlib.htm

Huntsville-Madison County Public Library
915 Monroe Street
Huntsville, AL 35801
(256) 532-5940
E-mail thru website
http://hpl.lib.al.us/

Irondale Public Library
105 20th St. South
Irondale AL 35210
(205) 951-1415
http://www.irondalelibrary.com/

Jefferson County Library Cooperative
2100 Park PL
Birmingham, AL 35203
(205) 226-3615
(205) 226-3617 Fax
pryan@bham.lib.al.us
http://www.jclc.org/

Luverne Public Library
148 E. Third Street
Luverne, AL 36049
(334) 335-5326
(334) 335-6402 Fax
library@luverne.org
http://library.luverne.org

Midfield Public Library
400 Breland Drive
Midfield, AL 35228
(205) 923-1027
jparsons@bham.lib.al.us
http://midfield.lib.al.us/

Mobile Public Library
700 Government Street
Mobile, AL 36602
(251) 208-7106
(251) 208-5865 Fax
mplboard@mplonline.org
http://www.mplonline.org/

Montgomery Public Library
P. O. Box 1950
Montgomery, AL 36102
(334) 240-4300
(334) 240-4977 Fax
jowes@mccpl.lib.al.us
http://www.mccpl.lib.al.us/
 Black History Collection

**Public Library of Anniston-
Calhoun County**
108 East 10th Street
Anniston, AL 36201
(256) 237-8501
http://www.anniston.lib.al.us/
 Ancestry resources

Rainbow City Public Library
3702 Rainbow Drive
Rainbow City, AL 35906
(256)442-8477
library@rbcalabama.com
http://www.rbclibrary.org/

Scottsboro Public Library
1002 S. Broad Street
Scottsboro, AL 35768
(256) 574-4335
(256) 259-4457 Fax
nselby@scottsboro.org
http://www.scottsborolibrary.
 com/#Your
Library100

Tuscaloosa Public Library
1801 Jack Warner Parkway
Tuscaloosa, AL 35401
(205) 345-5820
(205) 752-8300 Fax
http://www.tuscaloosa-library.org/

ALASKA

Anchorage Public Library
3600 Denali Street
Anchorage, AK 99503
(907) 343-2975
E-mail thru website
http://lexicon.ci.anchorage.ak.us

Cooper Landing Community Library
P. O. Box 517
Cooper Landing, AK 99572
(907) 595-1241
alibrary@arctic.net
http://www.arctic.net/~alibrary/

Cordova Public Library
622 First Street
Cordova, AK 99574
(907) 424-6667
http://www.cordovalibrary.org/

Delta Community Library
2291 Deborah Street
Delta Junction, AK 99737
(907) 895-4102
(907) 895-4375 Fax
city@ci.delta-junction.ak.us
http://www.ci.delta-junction.ak.us/
    city_information/library.htm

Dillingham Public Library
P. O. Box 870
Dillingham, AK 99576
(907) 842-5610
(907) 842-4237 Fax
librarian@dillinghamak.us
http://www.ci.dillingham.ak.us/
    library1.html

Fairbanks North Star Public Library
1215 Cowles Street
Fairbanks, AK 99701
(907) 459-1020
fairbanks@fnsblibrary.us
http://library.fnsb.lib.ak.us/

Haines Borough Public Library
P. O. Box 1089
Haines, AK 99827
(907) 766-2545
http://haineslibrary.org/

Homer Public Library
500 Hazel Avenue
Homer, AK 99603
(907) 235-3180
library@ci.homer.ak.us
http://library.ci.homer.ak.us/

Juneau Public Libraries
292 Marine Way
Juneau, Alaska 99801
(907) 586-5249
E-mail thru website
http://www.juneau.org/library/
    index.php

Kegoayah Kozga Library
P. O. Box 1168
Nome, AK 99762
(907) 443-6628
(907) 443-3762 Fax
library@ci.nome.ak.us
http://www.nomealaska.org/library/
    index.html

Kenai Community Library
163 Main Street Loop
Kenai, AK 99611
(907) 283-4378
(907) 283-2266 Fax
kenailibrary@ci.kenai.ak.us
http://www.kenailibrary.org/
Writers' Group

Ketchikan Public Library
629 Dock Street
Ketchikan, AK 99901
(907) 225-3331
library@firstcitylibraries.org
http://www.firstcitylibraries.org/

Kettleson Memorial Library
320 Harbor Drive
Sitka, AK 99835
(907) 747-8708
(907) 747-8755 Fax
library@cityofsitka.com
http://www.cityofsitka.com/dept/
   library/library.html

Martin Monsen
Regional Library
P. O. Box 147
Naknek, AK 99633
(907) 246-4465 (phone & fax)
library@theborough.com
http://www.theborough.com/
   library.html

Matanuska-Susitna Libraries
655 South Valley Way
Palmer, AK 99645
(907) 745-4690
plmrlib@mtaonline.net
http://www.matsulibraries.org/

Seward Community Library
P. O. Box 2389
Seward, AK 99664
(907) 224-4082
(907) 224-3521 Fax
plinville@cityofseward.net
http://www.cityofseward.net/library/
Historic Alaska photos

Soldotna Public Library
235 N. Binkley Street
Soldotna, AK 99669
(907) 262-4227
(907) 262-6856 Fax
tburdick@ci.soldotna.ak.us
http://www.cityofseward.net/library

Tuzzy Consortium Library
P. O. Box 2130
Barrow, AK 99723
1-800-478-6916
(907) 852-1729 Fax
E-mail thru website
http://www.tuzzy.org/
Regional information
Iñupiaq history/language/culture

Unalaska Public Library
P. O. Box 610
Unalaska, AK 99685
(907) 581-5060
(907) 581-5266 Fax
akunak@ci.unalaska.ak.us
http://www.unalaska-ak.
   us/index.asp?Type=B_
   BASIC&SEC={98F49855-AFED-
   4340-8915-4E9A7B314851}

Wasilla Public Library
391 N. Main Street
Wasilla, AK 99654
(907) 376-5913
library@ci.wasilla.ak.us
http://www.cityofwasilla.com/index.
   aspx?page=72

Wrangell Public Library
P. O. Box 679
Wrangell, AK 99929
(907) 874-3535
wrglib@aptalaska.net
http://www.wrangell.
   com/government/
   departments/articles/index.
   cfm?Department=22

ARIZONA

Apache Junction Public Library
1177 N. Idaho Rd.
Apache Junction, AZ 85219
(480) 474-8555
(480) 671-8037 Fax
lstaff@ajcity.net
http://www.ajpl.org/

Arizona State Library
Archives & Public Records
1700 W. Washington, Suite 200
Phoenix, AZ 85007
(602) 926-4035
(602) 256-7983 Fax
services@lib.az.us
http://www.lib.az.us/
Arizona history collection, includes
   photos and manuscripts
Federal publications

Avondale Public Library
495 E. Western Ave.
Avondale, AZ 85323
(623) 333-BOOK
(623) 333-0260 Fax
http://az-avondale.civicplus.com/
   index.asp?NID-26

Camp Verde Community Library
130 Black Bridge Loop Rd.
Camp Verde, Arizona 86322
(928) 567-3414
(928) 567-9583 Fax
library@cvaz.org
http://www.cvaz.org/library/

Casa Grande Public Library
449 N. Dry Lake Street
Casa Grande, AZ 85222
(520) 421-8710
http://www.casagrandeaz.gov/web/
   guest/library

Chandler Public Library
22 S. Delaware Street
Chandler, AZ 85225
(480) 782-2800
E-mail thru website
http://chandlerlibrary.org/
Biography reference bank
History reference center
Ancestry resources

Chino Valley Public Library
P. O. Box 1188
Chino Valley, AZ 86323
(928) 636-2687
(928) 636-9129 Fax
library@chinoaz.net
http://www.chinoaz.net/library/
   index.shtml

Cochise County Library District
Drawer AK
Bisbee, AZ 85603
(520) 432-8930
(520) 432-7339 Fax
lgilliland@cochise.az.gov
http://cochise.lib.az.us/cdistrict.html

Coolidge Library
92 W. Butte Avenue
Florence, AZ 85232
(520) 866-6457
(520) 866-6533 Fax
Denise.Keller@pinalcountyaz.gov
http://pinalcountyaz.gov/
   DEPARTMENTS/LIBRARY/Pages/
   Home.aspx

Desert Foothills Library
P. O. Box 4070
Cave Creek, AZ 85327
(480) 488-2286
(480) 595-8353 Fax
director@dfla.org
http://www.desertfoothillslibrary.org/

**Flagstaff City-Coconino County
Public Library**
300 West Aspen Avenue
Flagstaff, AZ 86001
(928) 779-7670
E-mail thru website
http://www.flagstaffpubliclibrary.org/

Glendale Public Library
5959 W. Brown Street
Glendale, AZ 85302
(623) 930-3531
E-mail thru website
http://www.glendaleaz.com/library/

Mesa Public Library
64 E. First St.
Mesa, AZ 85201
480-644-2207
mesalib.info@cityofmesa.org
http://www.mesalibrary.org/Home.
   aspx

Mohave County Library
P.O. Box 7000
Kingman, AZ 86402
(928) 692-BOOK
(928) 692-5762 Fax
http://mohavecountylibrary.info/

Navajo County Library District
P. O. Box 668
Holbrook, AZ 86025
(928) 524-4745
(928) 524-4747 Fax
gdurkee@navajo.lib.az.us
http://www.navajocountylibraries.
   org/navajo/

**Nogales-Santa Cruz
County Public Library**
518 N. Grand Avenue
Nogales, AZ 85621
(520) 287-3343
(520) 287-4823 Fax
webnogales@lib.az.us
http://nogales-santacruz.lib.az.us/

Page Public Library
P. O. Box 1776
Page, AZ 86040
(928) 645-4270
(928) 645-5804 Fax
debbie@cityofpage.org
http://www.youseemore.com/page/

Peoria Public Library
8463 W. Monroe Street
Peoria, AZ. 85345
623-773-7556
E-mail thru website
http://www.peoriaaz.gov/content2.
   asp?ID=10797

Phoenix Public Library
1221 N. Central Avenue
Phoenix, AZ 85004
(602) 262-4636
http://www.phoenixpubliclibrary.
  org/index.jsp
Regional collections

Pima Public Library
50 South 200 West
Pima, AZ 85543
(928) 485-2822
librarian@pimalibrary.org
http://www.pimalibrary.org/

Prescott Public Library
215 E. Goodwin Street
Prescott, AZ 86303
(928) 777-1500
E-mail thru website
http://www.prescottlibrary.info/

Prescott Valley Public Library
215 East Goodwin Street
Prescott Valley, AZ 86312
(928) 759-3040
tjohnson@pvaz.net
http://www.pvaz.net/Index.
  aspx?page=285

Quartzsite Public Library
P. O. Box 2812
Quartzsite, AZ 85346
(928) 927-6593
(928) 927-3593 Fax
qsitelib@hotmail.com
http://www.quartzsitelibrary.com/
Regional collection

Safford City Library
800 Seventh Avenue
Safford, AZ 85546
(928) 348-3202
(928) 348-3209 Fax
http://safford.govoffice.
  com/index.asp?Type=B_
  BASIC&SEC={0F8925CC-CB3B-
  407E-92F8-2A9D6BDABA16}

Scottsdale Public Library
3839 N. Drinkwater Boulevard
Scottsdale, AZ 85251
(480) 312-READ
rhamilton@scottsdaleaz.gov
http://library.ci.scottsdale.az.us/

Sedona Public Library
3250 White Bear Road
Sedona AZ 86336
(928) 282-7714
(928) 282-5789 Fax
director@sedonalibrary.org
http://www.sedonalibrary.org/

Show Low Public Library
180 North 9th Street
Show Low, AZ 85901
(928) 532-4070
http://ci.show-low.az.us/
  departments/library/

Sierra Vista Public Library
2600 E. Tacoma
Sierra Vista, AZ 85635
(520) 458-4225
(520) 458-5377 Fax
dgunckel@ci.sierra-vista.az.us
http://www.ci.sierravista.az.us/cms1//
  index.php?option=com_content&
  task=section&id=22&Itemid=162

Snowflake-Taylor Public Library
418 South 4th West
  Snowflake, AZ 85937
  (928) 536-7103, Ext. 245
  (928) 536-3057 Fax
  library@ci.snowflake.az.us
  http://www.ci.snowflake.az.us/res-
  library.htm

Sun City Library
16828 North 99th Avenue
Sun City, AZ 85351
(623) 974-2569
http://www.sclib.com/

Tempe Public Library
3500 S. Rural Road
Tempe, AZ 85282
(480) 350-5500
(480) 350-5544 Fax
tpladmin@tempe.gov
http://www.tempe.gov/library/

Tucson-Pima Public Library
101 N. Stone Ave.
Tucson, AZ 85701
(520) 594-5600
(520) 594-5621 Fax
E-mail thru website
http://www.lib.ci.tucson.az.us/

Yavapai County Library District
172 East Merritt Street, Suite E
Prescott, AZ 86301
(928) 771-3191
(928) 771-3113 Fax
http://www.yavapailibrary.org/

Yuma County Library
2951 South 1st Drive
Yuma, AZ 85364
(928) 782-1871
E-mail thru website
http://www.yumalibrary.org/

ARKANSAS

Arkansas River Valley Regional Library System
501 N. Front Street
Dardanelle, AR 72834
479-229-4418
arvrls@centurytel.net
http://www.arvrls.com/

Arkansas State Library
One Capitol Mall
Little Rock, AR 72201
(501) 682-2053
(501) 682-1529 Fax
aslref@asl.lib.ar.us
http://www.asl.lib.ar.us/

Baxter County Library
424 W. Seventh
Mountain Home, AR 72653
(870) 425-3598
questions@baxtercountylibrary.org.
http://www.baxtercountylibrary.org/

Bella Vista Library
11 Dickens Place
Bella Vista, AR 72714
(479) 855-1753
mfarner.bvpl@sbcglobal.net
http://www.bvpl.org/

Boone County Library
221 West Stephenson
Harrison, AR 72601
(870) 741-5913
info@boonecolib.com
http://bcl.state.ar.us/

Central Arkansas Library System
100 Rock Street
Little Rock, AR 72201
(501) 918-3000
http://www.cals.lib.ar.us/#
 Miller Aviation Collection

Corning Public Library
613 Pine Street
Corning, AR 72422
(870) 857-3453 Phone/Fax
clibrary@lycos.com
http://www.corninglibrary.org/

Craighead County Jonesboro Public Library
315 West Oak
Jonesboro, AR 72401
(870) 935-5133 Ext. 21 or 11
(870) 935-7987 Fax
reference@libraryinjonesboro.org
http://www.libraryinjonesboro.org/

Crawford County Library System
P. O. Box 724
Van Buren, AR 72956
(479) 471-3226
(479) 471-3227 Fax
crawfordcountylibrary@hotmail.com
http://www.crawfordcountylib.org/

Crossett Public Library
1700 S. Main Street
Crossett, AR 71635
(870) 364-2230
 Local history room
http://www.crossett.lib.
  ar.us/?refreshed

**Faulkner-Van Buren Regional
Library System**
1900 Tyler St.
Conway, AR 72032
(501) 327-7482
(501) 327-9098 Fax
webmaster@fcl.org (apparently
  goes to library)
http://www.fcl.org/#

Fayetteville Public Library
401 W. Mountain Street
Fayetteville, AR 72701
(479) 856-7000
(479) 571-0222 Fax
questions@faylib.org
http://www.faylib.org/

Forrest City Library
421 S. Washington Street
Forrest City, AR 72335
(870) 633-5646
(870) 633-5647 Fax
fcpl@forrestcitylibrary.org
http://www.forrestcitylibrary.org/
 The Annie B. Proctor
  Arkansas collection

Greene County Library
120 North 12th Street
Paragould, AR 72450
(870) 236-8711
(870) 236-1442 Fax
greencolibrarian@msn.com
http://www.greenecountylibrary.com/

Jackson County Library
P. O. Box 748
Newport, AR 72112
(870) 523-2952
(870) 523-5218 Fax
darby@jacksoncolibrary.net
http://www.jacksoncolibrary.net/
  library/

**Malvern-Hot Spring County
Library**
202 E Third Street
Malvern, AR 72104
(501) 332-5441
(501) 332-6679 Fax
hotspringcountylibrary@yahoo.com
http://www.hsc.lib.ar.us/

Piggott Public Library
361 West Main
Piggott, AR 72454
(870) 598-3666 Phone/Fax
piggottlibrary@yahoo.com
http://www.piggottlibrary.org/

**Pine Bluff/Jefferson County
Library System**
200 East 8th Avenue
Pine Bluff, AR 71601
(870) 534-4802
(870) 534-2159 (Fax)
pbjc-lib@pbjc-lib.state.ar.us (subj:
  Library)
http://pbjclibrary.state.ar.us/

Randolph County Public Library
201 Worth Street
Asheboro, NC 27203
(336) 318-6800
E-mail thru website
http://www.randolphlibrary.org/
The Randolph Room of local history

Rector Public Library
121 W 4th Street
Rector, AR 72461
(870) 595-2410
rectorlibrary@yahoo.com
http://www.rectorlibrary.org/

Rogers Public Library
711 S. Dixieland Road
Rogers, AR 72758
(479) 621-1152
rfinch@rogersark.org
http://library.rpl.lib.ar.us/

Saline County Library System
1800 Smithers Drive
Benton, AR 72015
1-800-476-4466
(501) 778-0536 Fax
administrator@saline.lib.ar.us
http://library.rpl.lib.ar.us/

Siloam Springs Library
401 West University
Siloam Springs, AR 72761
(479) 524-4236
(479) 524-3908 Fax
http://siloamlibrary.net
http://siloamsprings.com/
   departments/library/

Springdale Public Library
405 S. Pleasant Street
Springdale, AR 72764
(479) 750-8180
(479) 750-8182 Fax
E-mail thru website
http://www.springdalelibrary.org/

**Washington County Library
System**
1080 W. Clydesdale Drive
Fayetteville, AR 72701
(479) 442-6253
(479) 442-6812 Fax
info@wcls.lib.ar.us
http://www.wcls.lib.ar.us

**William F. Laman
Public Library**
2801 Orange Street
N. Little Rock, AR 72114
(501) 758-1720
(501) 758-3539 Fax
library.information@laman.net
http://www.laman.net/

CALIFORNIA

A K Smiley Public Library
125 W Vine Street
Redlands, Ca. 92373
(909) 798-7565
reference@akspl.org
http://www.akspl.org/
Carnegie Indian Collection
Manuscript collection
Oral Histories
Nordhoff - Morrison -
   Stillman Collection
Lincoln Memorial Site

Alameda County Library
2450 Stevenson Blvd.
Fremont, CA 94538
(510) 745-1500
E-mail thru website
http://www.aclibrary.org/

Alameda Free Library
1550 Oak Street
Alameda, CA 94501
(510) 747-7777
alamedafree@ci.alameda.ca.us
http://www.ci.alameda.ca.us/library/

Alhambra Civic Center Library
101 South 1st Street
Alhambra, CA 91801
(626) 570-5008
refstaff@alhambralibrary.org
http://www.alhambralibrary.org/

Alpine County Library
Markleeville Library & Archives
P. O. Box 187
Markleeville, CA 96120
(530) 694-2120
(530) 694-2408 Fax
library@alpinecountyca.gov
http://www.alpinecountyca.com/
   departments/library

Altadena Library
600 E. Mariposa Street
Altadena, CA 91001
(626) 798-0833
(626) 798-5351 Fax
E-mail thru website
http://library.altadena.ca.us/

Amador County Library
[no address given]
(209) 223-6400
library@co.amador.ca.us
http://www.co.amador.ca.us/depts/
   library/index.cfm?id=3

Anaheim Public Library
500 W. Broadway
Anaheim, CA 92805
(714) 765-1880
(714) 765-1730 Fax
E-mail thru website
http://www2.anaheim.net/custom.
   cfm?name=welcome_library.cfm

Arcadia Public Library
20 W. Duarte Road
Arcadia, CA 91006
(626)821-5567
E-mail thru website
http://www.ci.arcadia.ca.us/home/
    index.asp?page=664
Arcadia history collection
Government documents

Azusa City Library
729 N. Dalton Ave.
Azusa, CA, 91702
(626) 812-5232
(626)334-4868 Fax
atovar@ci.azusa.ca.us
http://www.ci.azusa.ca.us/index.
    asp?NID=191

Beaumont Library
125 E. 8th Street
Beaumont, CA 92223
(951) 845-1357
(951) 845-6217 Fax
E-mail thru website
http://bld.lib.ca.us/

Belvedere-Tiburon Library
1501 Tiburon Boulevard
Tiburon, CA 94920
(415) 789-2665
(415) 789-2650 Fax
refdesk@bel-tib-lib.org
http://bel-tib-lib.org/

Berkeley Public Library
2090 Kittredge Street
Berkeley, CA 94704
(510) 981-6100
E-mail thru website
http://berkeleypubliclibrary.org/

Beverly Hills Public Library
444 N. Rexford Drive
Beverly Hills, CA 90210
(310) 288.2244
E-mail thru website
http://www.beverlyhills.org/
    services/library/

**Blanchard/Santa Paula Public
Library**
119 North 8th Street
Santa Paula, CA 93060-2784
(805) 525-3615
(805) 933-2324 Fax
drobles@blackgold.org.
http://www.rain.org/~stapaula/
Collections include audiobooks

Buena Park Library District
7150 La Palma Avenue
Buena Park, CA 90620
(714) 826-4100
E-mail thru website
http://buenapark.lib.ca.us/

Burbank Public Library
110 North Glenoaks Boulevard
Burbank, CA 91502
(818) 238-5600
tlongcore@ci.burbank.ca.us
http://www.burbank.lib.ca.us/

Burlingame Public Library
480 Primrose Road
Burlingame, CA 94010
(650) 558-7400
bplref@plsinfo.org.
www.burlingame.org/library

Butte County Library
1108 Sherman Avenue
Chico, CA 95926
(530) 891-2762
chicolibrary@buttecounty.net
http://www.buttecounty.net/
  BCLibrary/

San Andreas Central Library
1299 Gold Hunter Road
San Andreas, CA 95249
(209) 754-6510
(209) 754-6512 Fax
E-mail via website
http://www.co.calaveras.ca.us/cc/
  Library.aspx

California State Library
P. O. Box 942837
Sacramento, CA 94237-0001
(916) 654-0174
(916) 654-0064 Fax
csl-adm@library.ca.gov
http://www.library.ca.gov

Camarena Memorial Library
850 Encinas Avenue
Calexico, CA 92231
(760) 768-2170
(760) 357-0404 Fax
stauler@calexico.ca.gov
http://www.calexicolibrary.org/

Cerritos Library
18025 Bloomfield Ave.
Cerritos, CA 90703
(562) 916-1350
http://menu.ci.cerritos.ca.us/
Book art collection
First ladies collection
Foundation materials
Local history collection

Commerce Central Library
5655 Jillson Street
Commerce, CA 90040
(323) 722-6660
Fax: (323) 724-1978
ReferenceL@ci.commerce.ca.us
http://ci.commerce.ca.us/centrallib.
  htm

Colusa Free Library
738 Market Street
Colusa, CA 95932
(530) 458-7671
colusalibrary@hotmail.com
http://www.colusanet.com/ccl/

Contra Costa County Library
1750 Oak Park Boulevard
Pleasant Hill, California • 94523
800-984-4636
Fax: 925.646.6461
libadmin@ccclib.org
http://ccclib.org/

Corona Public Library
650 S. Main Street
Corona, CA 92882
(951) 736-2381
E-mail thru website
http://www.coronapubliclibrary.org/

Coronado Public Library
640 Orange Avenue
Coronado, CA 92118
(619) 522-7390
(619) 435-4205 Fax
s.oakes@coronado.lib.ca.us
http://www.coronado.ca.us/library/

Covina Public Library
234 N. 2nd Avenue
Covina, CA 91723
(626) 967-3935
http://www.ci.covina.ca.us/contact/

Daly City Public Library
40 Wembley Drive
Daly City, CA 94015
(650) 991-8023
E-mail thru website
http://dalycitylibrary.org/

Dixon Public Library
230 North 1st Street
Dixon, CA 95620
(707) 678-5447
(707) 678-3515 Fax
reference@dixonlibrary.com
http://www.dixonlibrary.com/
Historical collections

Downey City Library
11121 Brookshire Avenue
Downey, CA 90241
(562) 904-7360
(562) 923-3763 Fax
questions@downeyca.org
http://www.downeylibrary.org/

El Centro Public Library
539 State Street
El Centro, CA 92243
(760) 337-4565
rbanks@ci.el-centro.ca.us
http://www.cityofelcentro.org/
   library/

El Dorado County Library
345 Fair Lane
Placerville, CA 95667
(530) 621-5540
(530) 622-3911 Fax
lib-pl@eldoradolibrary.org
http://www.eldoradolibrary.org/

El Segundo Public Library
111 West Mariposa Avenue
El Segundo, California 90245
(310) 524-2722
ecunningham@elsegundo.org
http://elsegundo.org/library/
   default.asp
Historic photos

Escondido Public Library
239 S. Kalmia Street
Escondido, CA 92025
(760) 839-4684
E-mail via website
http://www.ci.escondido.ca.us/library/

Folsom Public Library
Georgia Murray Building
411 Stafford Street
Folsom, CA 95630
(916) 355-7374
libstaff@folsom.ca.us
http://www.folsom.ca.us/depts/
   library_services/
default.asp

Fresno County Public Library
2420 Mariposa Street
Fresno, CA 93721
(559) 488-3195
E-mail thru website
http://www.fresnolibrary.org/
California history

Fullerton Public Library
353 W. Commonwealth Ave.
Fullerton, CA 92832
(714) 738-6334
(714) 447-3280 Fax
reference@fullertonlibrary.org
http://fullertonlibrary.org/

Glendale Central Public Library
222 E. Harvard St.
Glendale, CA 91205
818.548.2027
E-mail via website
http://www.ci.glendale.ca.us/
   librarydefault.asp
Glendale history
Cat Collection

Glendora Public Library
140 S. Glendora Ave.
Glendora, CA 91741
(626) 852-4891
(626) 852-4899 Fax
Library@glendoralibrary.org
http://ci.glendora.ca.us/library/

Harrison Memorial Library
P.O. Box 800
Carmel, CA 93921
(831) 624-7323
hml.reference@gmail.com
http://www.hm-lib.org/

Hayward Public Library
835 C Street
Hayward, CA 94541
(510) 293-8685
library@hayward-ca.gov
http://library.ci.hayward.ca.us/

Humboldt County Public Library
1313 Third Street
Eureka, CA 95501
(707) 269-1900
http://co.humboldt.ca.us/library/
Indian collection
Historical photos
Local history

Huntington Beach Public Library
7111 Talbert Avenue
Huntington Beach, CA 92648
(714) 842-4481
E-mail thru website
http://hbpl.org/

Imperial County Free Library
1125 Main Street
El Centro, CA 92243
(760) 339-6460
imperialcountylibrary@co.imperial.
   ca.us
http://www.imperialcounty.net/
   library/default.html

Inglewood Public Library
101 W. Manchester Blvd.
Inglewood, CA 90301
(310) 412-5380
(310) 412-8848 Fax
publiclibrary@cityofinglewood.org
http://www.cityofinglewood.org/
   depts/library/default.asp

Irwindale Public Library
5050 N. Irwindale Avenue
Irwindale, CA 91706
(626) 430-2229
(626) 430-2266 Fax
patricas@ci.irwindale.ca.us
http://www.ci.irwindale.ca.us/
   library.html

Kern County Library
701 Truxtun Avenue
Bakersfield, CA 93301
(661) 868-0700
(661) 868-0799 Fax
E-mail thru website
http://www.kerncountylibrary.org/

Kings County Library
401 N. Douty Street
Hanford, CA 93230
Phone: (559) 582-0261
Sherman.Lee@kingscountylibrary.org
http://www.kingscountylibrary.org/

Lake County Library
1425 N. High Street
Lakeport, CA 95453
707-263-8817
Library@co.lake.ca.us
http://www.co.lake.ca.us/Page386.
   aspx
Local history

Larkspur Public Library
400 Magnolia Avenue
Larkspur, CA 94939
(415) 927-5110
(415) 927-5022 Fax
library@larkspurcityhall.org
http://www.ci.larkspur.ca.us/209.html

Lincoln Public Library
485 Twelve Bridges Dr.
Lincoln CA, 95648
(916) 434-2410
www.libraryatlincoln.org

Livermore Public Library
1188 S. Livermore Avenue
Livermore, CA 94550
(925) 373-5500
lib@livermore.lib.ca.us
http://www.livermore.lib.ca.us/

Lodi Public Library
212 W. Pine St. (temporary)
201 W. Locust Street (permanent)
Lodi, CA 95240
(209) 333-5566
referencelib@lodilibrary.org
http://www.lodi.gov/library/

Long Beach Public Library
101 Pacific Avenue
Long Beach, CA 90822
(562) 570-7500
(562) 570-7408 Fax
LBPL_comments@lbpl.org
http://www.lbpl.org/

Los Angeles Public Library
630 W. 5th Street
Los Angeles, CA 90071
(213) 228-7272
(213) 228-7369 Fax
E-mail thru website
http://www.lapl.org/
Historic photo collection

Los Gatos Public Library
110 E. Main Street
Los Gatos, CA 95030
(408) 354-6891
(408) 399-5755 Fax
library@losgatosca.gov
http://www.losgatosca.gov/index.
   asp?NID=42
Historic collection

Madera County Library
121 North G Street
Madera, CA 93637
(559) 675-7871
http://www.maderacountylibrary.org/

Marin County Free Library
3501 Civic Center Drive
San Rafael, CA 94903
(415) 499-6051
(415) 499-3726 Fax
E-mail thru website
http://www.co.marin.ca.us/depts/
   lb/main/index.cfm

Mariposa County Library
PO Box 106
Mariposa, CA 95338
(209) 966-2140
(209) 742-7527 Fax
http://www.mariposalibrary.org/
California collection & local history

Mendocino County Library
499 Laurel Street
Fort Bragg, CA 95437
(707) 964 2020
(707) 961 2623 Fax
mendoref@co.mendocino.ca.us
http://www.co.mendocino.ca.us/
   library/

Menlo Park Library
800 Alma Street
Menlo Park, CA 94025
(650) 330.2500
mplref@plsinfo.org
http://www.menloparklibrary.org/

Mill Valley Public Library
375 Throckmorton Ave.
Mill Valley, CA 94941
(415) 389-4292
E-mail thru website
http://www.millvalleylibrary.org
Mill Valley Historic Photo Collection

Mission Viejo Library
100 Civic Center
Mission Viejo, CA 92691
(949) 830-7100
E-mail thru website
http://www.cmvl.org

Modoc County Library
212 West Third Street
Alturas, CA. 96101
(530) 233-6340
http://www.infopeople.org/modoc/
   index.html

Mono County Public Libraries
P. O. Box 1120
Mammoth Lakes, CA 93546
(760) 934-8670
(760) 934-6268 Fax
doldham@monocoe.k12.ca.us
http://www.monocolibraries.org/

Monterey County Free Libraries
17822 Moro Road
Salinas, CA 93907
(831) 663-2292
(831) 663-0203 Fax
E-mail thru website
http://www.co.monterey.ca.us/library/
Historical California collection

Monterey Park Bruggemeyer Library
318 S. Ramona Avenue
Monterey Park, CA 91754
(626) 307-1366
(626) 288-4251 Fax
Library@montereypark.ca.gov
http://montereyparklibrary.llwip.org/

Monterey Public Library
625 Pacific Street
Monterey, CA 93940
(831) 646.3932
(831) 656-5618 Fax
refdesk@ci.monterey.ca.us
http://www.monterey.org/library/

Moreno Valley City Library
25480 Alessandro Boulevard
Moreno Valley, CA 92553
(951) 413-3880
(951) 413-3750 Fax
http://www.moreno-valley.ca.us/
   resident_services/library/index_
   library.shtml

Mountain View Public Library
585 Franklin Street
Mountain View, CA 94041
(650) 903-6337
E-mail thru website
http://www.ci.mtnview.ca.us/city_
   hall/library/default.asp

Murrieta Public Library
Eight Town Square
Murrieta, CA 92562
Phone: (951) 304-BOOK
http://www.murrieta.org/services/
   library/

Napa City-County Library
580 Coombs Street
Napa, CA 94559
1-800-248-8402
(707) 253-4615 Fax
libref@co.napa.ca.us
http://www.co.napa.ca.us/library/

Nevada County Library
980 Helling Way
Nevada City CA 95959
(530) 265-1218
530-470-2748
Library.reference@co.nevada.ca.us
http://new.mynevadacounty.com/
   library/

Newport Beach Public Library
1000 Avocado Ave.
Newport Beach, CA 92660
(949) 717-3800
director@city.newport-beach.ca.us
http://www.city.newport-beach.
   ca.us/nbpl/

Oakland Public Library
125 14th Street
Oakland CA 94612
(510) 238-3134
jturbak@oaklandlibrary.org
http://www.oaklandlibrary.org/

Oceanside Public Library
330 N. Coast Highway
Oceanside, CA 92054
(760) 435-5580
public.library@ci.oceanside.ca.us
http://www.library.ci.ooceanside.
   ca.us/

Ontario City Library
215 East "C" Street
Ontario, CA 91764
(909) 395-2205
reference@ci.ontario.ca.us
http://www.ci.ontario.ca.us/index.
    cfm/6752
Robert E. Ellingwood Model Colony
    History Room

Orange County Public Libraries
[no address given]
(714) 566-3040
hefried@ocpl.org
http://egov.ocgov.com/ocgov/
    OC%20Public%20Libraries

Orange Public Library
407 E. Chapman Ave.
Orange, CA 92866
(714) 288-2400
247ref@cityoforange.org
http://www.cityoforange.org/depts/
    library/

Orland Free Library
333 Mill Street
Orland, CA 95963
(530) 865-1640
http://orlandfreelibrary.net/

Oxnard Public Library
251 South A Street
Oxnard, CA 93030
(805) 385-7532
library@ci.oxnard.ca.us
http://www.oxnard.org

Pacific Grove Public Library
550 Central Avenue
Pacific Grove, CA 93950
(831) 648-5760
(831) 373-3268 Fax
lmaddale@pacificgrove.lib.ca.us
http://www.pacificgrove.lib.ca.us/

Palm Springs Library
300 South Sunrise Way
Palm Springs, CA 92262
(760) 322-READ
E-mail thru website
http://www.palmsprings-ca.gov/
    index.aspx?page=78

Palmdale City Library
700 East Palmdale Blvd.
Palmdale, CA 93550
(661) 267-5600
(661) 267-5122 Fax
pcl@cityofpalmdale.org
http://www.cityofpalmdale.org/
    library/

Palo Alto Library
1213 Newell Road
Palo Alto, CA 94303
(650) 329-2436
pa.library@cityofpaloalto.org
http://www.city.palo-alto.ca.us/
    depts/lib/default.asp

Pasadena Public Library
285 E. Walnut Street
Pasadena, CA 91101
(626) 744-4066 (option 7)
E-mail thru website
http://www.ci.pasadena.ca.us/library

Paso Robles Library
1000 Spring Street
Paso Robles, CA 93446
(805) 237-3870
(805) 238-3665 Fax
library@prcity.com
http://www.prcity.com/
   government/departments/library/

Placer County Library
350 Nevada Street
   Auburn, CA 95603
   (530) 886-4550
   (530) 886-4555 (Fax)
   library@placerlibrary.org
http://www.placer.ca.gov/
   Departments/Library.aspx

Pleasanton Public Library
400 Old Barnal Avenue
Pleasanton, CA 94566
(925) 931-3400
(925) 846-8517 Fax
libweb@ci.pleasanton.ca.us
http://www.ci.pleasanton.ca.us/
   services/library/

Plumas County Library
445 Jackson
Quincy CA 95971
(530)283-6310
http://users.psln.com/PCLibQ/

Pomona Public Library
P. O. Box 2271
Pomona, CA 91769
(909) 620-2043
(909) 620-3713 Fax
library@ci.pomona.ca.us
The Laura Ingalls Wilder Collection

Rancho Cucamonga Library
7368 Archibald Avenue
Rancho Cucamonga, CA 91730
(909) 477-2720
(909) 477-2721 Fax
reference@cityofrc.com.
http://www.rcpl.lib.ca.us/

Redwood City Public Library
1044 Middlefield Road
Redwood City, CA 94063
650.780.7018
E-mail thru website
http://www.rcpl.info/

Richmond Public Library
325 Civic Center Plaza
Richmond, CA 94804
(510) 620-6555
Monique_leConge@ci.richmond.ca.us
http://www.ci.richmond.ca.us/index.
   asp?NID=105

Roseville Public Library
225 Taylor Street
Roseville, CA 95678
(916) 774-5221
library@roseville.ca.us
http://www.roseville.ca.us/library/
Roseville history collection
Digital collection

Sacramento Public Library
828 I Street
Sacramento, CA 95814
1-800-209-4627
E-mail thru website
http://www.saclibrary.org/

Salinas Public Library
350 Lincoln Ave.
Salinas, CA 93901
(831) 758-7311
http://www.salinas.lib.ca.us/

San Anselmo Public Library
110 Tunstead Ave.
San Anselmo, CA 94960
(415) 258-4656
sloyster@ci.san-anselmo.ca.us
http://sananselmolibrary.org/

San Benito County Free Library
470 Fifth Street
Hollister, CA 95023
(831) 636-4107
http://www.sanbenitofl.org/

San Bernardino County Library
104 W. 4th St
San Bernardino, CA 92415
(909) 387-5728
http://www.sbcounty.gov/library/
   home/

San Bernardino Public Library
Norman F. Feldheym Central
Library
555 West 6th Street
San Bernardino, CA 92410
(909) 381.8201
http://www.sbpl.org/
Historical photo collection

San Diego County Library
10433 Reserve Drive
San Diego, CA 92127
(858) 673-4697
jose.aponte@sdcounty.ca.gov
http://www.sdcl.org/

San Diego Public Library
820 E Street
San Diego, CA 92101
(619) 236-5800
weblibrary@sandiego.gov
http://www.sandiego.gov/public-
   library/

San Francisco Public Library
100 Larkin Street
San Francisco CA 94102-4733
(415) 557-4400
E-mail thru website
http://sfpl.lib.ca.us/
The Schmulowitz Collection of Wit
   & Humor

San Joaquin Valley Library
305 N. 4th Street
Coalinga CA 93210
(559) 935-1676
(559) 935-1058 Fax
http://www.coalingahuronlibrary.org
http://www.sjvls.org/
Song index
Regional photo heritage

San Jose Public Library
150 E. San Fernando St.
San José, CA 95112
(408) 808-2000
(408) 808-2355
admin.sjpl@sjlibrary.org
(408) 808-2176
publicinfo@sjlibrary.org
http://www.sjlibrary.org/
Asian-American Collection
Africana Collection

San Leandro Public Library
300 Estudillo Avenue
San Leandro, CA 94577
(510) 577-3971
(510) 577-3987 Fax
http://www.ci.san-leandro.ca.us/
   sllibrary.html

San Luis Obispo City-County
Library
P.O. Box 8107
San Luis Obispo, CA 93403
(805) 781 – 5785
http://slolibrary.org/

San Marino Public Library
1890 Huntington Drive
San Marino, CA 91108
(626) 300-0777
adallavalle@CityofSanMarino.org
http://sanmarinopl.org/

San Matao County Library
104 Hilton Way
Pacifica, CA 94044
(650) 355.5196
E-mail thru website
http://smcl.org/flash.html

San Matao Public Library
55 West 3rd Avenue
San Mateo, Ca 94402
(650) 522-7802
(650) 522-7801 Fax
bocon@cityofsanmateo.org
http://www.cityofsanmateo.org/
   index.asp?nid=507

Santa Ana Public Library
26 Civic Center Plaza
Santa Ana, CA 92701
(714) 647-5250
webmaster@ci.santa-ana.ca.us
http://www.ci.santa-ana.ca.us/
   library/

Santa Barbara Public Library
40 E. Anapamu Street
Santa Barbara, CA 93101
(805) 564-5608
(805) 564-5660 Fax
lmacias@SantaBarbaraCA.gov
http://www.sbplibrary.org/
Local history collection
Government documents
Edson Smith photograph collection
Choral scores

Santa Clara City Library
2635 Homestead Road
Santa Clara, CA 95051
(408) 615-2900
E-mail thru website
http://library.santaclaraca.gov/
Local history collection

Santa Clara County Library
14600 Winchester Blvd.
Los Gatos CA 95032
(408) 293-2326, Ext. 3001
melinda.cervantes@lib.sccgov.org
http://www.santaclaracountylib.org/

Santa Cruz Public Library
117 Union St.
Santa Cruz, CA 95060
(831) 420-5600
E-mail thru website
http://www.santacruzpl.org/
Local history collection

Santa Maria Public Library
421 S. McClelland Street
Santa Maria, CA 93454
1-800-354-9660.
(805) 928-8012 Fax
libraryreference@ci.santa-maria.ca.us
http://www.ci.santa-maria.ca.us/3091.
  html
Local history

Santa Monica Public Library
601 Santa Monica Boulevard
Santa Monica, CA 90401
(310) 458-8600
greg.mullen@smgov.net
http://www.smpl.org/

Sausalito Public Library
420 Litho Street
Sausalito, CA 94965
(415) 289-4121
mrichardson@ci.sausalito.ca.us
http://www.ci.sausalito.ca.us/Index.
  aspx?page=100
Sausalito newspaper on microfilm
  from 1885
Index to Marin Scope from 1990,
  obits & bios
Clipping file of articles related
  to Sausalito from the Marin
  Independent Journal & San
  Francisco Chronicle
A rare book collection primarily
  of California/Bay Area history &
  boating books
Alan Watts Collection

Signal Hill Library
1770 E. Hill Street
Signal Hill, CA 90755
(562) 989-7323
cmolloy@cityofsignalhill.org
http://www.citiofsignalhill.org/
  community_services/library.php

Siskiyou County Library
PO Box 632
Fort Jones, CA 96032
(530) 841-4175
siskiyoulibrary@snowcrest.net
http://www.snowcrest.net/
  siskiyoulibrary/

Solano County Library
1150 Kentucky Street
Fairfield, CA 94533
(707) 784-1500
E-mail thru website
http://www.solanolibrary.com/
Wine library
Local history

South Pasadena Public Library
1100 Oxley Street
South Pasadena CA 91030
(626) 403-7340
(626) 403-7331 Fax
http://www.ci.south-pasadena.
  ca.us/library/index.html

South San Francisco Library
840 West Orange Avenue
S. San Francisco, CA 94080
(650) 829-3860
ssfpladm@plsinfo.org
http://www.ssflibrary.net/

St. Helena Public Library
1492 Library Lane
St. Helena, CA 94574
(707) 963-5244
(707) 963-5264 Fax
director@shpl.org
http://www.shpl.org/

Stanislaus County Library
1500 "I" Street
Modesto, CA 95354
(209) 558-7800
E-mail thru website
http://www.stanislauslibrary.org/
Local history
Yearbooks

Stockton-San Joaquin County Public Library
605 N. El Dorado St
Stockton, CA 95202
(209) 937.8362
reference@ci.stockton.ca.us
http://www.stockton.lib.ca.us/

Sunnyvale Public Library
665 W. Olive Avenue
Sunnyvale, CA 94086
(408) 730-7300
(408) 730-7809 Fax
library@ci.sunnyvale.ca.us
www.sunnyvalelibrary.org

Tehama County Library
[online catalog]
http://tehamacountylibrary.org/

Thousand Oaks Public Library
1401 E. Janss Road
Thousand Oaks, CA 91362
(805) 449-2660
Library@toaks.org
http://www.toaks.org/library/
    default.asp

Torrance Public Library
3301 Torrance Boulevard
Torrance, CA 90503
(310) 618-5959
(310) 618-5952 Fax
pweiner@TorrNet.com
http://www.torrnet.com/
    Library/5465.htm

Trinity County Library
P. O. Box 1226
Weaverville, CA 96093
(530) 623-1373
(530) 623-4427 Fax
request_trinity@trinitycounty.org
http://www.youseemore.com/Trinity/
Trinity History Collection

Tulare County Library
200 West Oak Avenue
Visalia, CA 93291
(559) 713-2700
questions@tularecountylibrary.org
http://tularecountylibrary.org/
Historical Research Collection

Upland Public Library
450 N. Euclid Avenue
Upland, CA 91786
(909) 931-4200
E-mail thru website
http://uplandpl.lib.ca.us/asp/Site/
    Library/News/WhatsNew/index.asp

Ventura County Library
646 County Square Drive, #150
Ventura, CA 93003
(805) 477-7331
jackie.griffin@ventura.org
http://www.vencolibrary.org/

Watsonville Public Library
275 Main Street, Suite 100
Watsonville, CA 95076
(831) 768-3400
cheitzig @ ci.watsonville.ca.us
http://www.watsonvillelibrary.org/

Whittier Public Library
7344 Washington Avenue
Whittier, CA 90602
(562) 464-3450
lib@whittierlibrary.org
http://www.whittierlibrary.org/

Yolo County Library
226 Buckeye Street
Woodland, CA 95695
(530) 666-8005
(530) 666-8006 Fax
mel.russell@yolocounty.org
http://www.yolocounty.org/Index.
   aspx?page=189

Yorba Linda Public Library
18181 Imperial Highway
Yorba Linda, CA 92886
(714) 777-2873
http://ylpl.lib.ca.us/

[College Libraries]
UCLA Library
Performing & Visual Arts
Film & Television Books
~~1400 Public Policy~~
~~Los Angeles, CA 90230~~
(310) 825-3817
E-mail thru website
http://www.library.ucla.edu/
   libraries/special.cfm
Antiquarian books, score &
   manuscripts
UCLA Film & Television Archive
Film, Television & Theatre Archival
   Collections

USC Library
Cinematic Arts Library
Doheny Memorial Library, G4
3550 Trousdale Parkway
Los Angeles, CA 90089
(213) 740 3994
cin@usc.edu
http://www.usc.edu/libraries/
   locations/cinema_tv/
Constance McCormick Collection
Elmer Bernstein Collection
Dimitri Tiomkin Collection
Warner Brothers Archives
Performing Arts Archives

[Special]

The Margaret Herrick Library

333 S. La Cienega Boulevard
Beverly Hills, CA 90211
(310) 247-3020
E-mail thru website
http://www.oscars.org/library/index.
   html
Over 1,000 special collections
   related to the performing arts

Museum of Performance & Design

Veterans Building, 4th Floor
401 Van Ness Avenue, #402
San Francisco, CA 94102
(415) 255-4800
reference@mpdsf.org
http://www.sfpalm.org/
Stars of the Early San Francisco
   Stage exhibit
150 Years of Dance in California
San Francisco Stage 1900
San Francisco in Song

COLORADO

Arapahoe Library District
1471 S. Parker Road
Denver, CO 80231
(303) 542-7279
E-mail thru website
http://www.arapahoelibraries.org/

Aurora Public Library
14949 E. Alameda Parkway
Aurora, CO 80012
(303) 739-6600
library@auroragov.org
http://www.auroralibrary.org/

**Basalt Regional
Library District**
99 Midland Avenue
Basalt, CO 81621
(970) 927-4311
kristen_becker@marmot.org
http://www.basaltrld.org/

Bemis Public Library
6014 S. Datura St.
Littleton, CO 80120
(303) 795-3961
libms@littletongov.org
http://www.littletongov.org/bemis/

**Berthoud Community
Library District**
P. O. Box 1259
Berthoud, CO 80513
(970) 532-2757
(970) 532-4372 Fax
E-mail thru website
http://berthoud.colibraries.org/

Boulder Public Library
1001 Arapahoe Avenue
Boulder, CO 80302
(303) 441-3100
(303) 442-1808 Fax
E-mail thru website
http://www.boulder.lib.co.us/
 Writers groups

Bud Werner Memorial Library
1289 Lincoln Avenue
Steamboat Springs, CO 80487
(970) 879-0240
(970) 879-3476 Fax
cpainter@marmot.org
http://www.steamboatlibrary.org/

Buena Vista Public Library
P.O. Box 2019
Buena Vista, CO 81211
(719) 395-8700
(719) 395-6426 Fax
gnottingham@buenavistalibrary.org
http://www.youseemore.com/
    buenavista

Cañon City Public Library
516 Macon Ave.
Cañon City, CO 81212
(719)269-9020
(719)269-9031 Fax
ccpl@canoncity.org
http://www.ccpl.lib.co.us/

**E. Cheyenne County
Public Library**
P. O. Box 939
Cheyenne Wells, CO 80810
(719) 767-5138
(719) 767-5379 Fax
echeyennecountylibrary@yahoo.com
http://www.cwpl.org/

Cortez Public Library
202 North Park
Cortez, CO 81321
(970) 565-8117
http://www.cityofcortez.com/
   government/public_library

**Delta County Public
Library District**
211 West 6th Street
Delta, CO 81416
(970) 874-9630
(970) 874-8605 Fax
deltapl@sopris.net
http://dcpld.org/

Denver Public Library
10 W. Fourteenth Ave. Parkway
Denver, CO 80204
(720) 865-1111
E-mail thru website
http://denverlibrary.org/
  Western history
  African-American research

Dolores Public Library
1002 Railroad
Dolores, CO 81323
(970) 882-4127
(970) 882-2224 Fax
carole@fone.net
http://www.doloreslibrary.org/

Douglas County Libraries
100 S Wilcox
Castle Rock, CO 80104
(303) 791-READ
E-mail thru website
http://www.douglascountylibraries.
  org/

Durango Public Library
1900 East 3rd Avenue
Durango, CO 81301
(970) 375-3380
(970) 375-3398 Fax
armentdl@ci.durango.co.us
http://www.durangopubliclibrary.org/
  Local and state history

Eagle Valley Library District
PO Box 240
Eagle, CO 81631
(970) 328-8800
(970) 328-6901 Fax
E-mail thru website
http://www.evld.org/

East Morgan County Library
500 Clayton Street
Brush, CO 80723
(970) 842-4596
http://www.emcl-brush.org/

Elbert County Library District
P. O. Box 219
Elizabeth, CO 80107
(303) 646-3792
(303) 646-0315 Fax
director@elbertcountylibrary.org
http://www.elbertcountylibrary.org/

Englewood Public Library
1000 Englewood Parkway
Englewood, CO 80110
(303) 762-2550
epl@englewoodgov.org
http://www.ci.englewood.co.us/
     index.aspx?page=130

Estes Park Public Library
P. O. Box 1687
Estes Park, CO 80517
(970) 586-8166
(970) 586-0189 Fax
cperrault@esteslibrary.org
http://estes.lib.co.us/

Ft. Collins Public Library
Poudre River Public Library
201 Peterson Street
Fort Collins, CO 80524
(970) 221-6740
E-mail thru website
http://www.poudrelibraries.org/

Fort Morgan Public Library
414 Main Street
Fort Morgan, CO 80701
(970) 542-4000
pager@fmlibrary.org
http://www.fmlibrary.org/

**Garfield County Public
Library System**
76 S. 4th Street
Carbondale, CO 81623
(970)963-2889
(970)963-8573 Fax
ashipley@marmot.org
http://www.garfieldlibraries.org/
     GCLD/index.aspx

Gilpin County Public Library
15131 Highway 119
Golden, CO 80403
(303) 582-5777
gilpinlib@co.gilpin.co.us
http://www.gilpinlibrary.org/

Grand County Library District
P. O. Box 1050
Granby, CO 80446
(970) 887-9411
(970) 887-3227 Fax
adminoffice@gcld.org
http://www.gcld.org/

Gunnison County Public Libraries
Ann Zugelder Library
307 N. Wisconsin St.
Gunnison, CO 81230
(970) 641-3485
lmeredith@marmot.org
http://gunnisonlibrary.googlepages.
     com/home

High Plains Library District
Carbon Valley Regional Library
7 Park Avenue
Firestone, CO 80504
(720) 685-5100
(720) 685-5101 Fax
E-mail thru website
http://www.mylibrary.us/

Jefferson County Public Library
10200 W. 20th Avenue
Lakewood CO 80215
(303) 235-JCPL (5275)
E-mail thru website
http://www.jefferson.lib.co.us/

Lafayette Public Library
775 W. Baseline Road
Lafayette, CO 80026
(303) 665-5200
  library@cityoflafayette.com
http://www.cityoflafayette.com/
  SectionIndex.asp?SectionID=24

Longmont Public Library
409 Fourth Avenue
Longmont, CO 80501
(303) 651-8470
http://www.ci.longmont.co.us/
  library/index.htm

**[City of] Louisville
Public Library**
951 Spruce Street
Louisville, CO 80027
(303) 335-4849
(303) 335-4833 Fax
schumma@ci.louisville.co.us
http://www.louisville-library.org/

Loveland Public Library
300 N Adams
Loveland, Co 80537
(970) 962-2665
goodwp@ci.loveland.co.us
http://www.lovelandpubliclibrary.org/

**Mamie Doud Eisenhower
Public Library**
3 Community Park Road
Broomfield, CO 80020
(720) 887-2300
(720) 887-1384 Fax
library@broomfield.org
http://www.ci.broomfield.co.us/
  library/index.shtml

Mancos Public Library
P. O. Box 158
Mancos, CO 81328
(970) 533-7569
(970) 533-7600 Fax
E-mail thru website
http://www.mancos.lib.co.us/

**Manitou Springs
Public Library**
701 Manitou Avenue
Manitou Springs, CO 80829
(719) 685-5206
(719) 685-1169 Fax
E-mail thru website
http://manitousprings.colibraries.org/

**Mesa County Public Library
System**
530 Grand Avenue
Grand Junction, CO 81502
(970) 243-4442
http://www.mcpld.org/
State and local history

Moffatt County Libraries
570 Green Street
Craig, CO 81625
(970) 824-5116
(970) 824-2867 Fax
moffatlib@moffat.lib.co.us
http://www.moffat.lib.co.us/

**Montrose Regional Library
District**
320 South 2nd Street
Montrose, CO 81401
(970) 249-9656
(970) 240-1901 Fax
Reference@montroselibrary.org
http://www.montroselibrary.org/

Nederland Community Library
P.O. Box 836
Nederland, Colorado 80466
(303) 258-1101
library@nedlib.org
http://nederland.colibraries.org/

Pikes Peak Library District
P.O. Box 1579
Colorado Springs, CO 80901
(719) 531-6333
E-mail thru website
http://library.ppld.org/
1905 Carnegie Library photo collection
Regional history
Manuscripts & archives of local
    organizations and individuals
Newspaper archives

Pitkin County Library
120 North Mill Street
Aspen, CO 81611
(970) 429-1900
(970) 925-3935 Fax
libraryinfo@co.pitkin.co.us
http://www.pitcolib.org/page_1

Pueblo City-County Library District
100 E. Abriendo Avenue
Pueblo, CO 81004
(719) 562-5600
(719) 562-5610 Fax
E-mail thru website
http://www.pueblolibrary.org/

Rangeview Library District
11658 North Huron
Northglenn, CO 80234
(303) 288-2001
(303) 254-6998
psmith@rangeviewld.org
http://www.rangeviewld.org/

Red Feather Lakes Community Library
PO Box 123
Red Feather Lakes, Colorado 80545
970/881-2664
Fax: 970/881-2836
E-mail thru website
http://www.rfllibrary.org/

Rocky Ford Public Library
400 South 10th Street
Rocky Ford, CO 81067
(719) 254-6641
(719) 254-6647 Fax
E-mail thru website
http://rockyford.colibraries.org/

Salida Regional Library
405 'E' Street
Salida, CO 81201
(719) 539-4826
jdonlan@salidalibrary.org
http://www.salidalibrary.org/

Security Public Library
715 Aspen Drive
Colorado Springs, CO 80911
(719) 391-3191
hudsonb@wsd3.k12.co.us
http://www.securitypubliclibrary.org/

[Ruby M.] Sisson Memorial Library
P. O. Box 849
Pagosa Springs, CO 81147
(970) 264-2209
(970) 264-4764 Fax
E-mail thru website
http://pagosa.colibraries.org/

Southern Peaks Public Library
423 4th Street
Alamosa CO 81101
(719) 589-6592
(719) 589-3786 Fax
librarian@alamosalibrary.org
http://www.alamosalibrary.org/
San Luis Valley historical photos

Spanish Peaks Library District
323 Main Street
Walsenburg, CO 81089
(719) 738-2774
(719) 738-2468 Fax
librarian@spld.org
http://www.spld.org/

Sterling Public Library
420 North 5th Street
Sterling, CO 80751
(970) 522-2023
E-mail thru website
http://www.sterlingcolo.com/
   pages/dept/plr/library.php

Summit County Library
P. O. Box 770
Frisco, CO 80443
(970) 668-5555
(970) 668-5556 Fax
joyced@co.summit.co.us
http://www.co.summit.co.us/library/

[Town of] Vail Library
292 West Meadow Drive
Vail, CO 81657
(970) 479-2185
(970) 479-2192 Fax
info@vaillibrary.com
http://www.vaillibrary.com/

Westminster Public Library
3705 West 112th Avenue
Westminster, CO 80031
303-404-5555
jward@cityofwestminster.us
http://www.ci.westminster.co.us/44.
   htm

Wilkinson Public Library
P. O. Box 2189
Telluride, CO 81435
(970) 728-4519
(970) 728-3340 Fax
bbrattin@telluridelibrary.org
http://www.telluridelibrary.org/

**Windsor-Severance Library
District**
720 Third Street
Windsor, CO 80550
(970) 686-5603
E-mail thru website
http://www.youseemore.com/
   WindsorSeverance/

Woodruff Memorial library
522 Colorado Ave
La Junta, CO 81050-0479
(719) 384-4612
E-mail thru website
http://lajunta.colibraries.org/

CONNECTICUT

Acton Public Library
60 Old Boston Post Road
Old Saybrook, CT 06475
(860) 395-3184
(860) 395-2462 Fax
http://www.oldsaybrookct.org/
    Pages/OldSaybrookCT_Library/
    index

Aldrich Free Public Library
299 Main Street
Moosup, CT 06354
(860) 565-8760
(860) 564-8491 Fax
info@aldrichlibrary.org
http://www.aldrichlibrary.org/

Ansonia Public Library
53 South Cliff Street
Ansonia, CT 06401
(203) 734-6275
(203) 732-4551 Fax
http://www.biblio.org/ansonia/

Avon Free Public Library
281 Country Club Road
Avon, CT 06001
(860) 673-9712
(860) 675-6364 Fax
vvocelli@avonctlibrary.info
http://www.avonctlibrary.info/
Marion Hunter History Room

Babcock Library
25 Pompey Hollow Road
Ashford, CT 06278
(860) 487-4420
(860) 487-4438 Fax
librarian@babcocklibrary.org
http://www.babcocklibrary.com/

Bakerville Public Library
6 Maple Hollow Road
New Hartford, CT 06057
(860) 482-8806
http://bakervillelibrary.org/

Beacon Falls Public Library
10 Maple Avenue
Beacon Falls, Connecticut 06403
(203) 729 - 1441
marsha@bflib.org
http://www.bflib.org/

Beardsley & Memorial Library
40 Munro Place
Winsted, CT 06098
(860) 379-6043
director@beardsleyandmemorial.org
http://www.beardsleyandmemorial.
    org/

Berlin-Peck Memorial Library
234 Kensington Road
Berlin, CT 06037
(860) 828-7125
illbpml@libraryconnection.info
www.berlinpeck.lib.ct.us

Bethel Public Library
189 Greenwood Avenue
Bethel, CT 06801
(203) 794-8756
E-mail thru website
http://www.bethellibrary.org/

Bethlehem Public Library
32 Main Street South
Bethlehem, CT 06751
(203) 266-7792
http://ci.bethlehem.ct.us/Library/
   library.htm

Bill Memorial Library
240 Monument St.
Groton, CT 06340
(860) 445-0392
(860) 449-8971 Fax
info@billmemorial.org
http://www.billmemorial.org/

Bridgeport Public Library
925 Broad Street
Bridgeport, CT 06604
(203) 576-7777
(203) 333-0253 Fax
http://bportlibrary.org/
Blackstone Audio Collection
Historical collections

Bristol Public Library
5 High Street
Bristol, CT 06010
(860) 584-7787
(860) 584-7696 Fax
liblab@ci.bristol.ct.us
http://www.bristollib.com/
Local history

Brookfield Library
182 Whisconier Road
Brookfield, CT 06804
(203) 775-6241
(203) 740-7723 Fax
abarney@brookfieldlibrary.org
http://www.brookfieldlibrary.org/
 Writers group

Burlington Public Library
34 Library Lane
Burlington, CT 06013
(860) 673-3331
(860) 673-0897 Fax
bpl@libraryconnection.info
http://www.burlingtonctlibrary.info/

Canton Pubic Library
40 Dyer Avenue
Canton, CT 06019
(860) 693-5800
(860) 693-5804 Fax
rsimon@cantonpubliclibrary.org
http://www.cantonpubliclibrary.org/

Cheshire Public Library
104 Main Street
Cheshire, CT 06410
(203) 272-2245
(203) 272-7714 Fax
cheshire@cheshirelibrary.org
http://www.cheshirelib.org/

Connecticut State Library
231 Capitol Avenue
Hartford, CT 06106
1-866-886-4478
(860) 757-6503 Fax
isref@cslib.org
http://www.cslib.org/
State archives
Public records

Cora J. Belden Library
33 Church Street
Rocky Hills, CT 06067
(860) 258-7621
mhogan@ci.rocky-hill.ct.us
http://www.rockyhilllibrary.info/

Cragin Memorial Library
P.O. Box 508
Colchester, CT 06415
(860) 537-5752
(860) 537-4559 Fax
library@colchesterct.gov
http://www.colchesterct.gov/Pages/
    ColchesterCT_Dept/CML/index

Cromwell Belden Public Library
39 West Street
Cromwell, CT 06416
(860) 632-3460
E-mail thru website
http://www.cromwellct.com/
    library.htm

Danbury Public Library
170 Main Street
Danbury, CT 06810
(203) 797-4505
E-mail thru website
http://danburylibrary.org/

Darien Library
1441 Post Road
Darien, CT 06820
(203) 655-1234
lberry@darienlibrary.org
http://www.darienlibrary.org/

Deep River Public Library
150 Main Street
Deep River, CT 06417
(860) 526-6039
(860) 526-6040 Fax
http://deepriverct.com/library/

Derby Neck Library
307 Hawthorne Avenue
Derby, CT 06418
(203) 734-1492
headlibrarian@biblio.org
http://www.derbynecklibrary.org/

Derby Public Library
313 Elizabeth Street
Derby, CT 06418
(203) 736-1482
(203) 736-1419 Fax
http://www.derbypubliclibrary.org

Douglas Library
22 Main Street
Hebron, CT 06248
(860) 228-9312
(860) 228-4372 Fax
maryellen@douglaslibrary.org
http://www.douglaslibrary.org/

East Granby Public Library
P. O. Box G
E. Granby, CT 06026
(860) 653-3002
(860) 653-3936 Fax
eastgranbylibrary@egpl.org
http://www.egpl.org/
Historical Room with church, census,
    genealogical, and oral histories

E. Haddam Free Public Library
P. O. Box 372
Moodus, CT 06469
(860) 873-8248
(860) 873-1269 Fax
staff@ehfpl.org
http://www.ehfpl.org/

E. Hampton Public Library
105 Main Street
E Hampton, CT 06424
(860) 267-6621
E-mail thru website
http://www.easthamptonct.org/
   Pages/EastHamptonCT_Library/

E. Hartford Public Library System
840 Main Street
E. Hartford, CT 06108
(860) 289-6429
(860) 291-9166 Fax
pjones@libraryconnection.info
http://www.ehtfdlib.info/

E. Lyme Public Library
39 Society Road
Niantic, CT 06357
(860) 739-6926
(860) 691-0020 Fax
elpl@ely.lioninc.org
http://www.ely.lioninc.org/

Easton Public Library
691 Morehouse Road
Easton, CT 06612
(203) 261-0134
epl@eastonlibrary.org
www.eastonlibrary.org

Enfield Public Library
104 Middle Road
Enfield, CT 06082
(860) 763-7510
LibraryDirector@enfield.org
http://www.enfield-ct.gov/
   content/91/109/5403.aspx

Essex Library Association
33 West Avenue
Essex, CT 06426
(860) 767-1560
(860) 767-2500 Fax
http://www.essexlib.org/

Fairfield Public Library
1080 Old Post Road
Fairfield, CT 06824
(203) 256-3155
http://www.fairfieldpubliclibrary.org/

Farmington Libraries
6 Monteith Drive
Farmington, CT 06032
(860) 673-6791
(860) 675-7148 Fax
tinker@farmingtonlibct.org
http://www.farmingtonlibct.org/

Ferguson Public Library
One Public Library Plaza
Stamford, CT 06904
(203) 964-1000
E-mail thru website
http://www.fergusonlibrary.org/

Goshen Public Library
P. O. Box 180
Goshen, CT 06756
(860) 491-3234
(860) 491-0100 Fax
director@goshenpublib.org
http://www.goshenpublib.org/

Granby Public Library
15 N. Granby Road
Granby, CT 06035
(860) 844-5275
joanfox@granby-ct.gov
http://www.granby-ct.gov/Public_
    Documents/GranbyCT_Library/
    index

Greenwich Library
101 W. Putnam Avenue
Greenwich, CT 06830
(203) 622-7900
E-mail thru website
http://www.greenwichlibrary.org/
    default.asp

Groton Public Library
52 Newtown Road
Groton, CT 06340
(860) 441-6750
breiter@town.groton.ct.us
http://www.town.groton.ct.us/
    library/

Hagaman Library
227 Main Street
East Haven, CT 06512
(203) 468-3890
hagamanlib.easthaven@gmail.com
http://www.
    hagamanlibraryeasthavenct.org/

Hamden Library System
Miller Memorial Central Library
2901 Dixwell Avenue
Hamden, CT 06518
(203) 287-2680
E-mail thru website
http://www.hamdenlibrary.org/

Hartford Public Library
500 Main Street
Hartford, CT 06103
(860) 695-6300
(860) 722-6897 Fax
E-mail thru website
http://www.hartfordpl.lib.ct.us/

Harwinton Public Library
80 Bentley Drive
Harwinton, CT 06791
(860) 485-9113
staff@harwintonpl.org
http://www.harwintonpl.org/

Henry Carter Hull Library
10 Killingworth Turnpike
Clinton, CT 06413
(860) 669-2342
(860) 669-8318 Fax
E-mail thru website
http://www.hchlibrary.org/

Hotchkiss Memorial Library
P.O. Box 277
(860) 364-5041
(860) 364-6060 Fax
info@hotchkisslibrary.org
http://www.hotchkisslibrary.org/
Regional information

Ivoryton Library Association
P. O. Box 515
Ivoryton, CT 06442
(860) 767-1252
ivoryton@lioninc.org
http://www.ivoryton.com/

Blackstone Library
758 Main Street
Branford, CT 06405
(203) 488-1441
(203) 488-6077 Fax
library@blackstone.lioninc.org
http://www.blackstone.lioninc.org/

Kent Memorial Library
P. O. Box 127
Kent, CT 06757
(860) 927-3761
E-mail thru website
http://www.kentmemoriallibrary.org/

Killingly Public Library
25 Westcott Road
Danielson, CT 06239
(860) 779-5383
http://www.killinglypubliclibrary.org/
Regional resources

Killingworth Library
P. O. Box 725
Killingworth, CT 06419
(860) 663-2000
mail@killingworthlibrary.org
http://www.killingworthlibrary.org/

Ledyard Libraries
P. O. Box 225
Ledyard, CT 06339
(860) 464-9912
bradbury@ledyard.lioninc.org
http://www.lioninc.org/ledyard/

Levi E. Coe Library
P. O. Box 458
Middlefield, CT 06455
(860) 349-3857
(860) 349-2131 Fax
staff@leviecoe.com
http://www.leviecoe.com/Main/
  Home.html

**Licia & Mason Beekley
Community Library**
P. O. Box 247
New Hartf0rd, CT 06057
(860) 379-7235
(860) 379-5806 Fax
staff@beekleylibrary.org
http://www.newhartfordlibrary.org/

Lyme Public Library
482 Hamburg Road
Lyme, CT 06371
(860) 434-2272
staff@lymepl.org
http://www.lymepl.org/

Manchester Public Library
Mary Cheney Library
586 Main Street
Manchester, CT 06040
(860) 643-2471
Only e-mail available:
Book suggestions only accepted
  from city residents
http://library.ci.manchester.ct.us/

Mark Twain Library
P. O. Box 1009
Redding, CT 06875
(203) 938-2545
(203) 938-4026 Fax
asksam@marktwainlibrary.org
http://www.marktwainlibrary.org/

Meriden Public Library
105 Miller Street
Meriden, CT 06450
(203) 238-2344
kroesler@ci.meriden.ct.us
http://www.cityofmeriden.org/CMS/
    default.asp?CMS_AreaID=64

Milford Public Library
57 New Haven Avenue
Milford, CT 06460
(203) 783-3290
jtsang@ci.milford.ct.us
http://www.ci.milford.ct.us/Public_
    Documents/MilfordCT_Library/
    library
The Collection of Henry "Buster" Walsh

Mystic & Noank Library
40 Library Street
Mystic, CT 06355
(860) 536-7721
(860) 536-2350 Fax
mnl@juno.com
http://www.mysticnoanklibrary.com/

New Britain Public Library
20 High Street
New Britain, CT 06051
(860) 224-3155
cabrown@nbpl.info
http://www.nbpl.info/

New Canaan Library
151 Main Street
New Canaan, CT 06840
(203) 594-5000
(203) 594-5031 Fax
slaperla@newcanaanlibrary.org
http://newcanaanlibrary.org/

New Fairfield Public Library
P. O. Box F
New Fairfield, CT 06812
(203) 312-5679
(203) 312-5685 Fax
E-mail thru website
http://www.newfairfieldlibrary.org/

New Haven Free Public Library
133 Elm Street
New Haven, CT 06510
(203) 946-8130
khurley@nhfpl.org
http://www.cityofnewhaven.com/
    library/

Norfolk Library
P. O. Box 605
Norfolk, CT 06058
(860) 542-5075
(860) 542-1795 Fax
ryuran@biblio.org
http://www.norfolklibrary.org/

North Haven Memorial Library
17 Elm Street
North Haven, CT 06473
(203) 239-5803
(203) 234-9647 Fax
www.leaplibraries.org/nhaven
http://www.leaplibraries.org/nhaven/

Norwalk Public Library System
1 Belden Avenue
Norwalk, CT 06850
(203) 899-2780
(203) 866-7982 Fax
lkozerowitz@norwalkpubliclibrary.org
http://norwalklib.org/

Old Lyme Library
2 Library Lane
Old Lyme, CT 06371
(860) 434-1684
(860) 434-9547 Fax
mfiorell@oldlyme.lioninc.org
http://www.oldlyme.lioninc.org/

Oliver Wolcott Library
P. O. Box 187
Litchfield, CT 06759
(860) 567-8030
(860) 567-4784 Fax
awhite@owlibrary.org
http://www.owlibrary.org/

Otis Library
261 Main Street
Norwich, CT 06360
(860) 889-2365
(860) 886-4744 Fax
bfarwell@otis.lioninc.org
http://www.otislibrarynorwich.org/

Pequot Library
720 Pequot Avenue
Southport, CT 06890
(203) 259-0346
(203) 259-5602 Fax
ehanusovsky @ pequotlibrary.org
http://www.pequotlibrary.com/

Perrot Public Library
90 South Beach Avenue
Old Greenwich, CT 06870
(203) 637-1066
kmccarthy@perrotlibrary.org
http://www.perrotlibrary.org/

Plainville Public Library
56 East Main Street
Plainville, CT 06062
(860) 793-1446
(860) 793-2241 Fax
pchase@libraryconnection.info
http://plainvillelibrary.org/

Plumb Memorial Library
65 Wooster Street
Shelton, CT 06484
(203) 924-1580
(203) 924-8422 Fax
elydon@biblio.org
http://www.plumblibrary.org/

Portland Library
20 Freestone Avenue
Portland, CT 06480
(860) 342-6770
(860) 342-6778 Fax
jnocek@portlandct.org
http://www.portlandlibraryct.org/

Preston Public Library
389 Route 2
Preston, CT 06365
(860) 886-1010
(860) 886-4952 Fax
library@prestonlibrary.org
http://prestonlibrary.org/

Prospect Public Library
17 Center Street
Prospect, CT 06712
(860) 758-3001
(860) 758-0080 Fax
http://www.prospectct.com/library/

Prosser Public Library
1 Tunxis Avenue
Bloomfield, CT 06002
(860) 243-9721
(860) 242-1629 Fax
http://www.prosserlibrary.info/

Public Library of New London
63 Huntington Street
New London, CT 06320
(860) 447-1411
(860) 443-2083 Fax
peterc@lioninc.org
http://www.plnl.org/
Local history

Rathbun Free Library
P. O. Box G
East Haddam, CT 06423
(860) 873-8210
http://www.rathbun.lioninc.org/

Richmond Memorial Library
P. O. Box 387
Marlborough, CT 06447
(860) 295-6210
nwood@richmondlibrary.info
http://www.richmondmemoriallib.org/

Ridgefield Library Association
472 Main Street
Ridgefield, CT 06877
(203) 438-2282
cbnolan@ridgefieldlibrary.org
http://www.biblio.org/rdgfld/index.htm

Rowayton Library
33 Highland Avenue
Rowayton, CT 06853
(203) 838-5038
Library@Rowayton.org
http://www.rowayton.org/

Russell Library
123 Broad Street
Middleton, CT 06457
(860) 347-2528
(860) 347-4048 Fax
http://russelllibrary.org/

Salem Free Public Library
264 Hartford Road
Salem, CT 06420
(860) 859-1130
(860) 859-9961 Fax
salemctlibrary@yahoo.com
http://www.salem-ct-library.org/

Saxton B. Little Free Library
319 Route 87
Columbia, CT 06237
(860) 228-0350
(860) 228-1569 Fax
staff@columbiactlibrary.org
http://www.columbiactlibrary.org/

Scoville Memorial Library
38 Main Street
Salisbury, CT 06068
(860) 435-2838
(860) 435-8136 Fax
scovlibn@biblio.org
http://www.scovillelibrary.org/

Scranton Library
801 Boston Post Road
Madison, CT 06443
(203) 245-7365
scrantonlibrary@madisonct.org
http://www.scrantonlibrary.org/

Seymour Public Library
46 Church Street
Seymour, CT 06483
(203) 888-3903
(203) 888-4099 Fax
webmaster@seymourpubliclibrary.org
http://www.seymourpubliclibrary.org/

Silas Bronson Library
267 Grand Street
Waterbury, CT   06702
(203) 574-8222
(203) 574-8055 Fax
emcsweeney@waterburyct.org
http://www.bronsonlibrary.org/

Simsbury Public Library
725 Hopmeadow Street
Simsbury, CT   06070
(860) 658-7663
sbullock@simsburylibrary.info
http://www.simsburylibrary.info/
Writers Group

Somers Public Library
P. O. Box 278
Somers, CT 06071
(860) 763-3501
http://www.somersnow.com/library/

Southbury Public Library
100 Poverty Road
Southbury, CT 06488
(203) 262-0626.
kmostacero@biblio.org
http://www.southburylibrary.org/

Southington Library & Museum
255 Main Street
Southington, CT 06489
(860) 628-0947
(860)-628-0488 Fax
smaydas@southington.org
http://www.southingtonlibrary.org/

Stafford Library
P.O. Box 100
Stafford, CT 06075
(860) 684-2852
http://www.staffordlibrary.org/

Stonington Free Library
P.O. Box 232
Stonington, CT 06378
(860) 535-0658
(860) 535-3945 Fax
stonlib@stoningtonfreelibrary.org
http://www.stoningtonfreelibrary.org/

Stratford Library Association
2203 Main Street
Stratford, CT 06615
(203) 385-4164
E-mail thru website
http://www.stratford.lib.ct.us/index.
   html

Terryville Public Library
238 Main Street
Terryville, CT 06786
(860) 582-3121
(860) 585-4068 Fax
tplstaff@biblio.org
http://www.terryvillepl.info/

Thompson Public Library
934 Riverside Drive (Route 12)
North Grosvenordale, CT 06255
(860) 923-9779
aboutaugh@thompsonpubliclibrary.
    org
http://www.thompsonpubliclibrary.
    org/
Connecticut Collection
Foreign Language Materials
Parenting Collection
Local History

Torrington Library
12 Daycoeton Place
Torrington, CT 06790
(860) 489-6684
(860) 482-4664 Fax
info@torringtonlibrary.org
http://torringtonlibrary.org/

Trumbull Library System
33 Quality Street
Trumbull, CT 06611
(203) 452-5197
http://www.trumbullct-library.org/
shorton@trumbull-ct.org

United Valley Libraries
Ansonia Library
53 South Cliff Street
Ansonia, CT 06401
(203) 734-6275
(203) 732-4551 Fax
http://www.biblio.org/ansonia/

Wallingford Public Library
200 North Main Street
Wallingford, CT 06492
(203) 265-6754
E-mail thru website
http://www.wallingford.lioninc.org/

Waterford Public Library
49 Rope Ferry Road
Waterford, CT 06385
(860) 444-5805
http://www.waterfordpubliclibrary.org/

Watertown Library Association
470 Main Street
Watertown, CT 06795
(860) 945-5360
(860) 945-5367 Fax
wtnlib@watertownlibrary.org
http://www.watertownlibrary.org/

Welles-Turner Memorial Library
2407 Main Street
Glastonbury, CT 06033
(860) 652-7717
(860) 652-7721 Fax
barbara.bailey@glastonbury-ct.gov
http://www.wtmlib.com/

West Haven Public Library
300 Elm Street.
West Haven CT 06516
(203) 937-4233
dir@westhavenpl.org
http://www.westhavenpl.org/

Westport Public Library
Arnold Bernhard Plaza
20 Jesup Road
Westport, CT 06880
(203) 291-4800
(203) 227-3829 Fax
cclark@westportlibrary.org
http://www.westportlibrary.org/

Wheeler Library
P. O. Box 217
North Stonington, CT   06359
(860) 535-0383
(860) 535-8561 Fax
E-mail thru website
http://www.wheelerlibrary.org/

Willimantic Public Library
P. O. Box 218
Willimantic, CT 06226
(860) 465-3079
(860) 465-3083 Fax
http://www.biblio.org/willimantic/

**Willoughby-Wallace
Memorial Library**
146 Thimble Islands Road
Stony Creek, Ct 06405
(203) 488-8702
(203) 315-3347 Fax
librarystaff@branford-ct.gov
http://www.wwml.org/

Wilton Library Association
137 Old Ridgefield Road
Wilton, CT 06897
(203) 762-3950
(203) 834-1166 Fax
kcleeds@wiltonlibrary.org
http://www.wiltonlibrary.org/

Windsor Locks Public Library
28 Main Street
Windsor Locks, CT 06096
(860) 627-1495
epearce@libraryconnection.info
http://www.windsorlockslibrary.org/

Windsor Public Library
323 Broad Street
Windsor, CT 06095
(860) 285-1910
(860) 285-1889 Fax
rizzo@townofwindsorct.com
http://www.windsorlibrary.com/

Woodbridge Town Library
10 Newton Road
Woodbridge, CT 06525
(203) 389-3433
jvday@ci.woodbridge.ct.us
http://www.woodbridge.lioninc.org/

DELAWARE

**Corbit-Calloway
Memorial Library**
P.O. Box 128
Odessa, DE 19730
(302) 378-8838
(302) 378-7803 Fax
http://corbitlibrary.org/
Delmarva Collection (re history,
    culture, & literature)

Delaware Division of Libraries
[no address given]
302-739-4748, ext. 119
1-800-282-8696
marie.cunningham@state.de.us
http://www.state.lib.de.us/

Dover Public Library
45 South State Street
Dover, DE 19901
(302) 736-7030
(302) 736-5087 Fax
answerline_kent@lib.de.us
http://www.doverpubliclibrary.org/

Greenwood Public Library
P. O. Box 839
Greenwood, DE 19950
(302) 349-5309
greenwood.library@lib.de.us
http://www.greenwood.lib.de.us/

Kent County Levy Library
2319 S. DuPont Highway
Dover, DE 19901
(302) 698-6440
(302) 698-6441 Fax
http://www.co.kent.de.us/
    Departments/CommunitySvcs/
    Library/

Laurel Public Library
101 East 4th Street
Laurel, DE 19956
(302)875-3184
302)875-4519 Fax
normajean.fowler@lib.de.us
http://www.laurel.lib.de.us/

Lewes Public Library
111 Adams Avenue
Lewes, DE   19958
(302) 645-2733
leweslib@lib.de.us
http://www.leweslibrary.org/

Milford Public Library
11 SE Front Street
Milford, DE 19963
(302) 422-8996
info@milfordpubliclibrary.org
http://www.milfordpubliclibrary.
    org/index.htm

Milton Public Library
121 Union Street
Milton, DE 19968
(302) 684-8856
milton-director@lib.de.us
http://www.milton.lib.de.us/

Newcastle County Libraries
87 Reads Way
New Castle, DE 19720
(302)395-5555
(302) 395-5592 Fax
answerline_newcastle@lib.de.us (?)
http://www.co.new-castle.de.us/
   library/home/webpage1.asp

Rehoboth Beach Library
226 Rehoboth Avenue
Rehoboth Beach, DE 19971
(302) 227-8044
(302) 227-0597 Fax
E-mail thru website
http://www.rehobothlibrary.org/

Seaford District Library
402 North Porter ST
Seaford, Delaware 19973
(302) 629-2524
(302) 629-9181 Fax
amotta@lib.de.us
http://www.seaford.lib.de.us/

Selbyville Public Library
11 Main & McCabe Streets
Selbyville, DE 19975
(302) 436-8195
(302) 436-1508 Fax
http://www.selbyvillelibrary.org/

South Coastal Library
43 Kent Avenue
Bethany Beach, DE 19930
(302) 539-5231
SouthCoastal.Library@lib.de.us
http://www.southcoastal.lib.de.us/

**Sussex County
Department of Libraries**
P. O. Box 589
Georgetown, DE 19947
(302) 855-7890
(302) 855-7895 Fax
E-mail thru website
http://www.sussex.lib.de.us/

Wilmington Public Library
10th and Market Streets
Wilmington, DE 19801
(302) 571-7400
wilmref@lib.de.us
http://www.wilmlib.org/

DISTRICT OF COLUMBIA

District of Columbia
Public Library
901 G Street NW
Washington, DC 20001
(202) 727-0321
commentssuggestions.dcpl@dc.gov
http://www.dclibrary.org/dcpl/site/
    default.asp
Washingtoniana Collection
Black Studies Collection
Peabody Collection

FLORIDA

**Alachua County
Library District**
401 East University Avenue
Gainesville, Florida
352-334-3900
aref@aclib.us
http://www.acld.lib.fl.us/

Alamonte Springs Public Library
281 Maitland Avenue
Altamonte Springs, FL 32701
(407) 571-8830
http://www.altamonte.org/
   department/leisure/index.
   asp?ACTION=view&ID=15

Bartow Public Library
2150 S. Broadway Avenue
Bartow, FL 33830
(863) 534-0131
(863) 534-0913 Fax
bartowpubliclibrary@gmail.com
http://www.pclc.lib.fl.us/bartow/

Bay County Public Library
898 West 11th Street
Panama City, FL 32401
(850) 522-2100
(850) 522-2138 Fax
E-mail thru website
http://www.nwrls.lib.fl.us/index.html
Local History Collection

Boca Raton Public Library
200 NW Boca Raton Boulevard
Boca Raton, FL
(561) 393-7852
http://www.bocalibrary.org/

Boynton Beach City Library
208 South Seacrest Boulevard
Boynton Teach, FL 33435
(561) 742-6390
E-mail thru website
http://www.boyntonlibrary.org/

Brevard County Library System
201 Polk Avenue
Cape Canaveral, FL 32920
(321) 868-1101
iescapa@brev.org
http://www.brev.org/

Brockway Memorial Library
10021 NE Second Avenue
Miami Shores, FL 33138
(305) 758-8107
http://www.brockwaylibrary.
   org:8080/webopac/main?type=4
Miami Shores Archives

Charlotte County Library System
Port Charlotte Public Library
2280 Aaron Street
Port Charlotte, FL 33952
(941) 625-6470
(941) 743-4898 Fax
E-mail thru website
http://www.charlottecountyfl.com/
   library/

Citrus County Library System
425 W. Roosevelt Blvd.
Beverly Hills, FL 34465-4281
(352) 746-9077
(352) 746-9493 Fax
http://www.citruslibraries.org/

Clay County Public Library System
1895 Town Center Boulevard
Orange Park, FL 32003
(904) 278-3720
E-mail thru website
http://www.ccpl.lib.fl.us/

Clearwater Public Libraries
69 Bay Esplanade
Clearwater Beach, FL 33767
(727) 562-4970
E-mail thru website
http://www.clearwater-fl.com/cpl/

Collier County Public Library
2385 Orange Blossom Drive
Naples, FL 34109
(239) 593-3511
E-mail thru website
http://www.collier-lib.org/

Delray Beach Public Library
100 West Atlantic Avenue
Delray Beach, FL 33444
(561)266-9488
(561)266-9757 Fax
alan.kornblau@delraylibrary.org
http://www.delraylibrary.org/

East Lake Community Library
4125 East Lake Road
Palm Harbor, FL 34685
(727) 773-2665
eastlakelibrary@hotmail.com
http://www.eastlakelibrary.org/

Eustis Memorial Library
120 North Center Street
Eustis, FL 32726
(352) 357-6110
contactus@eustismemoriallibrary.
    org http://www.eustismemorial
    library.org

Flagler County Public Library
2500 Palm Coast Parkway NW
Palm Coast, FL 32137
(386) 446-6763
(386) 446-6773 Fax
E-mail thru website
http://www.flaglerlibrary.org/
John A. Clegg History Room

Franklin County Public Library
148 8th Street
Apalachicola, FL 32329
(850) 653-2784
ondra@franklin.lib.fl.us
http://www.fcpl.lib.fl.us/

Gulf Beaches Public Library
200 Municipal Drive
Madeira Beach, FL 33708
(727) 391-2828
E-mail thru website
http://gulfbeacheslib.org/

Gulfport Public Library
5501 28th Avenue South
Gulfport, FL 33707
(727) 893-1073
(727) 893-1072 Fax
gpublib@yahoo.com
http://www.tblc.org/gpl/

Heartland Library Cooperative
Avon Park Public Library
100 North Museum Avenue
Avon Park, FL 33825
(863) 452-3803
http://www.myhlc.org/apl/

Hendry County Library System
Clewiston Public Library
120 W. Osceola Avenue
Clewiston, FL 33440
(863) 983-1493
(863) 983-9194 Fax
clewiston@hendrylibraries.org
http://www.hendrylibraries.org/
   clewiston.htm

Hernando County Public Library
238 Howell Avenue
Brooksville, FL 34601
(352) 754-4043
hcplonline@tampabay.rr.com
http://www.hcpl.lib.fl.us/

Hillsborough County Public Library Cooperative
John F. Germany Public Library
900 North Ashley Drive
Tampa, Florida 33602
(813) 273-3652
http://www.hcplc.org/hcplc/
   liblocales/jfg/

Indian River County Library System
1600 21st Street
Vero Beach, FL 32960
(772) 770-5060
(772) 770-5066 Fax
http://www.irclibrary.org/

Jacksonville Public Library
303 N. Laura Street
Jacksonville, FL 32202
(904) 630-2665
E-mail thru website
http://jpl.coj.net/
The Freedom Shrine
International Languages Collection
Center Stage (opera on DVD)

Jefferson County Public Library
375 South Water St.
Monticello, Florida 32344
(850) 342-0205
(850) 342-0207 Fax
http://www.jefferson.lib.fl.us/

Lake County Library System
2401 Woodlea Road
Tavares, FL 32778
(352) 253-6180
E-mail thru website
http://www.lakeline.lib.fl.us/

Lake Park Public Library
529 Park Avenue
Lake Park, FL 33403
(561) 881-3330
askhere@lakeparkflorida.gov
http://www.lakepark-fl.gov/

Lake Wales Public Library
290 Cypress Gardens Lane
Lake Wales, FL 33853
(863) 678-4004
(863) 678-4051 Fax
peakt@pclc.lib.fl.us
http://www.cityoflakewales.com/
   library/index.shtml

Lake Worth Public Library
15 North M Street
Lake Worth, FL 33460
(561) 533-7354
(561) 586-1651 Fax
lwreference@lakeworth.org
http://lakeworth.govoffice.com/
    index.asp?Type=B_BASIC&SEC
    ={D4A82210-BB5D-4782-A298-
    DEA0789605CB}

Lakeland Public Library
100 Lake Morton Drive
Lakeland, FL 33801
(863) 834-4280
(863) 834-4293 Fax
lisa.lilyquist@lakelandgov.net
http://www.lakelandgov.net/library/
    home.html

Lee County Library System
Library Administration
2345 Union Street
Fort Myers, FL 33901
(239) 479-4636
E-mail thru website
http://www3.leegov.com/library/

Leesburg Public Library
100 East Main Street
Leesburg, FL 34748
(352) 728-9790
E-mail thru website
http://www.leesburgflorida.gov/library/

**LeRoy Collins Leon County Public
Library**
200 West Park Avenue
Tallahassee, FL 32301
(850) 606-2665
moellerh@leoncountyfl.gov
http://www.leoncountyfl.gov/library/

**Levy County Public Library
System**
P. O. Box 1210
Bronson, FL 32621
(352) 486-5552
(352) 486-5553 Fax
http://www.levy.lib.fl.us/rooms/
    portal/page/Sirsi_HOME

Liberty County Public Library
P. O. Box 697
Bristol, FL 32321
(850) 643-2247
(850) 643-2208 Fax
dseverance@nwrls.lib.fl.us
http://www.tfn.net/Liberty_Library/
    menu.html

Lynn Haven Library
901 Ohio Avenue
Lynn Haven, FL 32444
(850) 265-2781
(850) 265-7311 Fax
http://www.youseemore.com/
    lynnhaven/

Maitland Public Library
501 South Maitland Avenue
Maitland, FL 32751
(407) 647-7700
E-mail thru website
http://www.maitlandpubliclibrary.org/

Manatee County Library System
1301 Barcarrota Blvd. West
Bradenton, FL 34205
(941) 748-5555
(941) 749-7191 Fax
E-mail thru website
http://www.co.manatee.fl.us/library/
    master.html
Historic images

Martin County Library System
Blake Library
2351 S.E. Monterey Road
Stuart, FL 34996
(772) 288-5702
(772) 219-4959 Fax
library@martin.fl.us
http://www.library.martin.fl.us/

Miami-Dade Public Library
101 West Flagler Street
Miami, FL 33130
(305) 375-5184
E-mail thru website
http://www.mdpls.org/

Monroe County Library
700 Fleming Street
Key West, FL 33040
(305)292-3595
(305) 295-3626 Fax
dunn-christine@monroecounty-fl.gov
http://www.monroecounty-fl.gov/
    pages/MonroeCoFL_Library/index

Nassau Public Library System
Yulee Branch
FCCJ Campus
76346 William Burgess Boulevard
Yulee, FL 32097
(904) 548-4467
E-mail thru website
http://sirsi.nassau.lib.fl.us/

New Port Richey Public Library
5939 Main Street
New Port Richey, FL 34652
(727) 853-1279
(727) 853-1280 Fax
sddillinger@gmail.com
http://www.nprlibrary.org/home.html

New River Public Library Cooperative
103 North Lake Avenue
Lake Butler, FL 32054
(386) 496-2526
http://www.newriver.lib.fl.us/

Niceville Public Library
206 North Partin Drive
Niceville, FL 32578
(850) 729-4070
(850) 729-4053 Fax
sbishop@okaloosa.lib.fl.us
http://www.readokaloosa.org/
    details_nville.html
http://cityofniceville.org/library.html

North Indian River County Library
1001 Sebastian Boulevard (CR512)
Sebastian, FL 32958
(772) 589-1355
E-mail via blog linked to website
http://www.irclibrary.org/sebastian
    library/index.html

North Miami Public Library
835 NE 132nd Street
North Miami, FL 33161
(305) 891-5535
(305) 892-0843 Fax
library@northmiamifl.gov
http://www.northmiamifl.gov/
    community/library/

**Okaloosa County Public Library
Cooperative**
Niceville Public Library
206 North Partin Drive
Niceville, FL 32578
(850) 729-4070
(850) 729-4053 Fax
sbishop@okaloosa.lib.fl.us
http://www.readokaloosa.org/

Oldsmar Public Library
400 St. Petersburg Drive East
Oldsmar, FL 34677
(813) 749-1178
information@oldsmarlibrary.org
http://www.oldsmarlibrary.org/

**Orange County Library
System**
Orlando Public Library
101 E. Central Boulevard
Orlando, FL 32801
(407) 835-7323
(407) 835-7649 Fax
helpdesk@ocls.info.
http://www.ocls.lib.fl.us/Default.
   asp?bhcp=1

Osceola Library System
211 East Dakin Avenue
Kissimmee, FL 34741
(407) 742-8888
thelibrary@osceola.org
http://osceolalibrary.org/

Palm Beach County Library System
3650 Summit Boulevard
West Palm Beach, FL 33406
(561) 233-2600
E-mail thru website
http://www.pbclibrary.org/
Centennial Celebration

Palm Harbor Library
2330 Nebraska Avenue
Palm Harbor, FL 34683
(727) 784-3332
(727) 785-6543 Fax
gene@phlib.org
http://www.palmharborlibrary.org/

**Panhandle Public Library
Cooperative System**
2925 Optimist Drive
Marianna, FL 32448
(850) 482-9296
(850) 482-9297 Fax
Admin@pplcs.net
http://www.pplcs.net/

Pinellas Park Public Library
7770 52nd Street
Pinellas Park, FL 33781
(727) 541-0718
pnpkref01@tblc.org
http://pppl.tblc.lib.fl.us/

**Pinellas Public Library
Cooperative**
1330 Cleveland Street
Clearwater, FL 33755
(727) 441-8408
(727) 441-8938 Fax
http://www.pplc.us/
Wickman Collection (nautical)
Leadership Collection
Florida Collection
African-American Collection

Polk County Library Cooperative
2150 S. Broadway Avenue
Bartow, FL 33830
(863) 519-7958
(863) 534-0913 Fax
E-mail thru website
http://www.pclc.lib.fl.us/

Riviera Beach Public Library
600 West Blue Heron Boulevard
Riviera Beach, FL 33404
(561) 845-4195
(561) 881-7308 Fax
library@rivierabch.com
http://www.rivierabch.com/page.
   asp?PageId=52
African-American Room

Safety Harbor Public Library
101 Second Street North
Safety Harbor, FL 34695
(727) 724-1525
shplref@pplc.us
http://www.tblc.org/shpl/

Sanibel Public Library
770 Dunlop Road
Sanibel, FL 33957
(239) 472-2483
(239) 472-9524 Fax
http://www.sanlib.org/index2.html

Sarasota County Library System
1660 Ringling Boulevard
Sarasota, FL 34236
(941) 861-5468
libraryinfo@scgov.net
http://www.sclibs.net/Default.aspx

Seminole County Public Library
215 North Oxford Road
Casselberry, FL 32707
Phone: (407) 665-1505
Fax: (407) 665-1510
JPeterson@seminolecountyfl.gov
http://www.seminolecountyfl.gov/
   lls/library/

St. Lucie County Library System
7605 Santa Barbara Drive
Fort Pierce, FL 34951
(772) 462-6870
(772) 462-6874 Fax
ShroyerC@stlucieco.org
http://www.st-lucie.lib.fl.us/

St. Pete Beach Library
365 73rd Avenue
St. Pete Beach, FL 33706
(727) 363-9238
libadmin@stpetebeach.org
http://www.tblc.org/spb/
England/Eisle of Wright resources
Florida statutes
Morningstar Reports
SPB government documents

State Library of Florida
R.A. Gray Building
500 South Bronough Street
Tallahassee, FL 32399
(850) 245-6600
(850) 245-6651 Fax
cmoloney@dos.state.fl.us
http://dlis.dos.state.fl.us/library/
The Florida Collection
Florida Documents Collection
Federal Documents Collection

Suwannee River Regional Library
1848 Ohio/Dr. Martin Luther King
Jr. Ave S
Live Oak, FL 32064
(386) 362-2317
E-mail thru website
http://www.neflin.org/srrl/

**Tampa-Hillsborough County
Public Library System**
John F. Germany Public Library
900 North Ashley Drive
Tampa, Florida 33602
(813) 273-3652
http://www.thpl.org/

Tarpon Springs Public Library
138 East Lemon Street
Tarpon Springs, FL 34689
(727) 943-4922
(727) 943-4926 Fax
tslref@gmail.com
http://www.tblc.org/tarpon/

**Three Rivers Regional Library
System**
P.O. Box 1340
Mayo, FL 32066
(386) 294-3858
(386) 294-3861 Fax
shurd@neflin.org
http://www.3rivers.lib.fl.us/

Volusia County Public Library
1290 Indian Lake Road
Daytona Beach, FL 32124
(386) 248-1745
llcolee@co.volusia.fl.us
http://merlin.vcpl.lib.fl.us/
Environmental studies materials

Wakulla County Public Library
P. O. Box 1300
Crawfordville, FL 32326
(850) 926-7415
(850) 926-4513 Fax
E-mail thru website
http://www.wakullalibrary.org/

Walton County Library
3 Circle Drive
DeFuniak Springs, FL 32433
(850) 892-3624
(850) 892-4438 Fax
E-mail thru website
http://www.youseemore.com/walton/

West Florida Regional Library
200 West Gregory Street
Pensacola, Florida 32501
Main Number (850) 436-5060
(850) 436-5039 Fax
gfischer@ci.pensacola.fl.us
http://www.cityofpensacola.com/
  library/

West Palm Beach Public Library
411 Clematis Street
West Palm Beach, FL 33401
(561) 868-7701
(561) 868-7706 Fax
E-mail thru website
http://www.wpbpl.com/

**Wilderness Coast Public
Libraries**
1180 West Washington Street
Monticello, FL 32344
(850) 997-7400
(850) 997-7403 Fax
cturner@wildernesscoast.org
http://www.wild.lib.fl.us/

Winter Haven Public Library
325 Avenue A, NW
Winter Haven, FL 33881
(863) 291-5880
(863) 291-5889 Fax
jbeard@mywinterhaven.com
http://whpl.mywinterhaven.com/

Winter Park Public Library
460 E. New England Avenue
Winter Park, FL 32789
(407) 623-3300
rmelanson@wppl.org
http://www.wppl.org/

GEORGIA

Athens-Clarke County Library
2025 Baxter Street
Athens, Georgia 30606
(706) 613-3650
refdesk@athenslibrary.org
http://www.clarke.public.lib.ga.us/
Heritage Room (regional resources)

Atlanta-Fulton Public Library System
One Margaret Mitchell Square
Atlanta, GA 30303
(404) 730-1700
(404) 730-1989 Fax
referenceline@co.fulton.ga.us
http://www.afplweb.com/cms/

Bartow County Library System
429 West Main Street
Cartersville, GA 30120
(770) 382-4203
info@bartowlibrary.org
http://www.bartowlibraryonline.org/

Bartram Trail Regional Library System
Mary Willis Library
204 East Liberty Street
Washington, GA 30673
(706) 678-7736
(706) 678-1615 Fax
willism@btrl.net
http://www.wilkes.public.lib.ga.us/

Brooks County Public Library
404 Barwick Road
Quitman, GA 3
(229) 263-4412
(229) 263-8002 Fax
brookscpl@yahoo.com
http://brooks.public.lib.ga.us/

Chattahoochee Valley Libraries
3000 Macon Road
Columbus, GA 31906
(706) 243-2669
(706) 243-2710 Fax
contact@cvrls.net
http://www.thecolumbuslibrary.org/

Cherokee Regional Library
Dade County Library
P.O. Box 340
Trenton, GA 30752
(706) 657-7857
(706) 657-7860 Fax
jtrubey@chrl.org
http://www.walker.public.lib.ga.us/
Georgia History Room

Chestatee Regional Library System
Dawson County Library
342 Allen Street
Dawsonville, GA 30534
(706) 344-3690
cgibson@chestateelibrary.org
  http://www.chestateelibrary.org/
Local history

Clayton County Library System
865 Battle Creek Road
Jonesboro, GA 30236
(770) 473-3850
(770) 473-3858 Fax
E-mail thru website
http://www.claytonpl.org/index.asp

Coastal Plain Regional Library
2014 Chestnut Avenue
Tifton, GA 31794
(229) 386-3400
(229) 386-7007 Fax
http://www.cprl.org/

Cobb County Public Library
266 Roswell Street
Marietta, GA 30060
(770) 528-2320
evigil@speakeasy.net
http://www.cobbcat.org/
The Georgia Room

Conyers-Rockdale Library System
864 Green Street
Conyers, GA 30012
(770) 388-5041
(770) 388-5043 Fax
http://www.conyersrockdalelibrary.
  org/

DeKalb County Public Library
215 Sycamore Street
Decatur, GA 30030
(404) 370-8450
(404) 370-8469 Fax
E-mail thru website
http://www.dekalb.public.lib.ga.us/

Dougherty County Public Library
Central Library
300 Pine Avenue
Albany, GA 31701
(229) 420-3200
http://www.docolib.org/

East Central Georgia Regional Library
902 Greene Street
Augusta, GA 30901
(706) 821-2600
swintg@ecgrl.org
http://www.ecgrl.public.lib.ga.us/
Augusta Chronicle Archives

Forsyth County Public Library
585 Dahlonega Road
Cumming, GA 30040
(770) 781-9840
E-mail thru website
http://www.forsythpl.org/

Gwinnett County Public Library
1001 Lawrenceville Highway
Lawrenceville, GA 30045-4707
(770) 822-4522
(770) 822-5379 Fax
E-mail thru website
http://www.gwinnettpl.org/index.html

Hall County Library System
127 Main Street, NW
Gainesville, GA 30501
(770) 532-3311
amixson@hallcountylibrary.org
http://www.hallcountylibrary.org/
Black history photos
Historical photos

Hart County Library
150 Benson Street
Hartwell, GA 30643
(706) 376-4655
(706) 376-1157 Fax
info@hartcountylibrary.com
http://www.hartcountylibrary.com/
    modules/news

Henry County Library System
McDonough Public Library
1001 Florence McGarity Boulevard
McDonough, GA 30252
(770) 954-2806
(770) 954-2808 Fax
E-mail thru website
http://www.henry.public.lib.ga.us/

Houston County Public Library
1201 Washington Avenue
Perry, GA 31069
(478) 987-3050
E-mail thru website
http://www.houpl.org/

Jefferson County Library System
306 East Broad Street
Louisville, GA 30434
(478) 625-3751
(478) 625-7683 Fax
http://www.jefferson.public.lib.ga.us/

**Lake Blackshear Regional Library
System**
320 Tripp Street
Americus, GA 31709
(229) 924-8091
info@lbris.org
http://www.lbrls.org/

Lee County Library
245 Walnut Avenue, South
Leesburg, GA 31763
(229) 759-2369
(229) 759-2326 Fax
leavy@leecountylibrary.org
http://www.leecountylibrary.org/

Live Oak Public Libraries
2002 Bull Street
Savannah, GA 31401
(912) 652-3600
(912) 652-3638 Fax
E-mail thru website
http://www.liveoakpl.org/

**Middle Georgia Regional Library
System**
Washington Memorial Library
1180 Washington Avenue
Macon, GA 31201
(478) 744-0800
(478) 742-3161 Fax
jonest@bibblib.org
http://www.co.bibb.ga.us/library/
Middle Georgia Archives

Montezuma Public Library
506 North Dooly Street
Montezuma, GA 31063
(478) 472-9597 or 6095
(478) 472-5626 Fax
mgrlmo@mail.macon.public.lib.ga.us
http://www.montezuma-ga.org/
    library.htm

Mountain Regional Library System
P. O. Box 159
Young Harris, GA 30582
(706) 379-3732
(706) 379-2047 Fax
mountain@mountainregional
　library.org
http://www.mountainregional
　library.org/

Newnan-Coweta Public Library System
A. Mitchell Powell Jr. Public Library
25 Hospital Road
Newnan, GA 30263
(770) 253-3625
(770) 254-7262 Fax
referencedesk@newnan-coweta.org
http://www.newnan-coweta.org/

Newton County Library System
7116 Floyd Street
Covington, GA 30014
(770) 787-3231
(770) 784-2092 Fax
library@newtonlibrary.org
http://www.newtonlibrary.org/

Northwest Georgia Regional Library System
310 Cappes Street
Dalton, GA 30720
(706) 876-1360
suggestions@ngrl.org
http://www.ngrl.org/
Local history

Ocmulgee Regional Library System
531 Second Avenue
Eastman, GA 31023
(478) 374-4711
http://www.orls.org/

Oconee Regional Library
Laurens County Library
801 Bellevue Avenue
Dublin, GA 31021
(478) 272-5710
(478) 275-5381 Fax
http://www.ocrl.org/

Ohoopee Regional Library System
610 Jackson Street
Vidalia, GA 30474
(912) 537-9283
(912) 537-3735 Fax
vidalialib@ohoopeelibrary.org
http://www.toombs.public.lib.ga.us/

Peach Public Libraries
315 Martin Luther King Jr. Drive
Fort Valley, GA 31030
(478) 825-1640
(478) 825-2061 Fax
trippb@mail.peach.public.lib.ga.us
http://www.peach.public.lib.ga.us/

Roddenbery Memorial Library
320 North Broad Street
Cairo, GA 39828
(229) 377-3632
(229) 377-7204 Fax
rml@rmlibrary.org
http://www.rmlibrary.org/

Sara Hightower Regional Library System
205 RiverSide Parkway NE
Rome, GA 30161
(706) 236-4611
E-mail thru website
http://www.romelibrary.org/
Heritage Room

Satilla Regional Library System
200 S. Madison Avenue, Suite D
Douglas, GA 31533
(912) 384-4667
(912) 389-4365 Fax
douglib@srlsys.org
http://www.srlsys.org/

Screven-Jenkins Regional Library System
223 Daniel Street
Millen, GA 30442
(478) 982-4244
(478) 982-2192 Fax
http://www.sjrls.org/

Sequoya Regional Library System
116 Brown Industrial Parkway
Canton, GA 30114
(770) 479-3090
(770) 479-3069 Fax
kickern@seqlib.org
http://www.sequoyahregionalli
   brary.org/

South Georgia Regional Library
300 Woodrow Wilson Drive
Valdosta, GA 31602
(229) 333-0086
(229) 333-7669 Fax
sgrl@sgrl.org
http://www.sgrl.org/
Translated Japanese book collection

Southwest Georgia Regional Library System
Gilbert H. Gragg Library
301 South Monroe Street
Bainbridge, GA 39819
(229) 248-2665
(229) 248-2670 Fax
librarian@swgrl.org
http://www.swgrl.org/

Statesboro Regional Library System
124 South Main Street
Statesboro, GA 30458
(912) 764-1341
http://strl.info/

Three Rivers Regional Library System
Brunswick-Glynn County Public Library
208 Gloucester Street
Brunswick, GA 31520
(912) 267-1212
(912) 267-9597 Fax
http://www.trrl.org/

Troup-Harris Regional Library
LeGrange Memorial Library
115 Alford Street
LaGrange, GA 30240
(706) 882-7784
info@thclibrary.net
http://www.thclibrary.net/

Twin Lakes Library System
Mary Vinson Memorial Library
151 South Jefferson Street
Milledgeville, GA 31061
(478) 452-0677
barryreese@tllsga.org
http://www.twinlakeslibrarysystem.org/

Uncle Remus Regional Library System
1131 East Avenue
Madison, GA 30650
(706) 342-4974
(706) 342-4510 Fax
http://www.uncleremus.org/#

West Georgia Regional Library
710 Rome Street
Carrollton, GA 30117
(770) 836-6711
(770) 836-4787 Fax
cooperj@wgrl.net
http://www.wgrl.org/

HAWAII

IDAHO

Ada Community Library
10664 W. Victory Road
Boise, ID 83709
(208) 362-0181
askit@adalib.org
http://www.adalib.org/

Boise Public Library
715 S. Capitol Boulevard
Boise, ID 83702
(208) 384-4076
kbooe@cityofboise.org
http://www.boisepubliclibrary.org

Burley Public Library
1300 Miller Avenue
Burley, ID 83318
(208) 878-7708
E-mail thru website
http://www.bplibrary.org/

Clearwater Memorial Public Library
P. O. Box 471
Orofino, ID 83544
(208) 476-3411
email.cmp@valnet.org
http://orofinolibrary.org/

Coeur d'Alene Public Library
702 E. Front
Coeur d'Alene, ID 83814
(208)769-2315
(208)769-2381 Fax
info@cdalibrary.org
http://www.cdalibrary.org/

Council Valley Library
104 California Avenue
Council, ID 83612
(208) 253-6004
cvfl@ctcweb.net http://home.
  ctcweb.net/~cvfl/

Eagle Public Library
100 N Stierman Way
Eagle, ID 83616
(208) 939-6814
(208) 939-1359 Fax
eaglelibrary@cityofeagle.org
http://www.eaglepubliclibrary.org/

East Bonner County Library District
1407 Cedar Street
Sandpoint, ID 83864
(208) 263-6930
infodesk@ebcl.lib.id.us
http://www.ebcl.lib.id.us/ebcl/

Garden City Library
6015 Glenwood Street
Garden City, ID 83714
(208) 472-2940
E-mail thru website
http://gardencity.lili.org/

Grangeville Centennial Library
215 W. North Street
Grangeville, ID 83530
(208) 983-0951
(208) 983-2336 Fax
library@grangeville.us
http://www.centennial-library.org/

Hailey Public Library
7 West Croy
Hailey, ID 83333
(208) 788-2036
E-mail thru website
http://www.haileypubliclibrary.org/

Idaho Falls Public Library
457 W. Broadway
Idaho Falls, ID 83402
(208) 612-8460
library@ifpl.org
http://www.ifpl.org/

Idaho State Library
325 W. State Street
Boise, ID, 83702
(208) 334-2150
E-mail thru website
http://www.lili.org/portal/index.php

Kootenai-Shoshone Area Libraries
8385 N. Government Way
Hayden ID 83835
(208) 772-5612
hay@cin.kcl.org
http://ksalibraries.org/

Latah County Library District
110 S. Jefferson
Moscow, ID 83843
(208) 882-3925
annec@latahlibrary.org
http://www.latahlibrary.org/

Lewiston Public Library
428 Thain Road
Lewiston, ID 83501
(208) 743-6519
dwittman.lew@valnet.org
http://www.cityoflewiston.org/
   index.asp?nid=91

Marshall Public Library
113 S. Garfield Avenue
Pocatello, ID 83204
(208) 232-1263
(208) 232-9266 Fax
ref@marshallpl.org
http://www.marshallpl.org/

Meridian Library District
1326 W. Cherry Lane
Meridian, ID 83642
(208) 888-4451
director@mld.org
http://www.mld.org/

Mountain Home Public Library
790 North 10th East
Mountain Home, ID 83647
(208) 587-4716
(208) 580-2051
(208) 587-6645 Fax
E-mail thru website
http://mountainhome.lili.org/

Nampa Public Library
101 Eleventh Avenue S.
Nampa, ID 83651
(208) 468-5800
info@nampalibrary.org.
http://www.nampalibrary.org/

N. Bingham County District Library
[no address given]
(208) 357-7801
Librarian%3cheidir@ida.net%3e
(or thru website)
http://www.ida.net/org/nbcdl/

Oneida County Library
P. O. Box 185
Malad, ID 83252
(208) 766-2229 Phone/Fax
oclib@atcnet.net
http://www.maladidaho.org/library/

Portneuf District Library
5210 Stuart Avenue
Chubbuck, ID 83202
(208) 237-2192
E-mail thru website
http://portneuf.lili.org/

Post Falls Public Library
821 N. Spokane Street
Post Falls, ID 83854
(208) 773-1506
jreiss@cin.kcl.org
http://postfallslibrary.kcl.org/

Salmon River Public Library
126 N. Main Street
Riggins, ID 83549
(208) 628-3394
http://www.rigginsidaho.org/
   library.html
Book repair service

St. Maries Public Library
822 College Avenue
St. Maries, ID 83861
(208) 245-3732
smlibrary@smgazette.com http://
   www.stmariesidaho.com/library/

Sugar-Salem Community Library
#1 Digger Drive
Sugar City, ID 83448
(208) 356-0271
(208) 359-3167 Fax
http://www.sugarlib.org/

Twin Falls Public Library
201 Fourth Avenue E
Twin Falls, ID 83301
(208) 733-2964
E-mail thru website
http://twinfallspubliclibrary.org/

Weippe Public Library
P. O. Box 435
Weippe, ID 83553
(208) 435-4058
(208) 435-4374 Fax
weippelibrary@weippe.com
http://weippelibrary.org/

ILLINOIS

Acorn Public Library District
15624 South Central Avenue
Oak Forest, IL 60452
(708) 687-3700
(708) 698-3712 Fax
acorn@acornlibrary.org
http://www.acornlibrary.org/

Addison Public Library
4 Friendship Plaza
Addison, IL 60101
(630) 543-3617
(630) 543-7275 Fax
E-mail thru website
http://www.addisonlibrary.org/
Special collections in Spanish,
    Polish, Italian and Albanian
    languages

**Algonquin Area Public Library
District**
2600 Harnish Drive
Algonquin, IL 60102
(847) 458-6060
E-mail thru website
http://www.aapld.org

Alpha Park Public Library
3527 South Airport Road
Bartonville, IL 61607
(309) 697-3822
(309) 697-9681
alpha@alphapark.org
http://www.alphapark.org/

**Alsip-Merrionette Park Public
Library District**
11960 South Pulaski
Alsip, IL 60803
(708) 371-5666
(708) 371-5672 Fax
ampl@sslic.net
http://www.alsiplibrary.net/

**Arlington Heights Memorial
Library**
500 North Dunton Avenue
Arlington Heights, IL 60004
(847) 392-0100
(847) 506-2650 Fax
E-mail thru website
http://www.ahml.info/

Astoria Public Library District
220 West Broadway
Astoria, IL 61501
(309) 329-2423
(309) 329-2842 Fax
astorlib@astoriail.net
http://www.astoria.lib.il.us/

Aurora Public Library
1 East Benton Street
Aurora, IL 60505
(630) 264-4100
E-mail thru website
http://www.aurora.lib.il.us/

Barclay Public Library District
P. O. Box 349
Warrensburg, IL 62573
(217) 672-3621
(217) 672-8404 Fax
E-mail thru website
http://barclay.lib.il.us/

Barrington Public Library District
505 N. Northwest Highway
Barrington, IL 60010
(847) 382-1300
adultref@barringtonarealibrary.org
http://www.barringtonarealibrary.org/

Bartlett Public Library District
800 South Bartlett Road
Bartlett, IL 60103
(630) 837-2855
ideas@bartlett.lib.il.us
http://www.bartlett.lib.il.us/

Batavia Public Library District
10 South Batavia Avenue
Batavia, IL 60510
(630) 879-1393
(630) 879-9118 Fax
askus@bataviapubliclibrary.org
http://www.batavia.lib.il.us/home/
   bataviapubliclibraryhome.htm

Bedford Park Public Library District
7816 West 65th Place
Bedford Park, IL 60501
(708) 458-6826
http://www.bplib.net/

Bellwood Public Library
600 Bohland Avenue
Bellwood, IL 60104
(708) 547-7393
(708) 547-9352 Fax
bws@bellwoodlibrary.org
http://www.bellwoodlibrary.org/

Bensenville Community Public Library
200 South Church Road
Bensenville, IL 60106
(630) 766-4642
(630) 766-0788 Fax
bcplref@gmail.com
http://www.bensenville.lib.il.us/

Benton Public Library District
502 South Main Street
Benton, IL 62812
(618) 438-7511
erins@shawls.lib.il.us
http://www.benton.lib.il.us/

Berwyn Public Library
2701 South Harlem Avenue
Berwyn, IL 60402
(708) 795-8000
(708) 795-8101 Fax
http://www.berwynlibrary.org/

Bethalto Public Library District
321 South Prairie Street
Bethalto, IL 62010
(618) 377-8141
(618) 377-3520 Fax
bee@lcls.org
http://www.bethaltolibrary.org/

Bloomingdale Public Library
101 Fairfield Way
Bloomingdale, IL 60108
(630) 529-3120
(630) 529-3243 Fax
tjarzemsky@mybpl.org
http://www.mybpl.org/bpl/

Bloomington Public Library
P. O. Box 3308
Bloomington, IL 61702
(309) 828-6091
E-mail thru website
http://www.bloomingtonlibrary.org/

Blue Island Public Library
2433 York Street
Blue Island, IL 60406
(708) 388-1078
(708) 388-1143 Fax
E-mail thru website
http://www.blueislandlibrary.org/

Boubonnais Public Library District
250 W. John Casey Road
Boubonnais, IL 60914
(815) 933-1727
(815) 933-1961 Fax
kpierson@bourbonnais.lib.il.us
http://bourbonnais.lib.il.us/

Bradley Public Library District
296 North Fulton Avenue
Bradley, IL 60915
(815) 932-6245
info@bradleylibrary.org
http://www.bradleylibrary.org

Brimfield Public Library District
111 South Galena Street
Brimfield, IL 61517
(309) 446-9575
(309) 446-9357 Fax
psmith@brimfieldlibrary.org
http://brimfieldlibrary.org

Broadview Public Library District
2226 South 16th Avenue
Broadview, IL 60155
(708) 345-1325
(708) 345-5024 Fax
E-mail thru website
http://www.broadviewlibrary.org/

Brookfield Public Library
3609 Grand Boulevard
Brookfield, IL 60513
(708) 485-6917
(708) 485-5172 Fax
E-mail thru website
http://www.brookfieldpubliclibrary.
   info/

Bryan-Bennett Library
P. O. Box 864
Salem, IL 62881
(618) 548-3006
E-mail thru website
http://www.salembbl.lib.il.us/

Byron Public Library District
109 N. Franklin Street
Byron, IL 61010
(815) 234-5107
(815) 234-5582 Fax
library@byron.lib.il.us
http://www.byron.lib.il.us/

Cahokia Public Library
140 Cahokia Park Drive
Cahokia, IL 62206
(618) 332-1491
(618) 332-1104 Fax
E-mail thru website
http://cahokialibrary.org/

Calumet City Public Library
660 Manistee Avenue
Calumet City, IL 60409
(708) 862-6220,
http://www.calumetcitypl.org/

Carbondale Public Library
405 West Main
Carbondale, IL 62901
(618) 457-0354
(618) 457-0353 Fax
E-mail thru website
http://www.carbondale.lib.il.us/

Carol Stream Public Library
616 Hiawatha Drive
Carol Stream, IL 60188
(630) 653-0755
(630) 653-6809 Fax
cstream@cslibrary.org
http://www.cslibrary.org/

Carterville Public Library
117 South Division Street
Carterville, IL 62918
(618) 985-3298
http://www.carterville.lib.il.us/

Carthage Public Library District
500 Wabash Avenue
Carthage, IL 62321
(217) 357-3232
(217) 357-2392 Fax
cartlib@adams.net
http://www.carthage.lib.il.us/

Central Citizen's Library District
1134 East 3100 North Road, Suite C
Clifton, IL 60927
(815) 694-2800
(815) 694-3200 Fax
rwellborn@cusd4.org
http://www.ccld.org/

Centralia Regional Library District
515 E. Broadway
Centralia, IL 62801
(618) 532-5222
E-mail thru website
http://www.centralialibrary.org/

Centreville Public Library
P. O. Box 1260
Centreville, IL 62207
(618) 271-2040
(618) 271-6893 Fax
centreville@digitalesl.org
http://www.centrevillelibrary.org/

Chadwick Public Library District
P. O. Box 416
Chadwick, IL 61014
(815) 684-5215 Phone/Fax
jonellc@chadwicklibrary.org
http://chadwicklibrary.org/

Champaign Public Library
Clara Lane
200 West Green Street
Champaign, IL 61820
(217) 403-2070
(217) 403-2053 Fax
mgrove@champaign.org
http://www.champaign.org/

Charles B. Phillips Public Library District
P. O. Box 156
Newark, IL 60541
(815) 695-5851
(815) 695-5804 Fax
E-mail thru website
http://www.cbplib.us/

Charlston Carnegie Public Library
712 Sixth Street
Charlston, IL 61920
(217) 345-4913
(217) 348-5616 Fax
charlstonlibrary@yahoo.com
http://www.charlestonlibrary.org/
Local history
Historic photos

Chatham Area Public Library
600 East Spruce Street
Chatham, IL 62629
(217) 483-2713
E-mail thru website
http://www.chatham.lib.il.us/

Chenoa Public Library District
211 South Division
Chenoa, IL 61726
(815) 945-4253
(815) 945-4203 Fax
chenoapl@verizon.net
http://www.chenoapublic.lib.il.us/

Cherry Valley Public Library District
755 East State Street
Cherry Valley, IL 61016
(815) 332-5161
http://www.cherryvalley.lib.il.us/

Chester Public Library
733 State Street
Chester, IL 62233
(618) 826-3711
(618) 826-2733 Fax
graht@shawls.lib.il.us
chesterlibrary@shawls.lib.il.us
http://www.chester.lib.il.us/

Chicago Public Library
400 South State Street
Chicago, IL 60605
(312) 747-4070
http://www.chipublib.org/

Chicago Ridge Public Library
10400 South Oxford Avenue
Chicago Ridge, IL 60415
(708) 423-7753
(708) 423-2758 Fax
http://www.chicagoridge.lib.il.us/

Chillicothe Public Library District
430 North Bradley
Chillicothe, IL 61523
(309) 274-2719
(309) 274-3000 Fax
sdrissi@chillicothepubliclibrary.org
http://www.chillicothepubliclibrary.
  org/

City of Woodstock Public Library
414 West Judd Street
Woodstock, IL 60098
(815) 338-0542
library@woodstockil.gov
http://www.woodstockpublic
  library.org/

Clover Public Library District
440 North Division
Woodhull, IL 61490
(309) 334-2680
(309) 334-2378 Fax
wi_wood@winco.net
http://www.woodhull.lib.il.us/
  library/

Coal City Public Library District
85 North Garfield Street
Coal City, IL 60416
(815) 634-4552
(815) 634-2950 Fax
ccpld@coalcity.lib.il.us
http://coalcity.lib.il.us/
Local history

Collinsville Memorial Library Center
408 West Main Street
Collinsville, IL 62234
(618) 344-1112
(618) 345-6401 Fax
cve@lcls.org
http://www.collinsvillelibrary.org/

Columbia Public Library
106 North Metter Avenue
Columbia, IL 62236
(618) 281-4237
(618) 281-6977 Fax
ericapyle@lcls.org
http://www.columbialibrary.org/

Cook Memorial Public Library District
413 N. Milwaukee Ave.
Libertyville, IL 60048
(847) 362-2330
(847) 362-2354 Fax
E-mail thru website
http://www.cooklib.org/

Cortland Community Library
63 South Somonauk Road
Cortland, IL 60112
(815) 756-7274
114bc@tbcnet.com
http://www.cortlandlibrary.com/

Crab Orchard Public Library District
20012 Crab Orchard Road
Marion, IL 62959
(618) 982-2141
E-mail thru website
http://www.craborchard.lib.il.us/

Crete Public Library
1177 North Main Street
Crete, IL 60417
(708) 672-8017
schulten@sslic.net
http://www.cretelibrary.org/

Crystal Lake Public Library
126 Paddock Street
Crystal Lake, IL 60014
(815) 459-1687
(815) 459-9581 Fax
kmartens@crystallakelibrary.org
http://www.crystallakelibrary.org/

Danville Public Library
319 North Vermilion Street
Danville, IL 61832
(217) 477-5220
(217) 477-5230 Fax
bnolan@danville.lib.il.us
http://www.danville.lib.il.us/

Daugherty Public Library District
220 South Fifth Street
Dupo, IL 62239
(618) 286-4444
(618) 286-3636 Fax
E-mail thru website
http://www.dupolibrary.org/

Decatur Public Library
130 North Franklin Street
Decatur, IL 62523
(217) 424-2900
(217) 233-4071 Fax
lfisher@decatur.lib.il.us
http://www.decatur.lib.il.us/

Deerfield Public Library
920 Waukegan Road
Deerfield, IL 60015
(847) 945-3311
mpergander@deerfieldlibrary.org
http://www.deerfieldlibrary.org/
  deerfield/

**Des Plaines Valley Public Library
District**
Crest Hill Library Branch
1298 Theodore Street
Crest Hill, IL 60403
(815) 725-0234
(815) 725-3786 Fax
cresthill@dpvlib.org
http://www.dpvlib.org/

Dixon Public Library
221 South Hennepin Avenue
Dixon, IL 61021
(815) 284-7261
(815) 288-7323 Fax
roe@dixonpubliclibrary.org
http://www.dixonpubliclibrary.org/
Lincoln Collection
Local history, including Dixon
  Telegraph from 1851

Downers Grove Public Library
1050 Curtiss Street
Downers Grove, IL 60515
(630) 960-1200
(630) 960-9374 Fax
cbowen@downersgrovelibrary.org
http://www.downersgrovelibrary.org/

**Dundee Township Public Library
District**
555 Barrington Avenue
Dundee IL 60118
(847) 428-3661
(847) 428-0521 Fax
E-mail thru website
http://www.dundeelibrary.info/
  dundee/#

Earl Township Public Library
P. O. Box 420
Earlville, IL 60518
(815) 246-9543
(815) 246-6391 Fax
inquiry@earlvillelibrary.org
http://www.earlvillelibrary.org/

East Alton Public Library District
250 Washington Avenue
East Alton, IL 62024
(618) 259-0787
(618) 259-0788 Fax
eastaltonlibrary@gmail.org
http://www.eastaltonlibrary.org/

Ela Area Public Library District
275 Mohawk Trail
Lake Zurich, IL 60047
(847) 438-3433
E-mail thru website
http://www.eapl.org/

Ella Johnson Memorial Public Library
109 South State Street
Hampshire, IL 60140
(847) 683-4490
(847) 683-4493 Fax
library@ellajohnsonlibrary.org
http://www.ellajohnson.lib.il.us/

Eureka Public Library District
202 South Main Street
Eureka, IL 61530
(309) 467-2922
E-mail thru website
http://www.eurekapl.org/

Evanston Public Library
1703 Orrington Avenue
Evanston, IL 60201
(847) 448-8600
(847) 866-0313 Fax
director@epl.org
http://www.epl.org/

Fairfield Public Library
300 South East Second Street
Fairfield, IL 62837
(618) 842-4516
(618) 842-6708 Fax
mconard@shawls.lib.il.us
http://www.fairfield.lib.il.us

Forest Park Public Library
7555 Jackson Boulevard
Forest Park, IL 60130
(708) 366-7171
rbrayden@fppl.org
http://www.fppl.org/

Forsyth Public Library
P. O. Box 20
Forsyth, IL 62535
(217) 877-8174
(217) 877-3533 Fax
E-mail thru website
http://www.forsythlibrary.lib.il.us/
Donna Hoffman Memorial collection
   of children's books

Geneva Public Library
127 James Street
Geneva, IL 60134
(630) 232-0780
mteske@geneva.lib.il.us
http://www.geneva.lib.il.us/

Glencoe Public Library
320 Park Avenue
Glencoe, IL 60022
(847) 835-5056
(847) 835-5648 Fax
gckref@nsls.info
http://www.glencoe.lib.il.us/

Glenview Public Library
1930 Glenview Road
Glenview, IL 60025
(847) 729-7500
(847) 729-7682 Fax
E-mail thru website
http://www.glenviewpl.org/

Grande Prairie Public Library
3479 West 183rd Street
Hazel Crest, IL 60429
(708) 798-5563
(708) 798-5874 Fax
gpsreference@yahoo.com
http://www.grandeprairie.org/

Harrisburg District Library
2 West Walnut Street
Harrisburg, IL 62946
(618) 253-7455
(618) 252-1239 Fax
rmiller@shawls.lib.il.us
http://www.harrisburg.lib.il.us/
Local history

Harvey Public Library District
15441 Turlington
Harvey, IL 60426
(708) 331-0757
(708) 331-2835 Fax
has@harvey.lib.il.us
http://www.harvey.lib.il.us/

Hayner Public Library District
326 Belle Street
Alton, IL 62002
(618) 462-0677
(618) 462-0665 Fax
E-mail thru website
http://www.haynerlibrary.org/

Highland Park Public Library
494 Laurel Avenue
Highland Park, IL 60035
(847) 432-0216
(847) 432-9139 Fax
E-mail thru website
http://hppl.lib.il.us/

Hinsdale Public Library
20 East Maple Street
Hinsdale, IL 60521
(630) 986-1976
(630) 986-9654 Fax
administration@hinsdalelibrary.info
http://www.hinsdalelibrary.info/

Homewood Public Library
17917 Dixie Highway
Homewood, IL 60430
(708) 798-0121
hws@mls.lib.il.us
http://www.homewoodlibrary.org/

Kankakee Public Library
201 East Merchant Street
Kankakee, IL 60901
(815) 937-6901
sbertrand@lions-online.org
http://www.kankakee.lib.il.us/

Lillie M. Evans Library District
P. O. Box 349
Princeville, IL 61559
(309) 385-4540
(309) 385-2661 Fax
jcox@lmelibrary.org
http://www.lmelibrary.org/

The Lincoln Library
326 South 7th Street
Springfield, IL 62701
(217) 753-4900
nancy.huntley@lincolnlibrary.info
http://www.lincolnlibrary.info/
General collections (not just about
    Lincoln)

Macomb Public Library District
235 S. Lafayette
Macomb, Illinois 61455
(309) 833-2714
(309) 833-2714 Fax
library@macomb.com
http://www.macomb.lib.il.us/library/

Nauvoo Public Library
P. O. Box 276
Nauvoo, IL 62354
(217) 453-2707 Phone/Fax
nauvoopl@mchsi.com
http://www.nauvoo.lib.il.us/library/

Park Ridge Public Library
20 South Prospect
Park Ridge, IL 60068
(847) 825-3123
(847) 825-0001 Fax
librarydirector@prpl.org
http://www.parkridgelibrary.org/
Local history

Peoria Public Library
107 NE Monroe
Peoria, IL 61602
(309) 497-2000
E-mail thru website
http://www.peoriapubliclibrary.org/

Rolling Meadows Library
3110 Martin Lane
Rolling Meadows, IL 60008
(847) 259-6050
847-259-5319
david.ruff@rmlib.org
http://www.rmlib.org/

Roselle Public Library District
40 South Park Street
Roselle, IL 60172
(630) 529-1641
(630) 529-7579 Fax
lpoignant@roselle.lib.il.us
http://www.roselle.lib.il.us/

**Schaumburg Township District
Library**
130 South Roselle Road
Schaumburg, IL 60193
(847) 985-4000
(847) 923-3131
sarnoff@stdl.org
http://www.stdl.org/
Local history

Skokie Public Library
5215 Oakton Street
Skokie, IL 60077
(847) 673-7774
(847) 673-7797 Fax
CAnthony@skokielibrary.info
http://www.skokie.lib.il.us/

St. Charles Public Library
1 South 6th Avenue
St. Charles, IL 60174
(630) 584-007660174
    E-mail thru website
http://www.st-charles.lib.il.us/

Sugar Grove Public Library
P.O. Box 1049
Sugar Grove, Illinois 60554
(630) 466-4686
(630) 466-4189 Fax
director@sugargrove.lib.il.us
http://www.sugargrove.lib.il.us/site/
   modules/news/

Tremont District Library
P. O. Box 123
Tremont, IL 61568
(309) 925-5432
(309) 925-9953 Fax
trdl@dpc.net
http://www.tremont.lib.il.us/library/

Villa Park Public Library
305 South Ardmore Avenue
Villa Park, IL 60181
(630) 834-1164
vpplinfo@linc.lib.il.us
http://www.villapark.lib.il.us/

Westmont Public Library
428 North Cass
Westmont, IL 60559
(630) 969-5625
(630) 969-6490 Fax
http://westmontlibrary.org/

Wheaton Public Library
225 North Cross Street
Wheaton, IL 60187
(630) 668-1374
askref@wheatonlibrary.org
http://www.wheaton.lib.il.us/

Wilmette Public Library
1242 Wilmette Avenue
Wilmette, IL 60091
(847) 256-5025
(847) 256-6933 Fax
E-mail thru website
http://www.wilmette.lib.il.us/
Local history
Historical photos-

INDIANA

Akron Carnegie Public Library
P. O. Box 428
Akron, IN 46910
(574) 893-4113 Phone/Fax
http://www.akron.lib.in.us/

Alexandria-Monroe Public Library
117 East Church Street
Alexandria, IN 46001
(765) 724-2196
director@alex.lib.in.us
http://www.youseemore.com/
    alexandria-monroe/

Alexandrian Public Library
115 West Fifth Street
Mount Vernon, IN 47620
(812) 838-3286
(812) 838-9639 Fax
alexpl@evansville.net
http://www.apl.lib.in.us/

Allen County Public Library
900 Library Plaza
Fort Wayne, IN 46802
(260) 421-1200
(260) 421-1386
ask@acpl.info
http://www.acpl.lib.in.us/

Anderson Public Library
111 E. 12th Street
Anderson, IN 46016
(765) 641-2456
E-mail thru website
http://www.and.lib.in.us/

Argos Public Library
119 West Walnut Street
Argos, IN 46501
(574) 892-5818
(574) 892-5828 Fax
jehall@argos.lib.in.us
http://www.argos.lib.in.us/

Aurora Public Library District
414 Second Street
Aurora, IN 47001
(812) 926-0646
(812) 926-0665 Fax
weblib@eapld.org
http://www.eapld.net/

Avon-Washington Township Public Library
498 North State Road 267
Avon, IN 46123
(317) 272-4818
(317) 272-7302 Fax
reference@avon.lib.in.us
http://www.avon.lib.in.us/

Bartholomew County Public Library
536 Fifth Street
Columbus, IN 47201
(812) 379-1255
requests@barth.lib.in.us
http://www.barth.lib.in.us/

Batesville Memorial Public Library
131 North Walnut Street
Batesville, IN 47006
(812) 934-4706
reference@ebatesville.com
http://www.ebatesville.com/library/

Bedford Public Library
1323 K Street
Bedford, IN 47421
(812) 275-4471
smiller@bedlib.com
http://www.bedlib.org/

Beech Grove Public Library
1102 Main Street
Beech Grove, IN 46107
(317) 788-4203
(317) 788-0489 Fax
bgplreference@bgpl.lib.in.us
http://www.bgpl.lib.in.us/
(local) History Room

Berne Public Library
166 North Sprunger Street
Berne, IN 46711
(260) 589-2809
(260) 589-2940 Fax
bpl@bernepl.lib.in.us
heritage@bernepl.lib.in.us
http://www.bernepl.lib.in.us/

Bloomfield-Eastern Greene County Public Library
125 South Franklin Street
Bloomfield, IN 47424
(812) 384-4125
(812) 384-0820 Fax
bloomfield@bloomfield.lib.in.us
http://www.bloomfield.lib.in.us/
Local history

Brazil Public Library
204 North Walnut Street
Brazil, IN 47834
(812) 448-1981
(812) 448-3215 Fax
jill@brazil.lib.in.us
http://www.brazil.lib.in.us/

Bremen Public Library
304 North Jackson Street
Bremen, IN 46506
(574) 546-2849
(574) 546-4938 Fax
bremenpl@bremen.lib.in.us
http://www.bremen.lib.in.us/

Bristol Public Library
505 West Vistula Street
Bristol, IN 46507
(574) 848-7458
E-mail thru website
http://www.youseemore.com/
   BristolWash/default.asp

Brook-Iroquois-Washington Public Library
100 West Main Street
Brook, IN 47922
(219) 275-2471
(219) 275-8471 Fax
jwhaley@brook.lib.in.us
http://www.brook.lib.in.us/

Brookston-Prairie Township Public Library
111 West Second Street
Brookston, IN 47923
(765) 563-6511
(765) 563-6833 Fax
info@brookston.lib.in.us
http://www.brookstonlibrary.org/

Brown County Public Library
P.O. Box 8
Nashville, IN 47448
(812) 988-2850
(812) 988-8119 Fax
yoliger@browncounty.lib.in.us
http://www.browncounty.lib.in.us/

Brownsburg Public Library
450 South Jefferson Street
Brownsburg, IN 46112
(317) 852-3167
(317) 852-7734 Fax
reference@brownsburg.lib.in.us
http://www.brownsburg.lib.in.us/

Cambridge City Public Library
33 West Main Street
Cambridge City, IN 47327
(765) 478-3335
(765) 478-6144 Fax
ccitypl@yahoo.com
http://www.cclib.lib.in.us/

Carmel Clay Public Library
55 Fourth Avenue SE
Carmel, IN 46032
(317) 814-3900
http://www.carmel.lib.in.us/

**Carnegie Public Library of
Steuben County**
322 South Wayne Street
Angola, IN 46703
(260) 665-3362
info@steuben.lib.in.us
http://www.steuben.lib.in.us/

**Centerville Center Township
Public Library**
126 East Main Street
Centerville, IN 47330
(765) 855-5223
mbunch@cctpl.lib.in.us
http://www.cctpl.lib.in.us

**Charlestown-Clark County
Public Library**
51 Clark Road
Charlestown, IN 47111
(812) 256-3337
(812) 256-3890 Fax
E-mail thru website
http://www.clarkco.lib.in.us/
Local history

Churubusco Public Library
116 North Mulberry Street
Churubusco, IN 46723
(260) 693-6466
buscolibrary@verizon.net
http://buscolibrary.whitleynet.org/

Clinton Public Library
313 South 4th Street
Clinton, IN 47842
(765) 832-8349
cpl@clintonpl.lib.in.us
http://www.clintonpl.lib.in.us/

Crawford County Public Library
P. O. Box 159
English, IN 47118
(812) 338-2606
(812) 338-3034 Fax
libstaff@cccn.net
http://www.ccpl.lib.in.us/

Crawfordsville District Public Library
205 South Washington Street
Crawfordsville, IN 47933
(765) 362-2242
(765) 362-7986 Fax
http://www.cdpl.lib.in.us/

Culver-Union Township Public Library
107 North Main Street
Culver, IN 46511
(574) 842-2941
(574) 842-3441 Fax
E-mail thru website
http://www.culver.lib.in.us/

Danville Public Library
101 South Indiana Street
Danville, IN 46122
(317) 745-2604
(317) 745-0756 Fax
E-mail thru website
http://www.dpl.lib.in.us/

Decatur Public Library
Adams Public Library System
128 South 3rd Street
Decatur, IN 46733
(260) 724-2605
(260) 724-2877 Fax
http://www.decaturpl.lib.in.us/
    decatur_main_branch.htm

Delphi Public Library
222 East Main Street
Delphi, IN 46923
(765) 564-2929
(765) 564-4746 Fax
dplibrar@carrollnet.org
http://www.carlnet.org/dpl/

Dunkirk Public Library
127 West Washington Street
Dunkirk, IN 47336
(765) 768-6872 Phone/Fax
dunkirklibrary@netscape.net
http://www.dunkirkpubliclibrary.com/

East Chicago Public Library
2401 East Columbus Drive
East Chicago, IN 46312
(219) 397-2453
(219) 378-1591 Fax
mmontalvo@ecpl.org
http://www.ecpl.org/

Eckhart Public Library
603 South Jackson Street
Auburn, IN 46706
(260) 925-2414
reference@epl.lib.in.us
http://www.youseemore.com/eckhart/

Edinburgh Public Library
119 West Main Cross Street
Edinburgh, IN 46124
(812) 526-5487
(812) 526-7057 Fax
chamm@edinburgh.lib.in.us
http://www.edinburgh.lib.in.us/

Elkhart Public Library
300 South 2nd Street
Elkhart, IN 46516
(574) 522-2665
cjo@elkhart.lib.in.us
http://www.elkhart.lib.in.us/cgi-bin/
    index4.pl?&file=index7.pl

Evansville Vanderburg Public Library
200 SE Martin Luther King Jr. Boulevard
Evansville, IN 47713
(812) 428-8200
(812) 428-8397 Fax
E-mail thru website
http://www.evpl.org

Fairmount Public Library
217 South Main Street
Fairmount, IN 46928
(765) 948-3177
http://www.fairmountlibrary.com/

Fayette County Public Library
828 North Grand Avenue
Connersville, IN 47331
(765) 827-0883
Marilyn@fcplibrary.lib.in.us
http://www.fcplibrary.lib.in.us/

Flora-Monroe Township Public Library
109 North Center Street
Flora, IN 46929
(574) 967-3912
(574) 967-3671 Fax
floralib@flora.lib.in.us
http://www.flora.lib.in.us/

Frankfort Community/Clinton County Contractual Public Library
208 West Clinton Street
Frankfort, IN 46041
(765) 654-8746
(765) 654-8747 Fax
fcpl@accs.net
http://www.accs.net/fcpl/

Fremont Public Library
1004 West Toledo
Fremont, IN 46737
(260) 495-7157
(260) 495-7127 Fax
E-mail thru website
http://www.youseemore.com/
   Fremont/default.asp

Fulton County Public Library
320 West 7th Street
Rochester, IN 46975
(574) 223-2713
(574) 223-5102 Fax
director@fulco.lib.in.us
http://www.fulco.lib.in.us/

Garrett Public Library
107 West Houston Street
Garrett, IN 46738
(260) 357-5485
(260) 357-5170 Fax
http://www.gpl.lib.in.us/

Gary Public Library
220 West 5th Avenue
Gary, IN 46402
(219) 886-2484
(219) 886-6829 Fax
http://www.gary.lib.in.us/
Indiana Room

Gas City-Mill Township Public Library
135 East Main Street
Gas City, IN 46933
(765) 674-4718
(765) 674-5176 Fax
nlb723@yahoo.com
http://www.gcmtpl.lib.in.us/

Geneva Public Library
Adams Public Library
305 East Line Street
Geneva, IN 46740
(260) 368-7270
(260) 368-9776 Fax
geneva@apls.lib.in.us
http://www.genevapl.lib.in.us/
  geneva_branch.htm

Goshen Public Library
601 South 5th Street
Goshen, IN 46526
(574) 533-9531
(574) 533-5211 Fax
gpl@goshenpl.lib.in.us
http://www.goshenpl.lib.in.us/

**Greensburg-Decatur County
Public Library**
1110 East Main Street
Greensburg, IN 47240
(812) 663-2826
(812) 663-5617
aingmire@greensburg.lib.in.us
http://www.greensburglibrary.org/

Greenwood Public Library
310 South Meridian
Greenwood, IN 46143
(317) 881-1953
questions@greenwoodlibrary.us
http://www.greenwoodlibrary.us/

**Hagerstown Jefferson Township
Public Library**
10 West College Street
Hagerstown, IN 47346
(765) 489-5632
(765) 489-5808 Fax
info@hagerstown.lib.in.us
http://www.hagerstown.lib.in.us/

Hamilton East Public Library
Noblesville Library
1 Library Plaza
Noblesville, IN 46060
(317) 773-1384
AdultQuestions@hepl.lib.in.us
http://www.hepl.lib.in.us/
Indiana Room

Hammond Public Library
564 State Street
Hammond, IN 46320
(219) 931-5100
E-mail thru website
http://www.hammond.lib.in.us/
Local history

Hancock County Public Library
900 W. McKinzie Road
Greenfield, IN 46140
(317) 462-5141
(317) 462-5711 Fax
http://www.hancockpub.lib.in.us/

Harrison County Public Library
105 North Capitol Avenue
Corydon, IN 47112
(812) 738-5407
(812) 738-5408 Fax
hcpl@hcpl.lib.in.us
http://www.hcpl.lib.in.us/

Huntingburg Public Library
419 North Jackson Street
Huntingburg, IN 47542
(812) 683-2052
(812) 683-2056 Fax
klett@huntingburg.lib.in.us
http://www.huntingburg.lib.in.us/

**Huntington City-Township
Public Library**
200 West Market Street
Huntington City, IN 46750
(260) 356-0824
(260) 356-3073 Fax
http://www.huntingtonpub.lib.in.us/
Indiana History Room

**Hussey-Mayfield Memorial
Public Library**
250 North 5th Street
Zionsville, IN 46077
(317) 873-3149
(317) 873-8339 Fax
E-mail thru website
http://www.zionsville.lib.in.us/
   hmmpl/page/main
Local history

Indiana State Library
315 West Ohio Street
Indianapolis, IN 46202
(866) 683-0008
(317) 232-3728 Fax
E-mail thru website
http://www.in.gov/library/
Indiana collection
Manuscripts

**Indianapolis-Marion County
Public Library**
P. O. Box 211
Indianapolis, IN 46206
(317) 275-4100
E-mail thru website
http://www.imcpl.org/

Jackson County Public Library
303 West 2nd Street
Seymour, IN 47274
(812) 522-3412
bbb@myjclibrary.org
http://www.myjclibrary.org/

Jasper County Public Library
208 West Susan Street
Rensselaer, IN 47978
(219) 866-5881
lpoortenga@jasperco.lib.in.us
http://www.jasperco.lib.in.us/

Jay County Public Library
315 North Ship Street
Portland, IN 47371
(260) 726-7890
(260) 726-7317 Fax
http://www.jaycpl.lib.in.us/library/

**Jeffersonville Township
Public Library**
211 East Court Avenue
Jeffersonville, IN 47130
(812) 285-5630
http://jefferson.lib.in.us/

Jennings County Public Library
2375 North State Highway 3
North Vernon, IN 47265
(812) 346-2091
(812) 346-2127 Fax
Mary.Hougland@jenningslib.org
http://www.jenningscounty.lib.in.us/

Johnson County Public Library
401 State Street
Franklin, IN 46131
(317) 738-2833
(317) 738-9635 Fax
aalexander@jcplin.org
http://www.jcplin.org/

Kendallville Public Library
221 South Park Avenue
Kendallville, IN 46755
(260) 343-2010
(260) 343-2011 Fax
info@kendallvillelibrary.org
http://www.kendallvillelibrary.org/

Kentland Public Library
210 East Graham Street
Kentland, IN 47951
(219) 474-5044
http://kentland.lib.in.us/

Kirklin Public Library
115 North Main
Kirklin, IN 46050
(765) 279-8308
(765) 279-8258 Fax
E-mail thru website
http://www.kirklinlibrary.com/

Knox County Public Library
502 North 7th Street
Vincennes, IN 47591
(812) 886-4380
publib@kcpl.lib.in.us
http://www.kcpl.lib.in.us/kclib/

**Kokomo Howard County
Public Library**
220 North Union Street
Kokomo, IN 46901
(765) 457-3242
(765) 457-3683 Fax
info@khcpl.org
http://www.kokomo.lib.in.us/
Hoosier Art Collection

**Ladoga Clark Township
Public Library**
P.O. Box 248
Ladoga, IN 47954
(765) 942-2456
ladogapl@sbcglobal.net
http://www.ladoga.lib.in.us/

LeGrange County Public Library
203 West Spring Street
LaGrange, IN 46761
(260) 463-2841 Phone/Fax
info@lagrange.lib.in.us
http://www.lagrange.lib.in.us/

Lake County Public Library
1919 West 81st Avenue
Merrillville, IN 46410
(219) 769-3541
(219) 756-9358 Fax
E-mail thru website
http://www.lakeco.lib.in.us/

LaPorte County Public Library
904 Indiana Avenue
LaPorte, IN 46350
(219) 362-6156
reference@lapcat.org
http://www.lapcat.org/

**Lawrenceburg Public
Library District**
150 Mary Street
Lawrenceburg, IN 47025
(812) 537-2775
(812) 537-2810
lawplib@lpld.lib.in.us
http://www.lpld.lib.in.us/

Lebanon Public Library
104 East Washington Street
Lebanon, IN 46052
(765) 482-3460
(317) 873-5059 Fax
kay@leblib.org
http://www.bccn.boone.in.us/LPL/

Ligonier Public Library
300 South Main Street
Ligonier, IN 46767
(260) 894-4511
(260) 894-4509 Fax
jnesbitt@ligonier.lib.in.us
http://www.ligonier.lib.in.us/

Lincoln Heritage Public Library
P. O. Box 784
Dale, IN 47523
(812) 937-7170
(812) 937-7102 Fax
http://www.lincolnheritage.lib.in.us/
Indiana Room

**Logansport-Cass County
Public Library**
616 East Broadway
Logansport, IN 46947
(574) 753-6383
(574) 722-5889
library@logan.lib.in.us
http://www.logan.lib.in.us/

Lowell Public Library
1505 East Commercial Avenue
Lowell, IN 46356
(219) 696-7704
(219) 696-5280 Fax
http://www.lowellpl.lib.in.us/

**Madison-Jefferson County
Public Library**
420 West Main Street
Madison, IN 47250
(812) 265-2744
(812) 265-2217 Fax
contact@mjcpl.org
http://www.mjcpl.org/

Marion Public Library
600 South Washington Street
Marion, IN 46953
(765) 668-2900
(765) 668-2911 Fax
meckerle@marion.lib.in.us
http://www.marion.lib.in.us/default.
  htm

Melton Public Library
8496 West College Street
French Lick, IN 47432
(812) 936-2177
carol@melton.lib.in.us
http://www.melton.lib.in.us/

Bell Memorial Public Library
P. O. Box 368
Mentone, IN 46539
(574) 353-7234
(574) 353-1307 Fax
lklein@bell.lib.in.us
http://www.bell.lib.in.us/

Michigan City Public Library
100 East 4th Street
Michigan City, IN 46360
(219) 873-3050
reference@mclib.org
http://www.mclib.org/
Lincoln exhibit
Local history

Middlebury Community Public Library
P. O. Box 192
Middlebury, IN 46540
(574) 825-5601
(574) 825-5150 Fax
E-mail thru website
http://www.mdy.lib.in.us/

Milford Public Library
101 North Main Street
Milford, IN 46542
(574) 658-4312
(574) 658-9454 Fax
jfrew@milford.lib.in.us
http://www.milford.lib.in.us/

Mishawaka-Penn-Harris Public Library
209 Lincoln Way East
Mishawaka, IN 46544
(574) 259-5277
(574) 255-8489 Fax
(574) 254-5585 Fax
d.eisen@mphpl.org
http://www.mphpl.org/

Mitchell Community Public Library
804 Main Street
Mitchell, IN 47446
(812) 849-2412
mitlib@mitlib.org
http://www.mitlib.org/

Monon Town and Township Public Library
P. O. Box 305
Monon, IN 47959
(219) 253-6517
(219) 253-8373 Fax
mononplstaff@yahoo.com
http://www.monon.lib.in.us/

Monroe County Public Library
303 East Kirkwood Avenue
Bloomington, IN 47408
(812) 349-3050
E-mail thru website
http://www.monroe.lib.in.us/
Indiana Room

Mooresville Public Library
220 West Harrison Street
Mooresville, IN 46158
(317) 831-7323
(317) 831-7383 Fax
wecare@mooresville.lib.in.us
http://www.mooresvillelib.org/

Morgan County Public Library
110 South Jefferson Street
Martinsville, IN 46151
(765) 342-3451
(765) 342-9992 Fax
E-mail thru website
http://morg.lib.in.us/

Morrisson-Reeves Library
80 North 6th Street
Richmond, IN 47374
(765) 966-8291
(765) 962-1318 Fax
mckey@mrlinfo.org
http://www.mrlinfo.org/

Muncie Public Library
2005 South High Street
Muncie, IN 47302
(765) 7·.·'-8200
gnilles@munpl.org
http://www.munpl.org/
Local history

Nappanee Public Library
157 North Main Street
Nappanee, IN 46550
(574) 773-7919
(574) 773-7910 Fax
readmore@nappanee.lib.in.us
http://www.nappanee.lib.in.us/

New Albany Floyd County Public Library
180 West Spring Street
New Albany, IN 47150
(812) 944-8464
(812) 949-3532 Fax
E-mail thru website
http://www.nafclibrary.org/#

New Carlisle-Olive Township Public Library
408 South Bray Street, Box Q
New Carlisle, IN 46552
(574) 654-3046
(574) 654-8260 Fax
sboggs@ncpl.info
http://www.ncpl.lib.in.us/

New Castle-Henry County Public Library
376 South 15th Street
New Castle, IN 47362
(765) 529-0362
(765) 521-3581 Fax
winniep@nchcpl.lib.in.us
http://www.nchcpl.lib.in.us/rooms/
    portal/page/Sirsi_HOME

North Manchester Public Library
405 North Market Street, North Manchester, IN 46962
(260) 982-4773
(260) 982-6342 Fax
nmpl@nman.lib.in.us
http://www.nman.lib.in.us/

Ohio Township Public Library System
4111 Lakeshore Drive
Newburgh, IN 47630
(812) 853-5468
(812) 853-6377 Fax
sthomas@ohio.lib.in.us
http://www.ohio.lib.in.us/

Owen County Public Library
10 South Montgomery Street
Spencer, IN 47460
(812) 829-3392
(812) 829-6165 Fax
http://www.owencpl.blogspot.com/

Peru Public Library
102 East Main Street
Peru, IN 46970
(765) 473-3069
(765) 473-3060 Fax
perupubliclibrary@yahoo.com
http://www.peru.lib.in.us/

Plainfield/Guilford Township Public Library
1120 Stafford Road
Plainfield, IN 46168
(317) 839-6602
(317) 838-3805 Fax
E-mail thru website
http://www.plainfieldlibrary.net/
Indiana Room

Plymouth Public Library
201 North Center Street
Plymouth, IN 46563
(574) 936-2324
(574) 936-7423 Fax
http://www.plymouth.lib.in.us/

Roanoke Public Library
P. O. Box 249
Roanoke, IN 46783
(260) 672-2989
(260) 672-3306 Fax
director@roanoke.lib.in.us
http://www.youseemore.com/
   roanoke/

Rushville Public Library
130 West 3rd Street
Rushville, IN 46173
(765) 932-3496
(765) 932-4528 Fax
rpl@rpl.lib.in.us
http://www.rushcounty.com/library/

Spencer County Public Library
210 Walnut Street
Rockport, IN 47635
(812) 649-4866
(812) 649-4018 Fax
http://www.rockport-spco.lib.in.us/

St. Joseph County Public Library
304 South Main Street
South Bend, IN 46601
(574) 282-4646
donald.napoli@sicpl.org
http://www.sjcpl.lib.in.us/

Sullivan County Public Library
100 South Crowder
Sullivan, IN 47882
(812) 268-4957
(812) 268-5370 Fax
rcole@sullivan.lib.in.us
http://www.sullivan.lib.in.us/

Tell City-Perry County Public Library
2328 Tell Street
Tell City, IN 47586
(812) 547-2661
(812) 547-3038 Fax
library@tcpclibrary.org
http://www.tcpclibrary.org/

Tippecanoe County Public Library
627 South Street
Lafayette, IN 47901
(765) 429-0100
E-mail thru website
http://www.tcpl.lib.in.us/

Tyson Library
P. I. Box 769
Versailles, IN 47042
(812) 689-5894
(812) 689-7401 Fax
tysonlib@seidata.com
http://www.tysonlibrary.org/
Indiana resources
U.S. resources

Union County Public Library
2 East Seminary
Liberty, IN 47353
(756) 458-5355 or 6227
(765) 458-9375 Fax
ucplwebsite@hotmail.com
http://www.union-county.lib.in.us/

Vigo County Public Library
1 Library Square
Terre Haute, IN 47807
(812) 232-1113
questions@vigo.lib.in.us
http://www.vigo.lib.in.us/

Wakarusa Public Library
P.O. Box 485
Wakarusa, IN 46573
(574) 862-2465
(574) 862-4156 Fax
info@wakarusa.lib.in.us
http://www.wakarusa.lib.in.us/

Westchester Public Library
200 West Indiana Avenue
Chesterton, IN 46304
(219) 926-7696
wpldir@wpl.lib.in.us
http://wpl.lib.in.us/

**Westfield Washington
Public Library**
333 West Hoover Street
Westfield, Indiana 46074
(317) 896-9391
(317) 896-3702 Fax
librarian@wwpl.lib.in.us
http://www.westfieldlibrary.lib.in.us/

Whiting Public Library
1735 Oliver Street
Whiting, IN 46394
(219) 473-4700 or 659-0269
(219) 659-5833 Fax
cyh@whiting.lib.in.us
http://www.whiting.lib.in.us/

Willard Library
21 First Avenue
Evansville, IN 47710
(812) 425-4309
willard@willard.lib.in.us
http://www.willard.lib.in.us/
Ghost of the Gray Lady spotted by
   many here

IOWA

Ames Public Library
515 Douglas Avenue
Ames, IA 50010
(515) 239-5656
E-mail thru website
http://www.ames.lib.ia.us/

Anita Public Library
P. O. Box 366
Anita, IA 50020
(712) 762-3639
(712) 712-3178 Fax
anitapl@midlands.net
http://www.anita.swilsa.lib.ia.us/

Atlantic Public Library
507 Poplar Street
Atlantic, IA 50022
(712) 243-5466
(712) 243-5011 Fax
cstanger@atlantic.lib.ia.us
http://www.atlantic.lib.ia.us/

Burlington Public Library
210 Court Street
Burlington, IA 52601
(319) 753-1647
(319) 753-5316 Fax
HelpDesk@burlington.lib.ia.us
http://www.burlington.lib.ia.us/

Carnegie-Stout Public Library
360 West 11th Street
Dubuque, IA 52001
(563) 589-4225
(563) 589-4217 Fax
E-mail thru website
http://www.dubuque.lib.ia.us/
Iowa resources

Cedar Falls Public Library
524 Main Street
Cedar Falls, IA 50613
(319) 273-8643
(319) 273-8648 Fax
cedarfallslibrary@gmail.com
http://www.cedar-falls.lib.ia.us/

Cedar Rapids Public Library
Westgate Mall
2600 Edgewood Road SW
Cedar Rapids, IA 52404
(319) 398-5123
gliset@crlibrary.org
http://www.crlibrary.org/

Coralville Public Library
1401 Fifth Street
Coralville, IA 52241
(319) 248-1850
(319) 248-1890 Fax
agalstad@coralville.lib.ia.us
http://www.coralvillepubliclibrary.org/

Council Bluffs Public Library
400 Willow Avenue
Council Bluffs, IA 51503
(712) 323-7553
bpeterson@cbpl.lib.ia.us
http://www.cbpl.lib.ia.us/
Civil War collections
Local history collections
Historical photograph collection

Davenport Public Library
321 Main Street
Davenport, IA 52801
(563) 326-7832
(563) 326-7809 Fax
lroudebush@davenportlibrary.com
http://www.davenportlibrary.com/

Decorah Public Library
202 Winnebago Street
Decorah, IA 52101
(563) 382-3717
(563) 382-4524 Fax
dpllib@decorah.lib.ia.us
http://www.decorah.lib.ia.us/

Des Moines Public Library
1000 Grand
Des Moines, IA 50309
(515) 283-4152
sjamdursky@desmoineslibrary.com
http://www.pldminfo.org/

Dubuque County Library
P. O. Box 10
Farley, IA 52046
(563) 744-3577
(563) 744-3816 Fax
library@dubcolib.lib.ia.us
http://www.dubcolib.lib.ia.us/

Fairfield Public Library
104 West Adams
Fairfield, IA 52556
(641) 472-6551
(641) 472-3249 Fax
E-mail thru website
http://www.youseemore.com/
    fairfield/default.asp

Fort Dodge Public Library
424 Central Avenue
Fort Dodge, IA 50501
(515) 573-8167
(515) 573-5422 Fax
fdplinfo@fortdodge.lib.ia.us
http://www.fortdodgeiowa.org/
    department/index.asp?fDD=11-0

Grimes Public Library
P. O. Box 290
Grimes, IA 50111
(515) 986-3551
(515) 986-9553 Fax
library@grimes.lib.ia.us
http://www.grimes.lib.ia.us/

Indianola Public Library
207 North B Street
Indianola, IA 50125
(515) 961-9418
(515) 961-9419 Fax
jgodwin@indianola.lib.ia.us
http://www.indianola.lib.ia.us/

Iowa City Public Library
123 South Linn Street
Iowa City, IA 52240
(319) 356-5200
(319) 356-5494 Fax
E-mail thru website
http://www.icpl.org/

Johnston Public Library
P. O. Box 327
Johnston, IA 50131
(515) 278-5233
goers@johnstonlibrary.com
http://www.johnstonlibrary.com/

Kirkendall Public Library
1210 NW Prairie Ridge Drive
Ankeny, IA 50023
(515) 965-6460
manderson@ankenyiowa.gov
http://www.ankenyiowa.gov/Index.
  aspx?page=75

Marion Public Library
1095 Sixth Avenue
Marion, IA 52302
(319) 377-3412
(319) 377-0113 Fax
mplinfo@library.ci.marion.ia.us
http://cityofmarion.org/mlibrary

Mason City Public Library
225 Second Street SE
Mason City, IA 50401
(641) 421-3668
(641) 423-2615 Fax
malmarkwalter@yahoo.com
http://www.mcpl.org/
Lee P. Loomis Archive (photographic
  & resources re Iowa and local
  history)

Pocahontas Public Library
14 Second Avenue NW
Pocahontas, IA 50574
(712) 335-4471
(712) 335-4471 Fax
pocahontaspl@pocahontas.lib.ia.us
http://www.pocahontas.lib.ia.us/

Sioux City Public Library
529 Pierce Street
Sioux City, IA 51101
(712) 255-2933
E-mail thru website
http://www.siouxcitylibrary.org/

Spencer Public Library
21 East 3rd Street
Spencer, IA 51301
(712) 580-7290
(712) 580-7468 Fax
info@spencerlibrary.com
http://spencerlibrary.com/

State Library of Iowa
1112 E. Grand Ave.
Des Moines, IA 50319-0233
1-800-248-4483
(515) 281-6191 Fax
annette.wetteland@lib.state.ia.us
http://www.statelibraryofiowa.org/
State data

Urbandale Public Library
3520 Eighty-Sixth Street
Urbandale, IA 50322
(515) 278-3945
(515) 278-3918 Fax
E-mail thru website
http://www.urbandalelibrary.org/

Waterloo Public Library
415 Commercial Street
Waterloo, IA 50701
(319) 291-4480
(319) 291-6736 Fax
infowiz.wpl@gmail.com
http://www.waterloo.lib.ia.us/

West Des Moines Public Library
4000 Mills Civic Parkway
West Des Moines, IA 50265
(515) 222-3400
(515) 222-3401 Fax
library@wdm-ia.com
http://www.wdmlibrary.org/

Winfield Public Library
112 West Ash
Winfield, IA 52649
(319) 257-3247 Phone/Fax
director47@winfield.lib.ia.us
http://www.winfield.lib.ia.us/

KANSAS

Abilene Public Library
1204 NW Third
Abilene, KS 67410
(785) 263-3082
http://abilene.mykansaslibrary.org/

Arkansas City Public Library
120 East 5th Avenue
Arkansas City, KS 67005
(620) 442-1280
arkcitypl @ acpl.org
http://arkcity.org/index.aspx?ID=228

Atchinson Library
401 Kansas Avenue
Atchison, KS 66002
(913) 367-1902
hammer@atchison.lib.ks.us
http://www.atchisonlibrary.org/

Belleville Public Library
1327 Nineteenth Street
Belleville, KS 66935
(785) 527-5305 Phone/Fax
leahkrotz@nckcn.com
http://www.bellevillelibrary.org
Local history
WPA art collection

Bonner Springs City Library
200 East Third Street
Bonner Springs, KS 66012
(913) 441-2665
(913) 441-2660 Fax
bsclib@bonnerlibrary.org
http://www.bonnerlibrary.org/

Columbus Public Library
205 North Kansas
Columbus, KS 66725
(620) 429-2086
(620) 429-1950 Fax
columbuslibrary@yahoo.com
http://skyways.lib.ks.us/library/
  columbus/

Council Grove Public Library
829 West Main Street
Council Grove, KS 66846
(620) 767-5716
(620) 767-7312
cglib@cgtelco.net
http://cgpl.mykansaslibrary.org/

Emporia Public Library
110 East 6th Avenue
Emporia, KS 66801
(620) 340-6462
(620) 340-6444 Fax
olsonlyn@emporialibrary.org
http://skyways.lib.ks.us/library/
  emporia/

Fredonia Public Library
807 Jefferson Street
Fredonia, KS 66736
(620) 378-2863
(620) 378-2645 Fax
fredodir@twinmounds.com
http://skyways.lib.ks.us/library/
  fredonia/

Goodland Public Library
812 Broadway
Goodland, KS 67735
(785) 899-5461 Phone/Fax
karen@gplibrary.org
http://www.goodlandlibrary.org/

Hutchinson Public Library
901 North Main
Hutchinson, KS 67501
(620) 663-5441
(620) 663-1583 Fax
gwamsley@hutchpl.org
http://www.hutchpl.org/

Iola Public Library
218 East Madison
Iola, KS 66749
(620) 365-3262
(620) 365-5137 Fax
iolaref@sekls.org
http://www.iola.lib.ks.us/

Johnson County Library
9875 West 87th Street
Overland Park, KS 66212
(913) 495-2400
(913) 495-2460 Fax
E-mail thru website
http://www.jocolibrary.org/

Kansas City Public Library
625 Minnesota Avenue
Kansas City, KS 66101
(913) 551-3280
(913) 279-2032 Fax
http://www.kckpl.lib.ks.us/

Lawrence Public Library
707 Vermont Street
Lawrence, KS 66044
(785) 843-3833
(785) 843-3368 Fax
bflanders@lawrence.lib.ks.us
http://www.lawrence.lib.ks.us/
Helen Osma Room (Lawrence and
   Douglas County history)

Manhattan Public Library
629 Poyntz Avenue
Manhattan, KS 66502
(785) 776-4741
(785) 776-1545 Fax
fdatch@manhattan.lib.ks.us
http://www.manhattan.lib.ks.us/
   general/index.shtml

Mulvane Public Library
101 East Main
Mulvane, KS 67110
(316) 777-1211
http://skyways.lib.ks.us/kansas/
   towns/Mulvane/library.html

Newton Public Library
720 North Oak
Newton, KS 67114
(316) 283-2890
(316) 283-2916 Fax
library @ newtonplks.org
http://www.newtonplks.org/

Ottawa Library
105 South Hickory
Ottawa, KS 66067
(785) 242-3080
ottawalibraryreference@yahoo.com
http://www.ottawalibrary.org/

Salina Public Library
301 West Elm
Salina, KS 67401
(785) 825-4624
http://www.salpublib.org/

Smith Center Public Library
117 West Court
Smith Center, KS 66967
(785) 282-3361
(785) 282-6740 Fax
smcntpl@ruraltel.net
http://skyways.lib.ks.us/library/
   smithcenter/
Hospice library
Kansas Collection

**Topeka and Shawnee County
Public Library**
1515 Southwest 10th Avenue
Topeka, KS 66604
(785) 580-4400
E-mail thru website
http://www.tscpl.org/

Wichita Public Library
223 South Main
Wichita, KS 67202
(316) 261-8500
admin@wichita.lib.ks.us
http://www.wichita.lib.ks.us/

Winfield Public Library
605 College Street
Winfield, KS 67156
(620) 221-4470
library@wpl.org
http://www.wpl.org/

KENTUCKY

Allen County Public Library
106 West Main
Scottsville, KY 42164
(270) 237-3861
(270) 237-4095 Fax
sstovall@allencountylibrary.com
http://www.youseemore.com/allen/

Boone County Public Library
1786 Burlington Park
Burlington, KY 41005
(859) 342-2665
(859) 689-0435 Fax
E-mail thru website
http://www.bcpl.org/

Bowling Green Public Library
Warren County Public Library
1225 State Street
Bowling Green, KY 42101
(270) 781-4882
(270) 781-3699 Fax
Lisar@warrenpl.org
http://www.bgpl.org/

Boyd County Public Library
1740 Central Avenue
Ashland, KY 41101
(606) 329-0518
(606) 329-0578 Fax
dcosper@thebookplace.org
http://www.thebookplace.org/

Boyle County Public Library
307 West Broadway
Danville, KY 40422
(859) 236-8466
(859) 236-7692 Fax
library@boylepublib.org
http://www.boylepublib.org/

Bullitt County Public Library
Ridgeway Memorial library
P. O. Box 99
Shepherdsville, KY 40165
(502) 543-7675
(502) 543-5487 Fax
randy@bcplib.org
http://www.bcplib.org/

Campbell County Public Library
3920 Alexandria Pike
Cold Spring, KY 41076
(859) 781-6166
http://www.cc-pl.org/

Carroll County Public Library
136 Court Street
Carrollton, KY 41008
(502) 732-7020
(502) 732-7122 Fax
information@carrollcountylibrary.org
http://www.youseemore.com/Carroll/

Casey County Public Library
238 Middleburg Street
Liberty, KY 42539
(606) 787-9381
(606) 787-7720 Fax
info@caseylibrary.org
http://www.caseylibrary.org/

Clark County Public Library
370 South Burns Avenue
Winchester, KY 40391
(859) 744-5661
clarkbooks@gmail.com
ccpl40391@yahoo.com
http://www.clarkpublib.org/

Daviess County Public Library
2020 Frederica Street
Owensboro, KY 42301
(270) 684-0211
(270) 684-0218 Fax
ref450@dcplibrary.org
http://www.dcplibrary.org/
Kentucky Room

Fleming County Public Library
202 Bypass Boulevard
Flemingsburg, KY 41041
(606) 845-7851
(606) 845-7045 Fax
flemingcountylibrary@yahoo.com
http://www.youseemore.com/
   fleming/
Harriet Dudley Grannis Collection
Franklin Sousley Collection
Henry Chittison History/Music
   Collection

Floyd County Public Library
161 North Arnold Avenue
Prestonsburg, KY 41653
(606) 886-2981
E-mail thru website
http://www.fclib.org/news.php

Gallatin County Public Library
P. O. Box 848
Warsaw, KY 41095
(859) 567-2786
(859) 567-4750 Fax
info@gallatincountylibrary.org

Garrard County Public Library
101 Lexington Street
Lancaster, KY 40444
(859) 792-3424
(859) 792-2366 Fax
garrardcountypubliclibrary@yahoo.
   com
http://garrardpublib.state.ky.us/

Grant County Public Library
201 Barnes Road
Williamstown, KY 41097
(859) 824-2080
grantcountypubliclibrary@fuse.net
http://www.youseemore.com/
   GrantCounty/

Graves County Public Library
601 North 17th Street
Mayfield, KY 42066
(270) 247-2911
dianegcpl@bellsouth.net
http://www.gcpl.org/

Grayson County Public Library
130 East Market Street
Leitchfield, KY 42754
(270) 259-5455
(270) 259-4552 Fax
gillespie@graysoncountylibrary.org
http://www.youseemore.com/
   grayson/

Green County Public Library
112 West Court Street
Greensburg, KY 42743
(270) 932-7081 Phone/Fax
shelleypruitt@kyol.net
http://www.youseemore.com/
  greenco/

Harlan County Public Libraries
107 North 3rd Street
Harlan, KY 40831
(606) 573-5220 Phone/Fax
harlanlibrary@bellsouth.net
http://www.harlancountylibraries.org/

Hart County Public Library
500 East Union Street
Munfordville, KY 442765
(270) 524-1953
(270) 524-7323 Fax
library@hartcountypubliclibrary.org
http://www.hartcountypubliclibrary.
  org/

Henderson County Public Library
101 South Main Street
Henderson, KY 42420
(270) 826-3712
(270) 827-4226 Fax
http://www.hcpl.org/

Henry County Public Library
172 Eminence Terrace
Eminence, KY 40019
(502) 845-5682
(502) 845-4807 Fax
info@henrylibrary.org
http://www.youseemore.com/henry/

**Hopkins County-Madisonville
Public Library**
31 South Main Street
Madisonville, KY 42431
(270) 825-2680
(270) 825-2777 Fax
library@publiclibrary.org
http://www.publiclibrary.org/

Jessamine County Public Library
600 South Main Street
Nicholasville, KY 40356
(859) 885-3523
(859) 885-5164 Fax
jcplcirculation@jesspublib.org
http://www.jesspublib.org/

Kenton County Public Library
502 Scott Boulevard
Covington, Ky 41011
(859) 962-4060
E-mail thru website
http://www.kenton.lib.ky.us/

Laurel County Public Library
120 College Park Drive
London, KY 40741
(606) 864-5759
(606) 862-8057 Fax
E-mail thru website
http://laurellibrary.org/

Lawrence County Public Library
P. O. Box 600
Louisa, KY 41230
(606) 638-4497 or 0554
(606) 638-1293 Fax
marymcguire@lcplky.org
http://www.lcplky.org/

Letcher County Public Library District
Harry M. Caudill Memorial Library
220 Main Street
Whitesburg, KY 41858
(606) 633-7547
(606) 633-3407 Fax
hmclib@lcld.org
http://www.lcld.org/
Kentucky and Appalachian books

Lexington Public Library
140 East Main Street
Lexington, KY 40507
(859) 231-5530
kimhoff@lexpublib.org
http://www.lexpublib.org/
Kentucky Room

Logan County Public Library
201 West 6th Street
Russellville, KY 42276
(270) 726-6129
(270) 726-6127 Fax
linda@loganlibrary.org
http://www.loganlibrary.org/

Louisville Free Public Library
301 York Street
Louisville, KY 40203
(502) 574-1611
E-mail thru website
http://lfpl.org/

Madison County Public Library
319 Chestnut Street
Berea, KY 40403
(859) 986-7112
(859) 986-7208 Fax
berea@madisonlibrary.org
http://www.madisonlibrary.org/

Marshall County Public Library
1003 Poplar Street
Benton, KY 42025
(270) 527-9969
(270) 527-0506 Fax
http://www.marshallcolibrary.org/

Mason County Public Library
218 East 3rd Street
Maysville, KY 41056
(606) 564-3286
masoncolibrary@bellsouth.net
http://www.masoncountylibrary.com/

McCracken County Public Library
555 Washington Street
Paducah, KY 42003
(270) 442-2510
http://www.mclib.net/

McCreary County Public Library
P. O. Box 8
Whitley City, KY 42653
(606) 376-8738
(606) 376-3631 Fax
mcpl@highland.net
http://www.mccrearylibrary.org/

Meade County Public Library
400 Library Place
Brandenburg, KY 40108
(270) 422-2094
(270) 422-3133 Fax
askus@kynet.org
http://www.meadereads.org/

Mercer County Public Library
109 West Lexington Street
Harrodsburg, KY 40330
(859) 734-3680
(859) 734-7524 Fax
http://www.mcplib.info/

Mt. Sterling-Montgomery County Library
241 West Locust Street
Mt. Sterling, KY 40353
(859) 498-2404
(859) 498-7477 Fax
mtsterlinglibrary@yahoo.com
http://www.youseemore.com/
   mtsterling/

Muhlenberg County Public Libraries
108 East Broad Street
Central City, KY 42330
(270) 754-4630
cclib@mcplib.org
http://www.mcplib.org/

Nelson County Public Library
201 Cathedral Manor
Bardstown, KY 40004
(502) 348-3714
(502) 348-5578 Fax
nelsoncopublib@hotmail.com
http://www.nelsoncopublib.org/

Nicholas County Public Library
223 North Broadway
Carlisle, KY 40311
(859) 289-5595
(859) 289-4340 Fax
becky@nicholascountylibrary.com
http://www.nicholascountylibrary.com/

Ohio County Public Library
413 Main Street
Hartford, KY 42347
(270) 298-3790
(270) 298-4214 Fax
info@ohiocountypubliclibrary.org
http://www.
   ohiocountypubliclibrary.org/

Oldham County Public Library
308 Yager Avenue
LaGrange, KY 40031
(502) 222-9713
(502) 222-1141 Fax
susane@oldhampl.org
http://www.youseemore.com/
   oldham/
Kentucky Collection
DAR Collection
Civil War History Collection

Owen County Public Library
118 North Main Street
Owenton, KY 40359
(502) 484-3450
(502) 484-3463 Fax
jennifernippert@bellsouth.net
http://www.youseemore.com/owen/

Paris-Boubon County Library
701 High Street
Paris, KY 40361
(859) 987-4419
(859) 987-2421 Fax
http://www.bourbonlibrary.org/

Paul Sawyier Public Library
319 Wapping Street
Frankfort, KY 40601
(502) 352-2665
(502) 227-2250 Fax
E-mail thru website
http://www.pspl.org/

**Pike County Public
Library District**
119 College Street
Pikeville, KY 41502
(606) 432-9977
(606) 432-9908 Fax
http://www.pikelibrary.org/

Powell County Public Library
725 Breckenridge Street
Stanton, KY 40380
(606) 663-4511
(606) 663-4346 Fax
powell_library@bellsouth.net
http://www.geocities.com/
   powellcountylibrary/

Pulaski County Public Library
304 South Main Street
Somerset, KY 42501
(606) 679-8401
(606) 679-1779 Fax
pulaski.library@pulaskilibrary.com
http://www.pulaskipubliclibrary.
   org/index.htm

Robertson County Public Library
P. O. Box 282
Mount Olivet, KY 41064
(606) 724-2015
(606) 724-5746 Phone/Fax
contact@robertsonlibrary.com
http://www.robertsonlibrary.com/

Rowan County Public Library
185 East 1st Street
Morehead, KY 40351
(606) 784-7137
(606) 784-3917 Fax
http://www.youseemore.com/rowan/

Spencer County Library
168 Taylorsville Road
Taylorsville, KY 40071
(502) 477-8137
http://members.iglou.com/scpl/

Wolfe County Public Library
P. O. Box 10
Campton, KY 41301
(606) 668-6571
(606) 668-6561 Fax
http://www.
   wolfecountypubliclibrary.org/

Woodford County Library
115 North Main Street
Versailles, KY 40383
(859) 873-5191
E-mail thru website
http://woodfordcountylibrary.org/

LOUISIANA

Acadia Parish Library
1125 North Parkerson Avenue
Crowley, LA 70526
(337) 788-1880
http://www.acadia.lib.la.us/
Historic photographs

Allen Parish Libraries
P. O. Box 400
Oberlin, LA 70655
1-800-960-3015
(337) 639-2654 Fax
tpatters@pelican.state.lib.la.us
http://www.allen.lib.la.us/

Ascension Parish Library
708 South Irma Boulevard
Gonzales, LA 70737
(225) 647-3955
E-mail thru website
http://www.myapl.org

Audubon Regional Library
P. O. Box 8389
Lawyers Row
Clinton, LA 70722
(225) 634-7408
E-mail thru website
http://www.youseemore.com/
   Audubon/

Avoyelles Parish Libraries
104 North Washington
Marksville, LA 71351
(318) 253-7559
http://www.avoyelles.lib.la.us/

Beauregard Parish Public Library
205 South Washington Avenue
DeRidder, LA 70634
(337) 463-6217
(337) 462-5434 Fax
admin@beau.org
http://www.beau.lib.la.us/lib/index.
   html

Bienville Parish Library
2768 Maple Street
Arcadia, LA 71001
(318) 263-7410
(318) 263-7428 Fax
http://www.bienville.lib.la.us/

Bossier Parish Library
2206 Beckett Street
Bossier City, LA 71111
(318) 746-1693
(318) 746-7768 Fax
amadison@state.lib.la.us
http://www.bossierlibrary.org/

Calcasieu Parish Public Library
301 West Claude Street
Lake Charles, LA 70605
(337) 721-7116
msawyer@calcasieu.lib.la.us
http://www.calcasieu.lib.la.us/

Cameron Parish Public Library
P. O. Box 1130
Cameron, LA 70631
(337) 598-5950
(337) 598-5949 Fax
ctroscla@pelican.state.lib.la.us
http://www.cameron.lib.la.us/

Concordia Parish Library
1609 Third Street
Ferriday, LA 71334
(318) 757-3550
admin.t1cn@pelican.state.lib.la.us
http://www.concordia.lib.la.us/

DeSoto Parish Library System
109 Crosby Street
Mansfield, LA 71052
(318) 872-6100
(318) 872-6120 Fax
wberry@pelican.state.lib.la.us
http://www.desotoparish.net/svcs/
    library/index.asp

East Baton Rouge Parish Library
7711 Goodwood Boulevard
Baton Route, LA 70806
(225) 231-3750
dfarrar@ebr.lib.la.us
http://www.ebr.lib.la.us/
Louisiana Collection
Black Heritage Collection
Baton Rouge Room

East Carroll Parish Library
109 Sparrow Street
Lake Providence, LA 71254
(318) 559-2615
(318) 559-4635 Fax
admin.t1ec@pelican.state.lib.la.us
http://www.ecarroll.lib.la.us/

Evangeline Parish Library
242 West Main Street
Ville Platte, LA 70586
(337) 363-1369
(337) 363-2353 Fax
mfoster2@state.lib.la.us
http://www.evangeline.lib.la.us/

Grant Parish Library
300 Main Street
Colfax, LA 71417
(318) 627-9920
(318) 627-9900 Fax
dlively@pelican.state.lib.la.us
http://www.grant.lib.la.us/

Iberia Parish Library
445 East Main Street
New Iberia, LA 70560
(337) 364-7024
(337) 364-7042 Fax
newiberialib@yahoo.com
http://www.iberia.lib.la.us/
Bunk Johnson Collection
I.A. & Carroll Martin historical
    photograph collection

Iberville Parish Library
P. O. Box 736
Plaquemine, LA 70764
(225) 687-2520 or 687-4397
(225) 687-9719 Fax
dball@pelican.state.lib.la.us
http://catalog.iberville.lib.la.us/

Jackson Parish Library
614 South Polk Avenue
Jonesboro, LA 71251
(318) 259-5697
(318) 259-8984 Fax
admin.t1ja@state.lib.la.us
http://www.youseemore.com/
    JacksonParish/default.asp

Jefferson Davis Parish Library
118 West Plaquemine Street
Jennings, LA 70546
(337) 824-1210
(337) 824-5444 Fax
http://www.jefferson-davis.lib.la.us/

Jefferson Parish Library
4747 West Napoleon Avenue
Metairie, LA 70001
(504) 838-1100
(504) 838-1110 Fax
helpdesk@jefferson.lib.la.us
http://www.jefferson.lib.la.us/

Lafayette Public Library
301 West Congress Street
Lafayette, LA 70501
(337) 261-5775
http://www.lafayette.lib.la.us/

Lafourche Parish Public Library
303 West 5th Street
Thibodaux, LA 70301
(985) 446-1163
(985) 446-3848 Fax
slebouef@lafourche.org
http://www.lafourche.org/newsite/

LaSalle Parish Library
3108 North 1st Street
Jena, LA 71342
(318) 992-5675
(318) 992-7374 or 7394 Faxes
admin.h1ls@pelican.state.lib.la.us
   http://www.lasalle.lib.la.us/
Louisiana Collection

Livingston Parish Library
P. O. Box 397
Livingston, LA 70754
(225) 686-2436
http://www.livingston.lib.la.us/

Morehouse Parish Library
524 East Madison Avenue
Bastrop, LA 71220
(318) 281-3696
(318) 281-3683 Fax
tlmh@state.lib.la.us
http://www.youseemore.com/
   morehouse/

Natchitoches Parish Library
450 Second Street
Natchitoches, LA 71457
(318) 357-3280
(318) 357-7073 Fax
info@natchitoches.lib.la.us
http://www.youseemore.com/
   natchitoches/

New Orleans Public Library
219 Loyola Avenue
New Orleans, LA 70112
(504) 596-2560
tbarnes@gno.lib.la.us
http://nutrias.org/
African-American resources
Louisiana resources

Ouachita Parish Public Library
1800 Stubbs Avenue
Monroe, LA 71201
(318) 327-1490
(318) 327-4057 Fax
mouliere@oplib.org
http://www.ouachita.lib.la.us/

Pointe Coupee Parish Library
201 Claiborne Street
New Roads, LA 70760
(225) 638-9841
(225) 638-9847 Fax
mkhymel@yahoo.com
http://www.pointe-coupee.lib.la.us/

Rapides Parish library
411 Washington Street
Alexandria, LA 71301
(318) 442-1858
(318) 445-6478 Fax
lrgreen@rpl.org
http://www.rpl.org/

Richland Parish Library
1410 Louisa Street
Rayville, LA 71269
(318) 728-4806
bdoran@pelican.state.lib.la.us
http://www.youseemore.com/
   Richland/default.asp

Sabine Parish Library
705 Main Street
Many, LA 71449
(318) 256-4150
E-mail thru website
http://www.sabine.lib.la.us/

Shreve Memorial Library
424 Texas Avenue
Shreveport, LA 71101
(318) 226-5897
(318) 226-4780 Fax
pevans@shreve-lib.org
http://www.shreve-lib.org/

South St. Landry Community Library
235 Marie Street
Sunset, LA 70584
(337) 662-3442
(337) 662-3475 Fax
bmalbrue2@pelican.state.lib.la.us
http://www.southstlandrylibrary.com/

St. Charles Parish Library
P. O. Box 949
Luling, LA 70070
(985) 785-8471
(985) 785-8499 Fax
http://www.stcharles.lib.la.us/

St. James Parish Library
1879 West Main Street
Lutcher, LA 70071
(225) 869-3618
(225) 869-8435 Fax
http://www.stjames.lib.la.us/

St. John the Baptist Parish Library
2920 New Highway 51
LaPlace, LA 70068
(985) 652-6857 or 2225
(985) 652-8005 Fax
randy.desoto@email.address
http://www.stjohn.lib.la.us/

St. Martin Parish Library
201 Porter Street
St. Martinville, LA 70582
(337) 894-2207
http://www.stmartin.lib.la.us/

St. Tammany Parish Library
310 West 21st Avenue
Covington, LA 70433
(985) 871-1219
(985) 871-1224 Fax
covington@mail.sttammany.lib.la.us
http://www.sttammany.lib.la.us/
   home_flash.html
Louisiana State Depository
Bayou Bonfouca Superfund Project
   and the Southern Shipbuilding
   Corporation Superfund Project

State Library of Louisiana
P. O. Box 131
Baton Rouge, LA 70821
(225) 342-4923
(225) 219-4804 Fax
admin@state.lib.la.us
http://www.state.lib.la.us/
Government documents
State materials

Tangipahoa Parish Library
200 East Mulberry Street
Amite, LA 70422
(985) 748-7559
(985) 748-2812 Fax
bbradford@state.lib.la.us
http://www.tangipahoa.lib.la.us/

Terrebonne Parish Library System
151 Library Drive
Houma, LA 70360
(985) 876-5861
(985) 876-5864 Fax
ghebert@terrebonne.lib.la.us
http://www.terrebonne.lib.la.us/

Union Parish Library
202 West Jackson Street
Farmerville, LA 71241
(318) 368-9226
(318) 368-9224 Fax
t1un@pelican.state.lib.la.us
http://www.youseemore.com/
   unionparish/

Vermilion Parish Library
P. O. Drawer 640
Abbeville, LA 70510
(337) 893-2674 or 2655
(337) 898-0526 Fax
abbeville@vermilion.lib.la.us
http://www.vermilion.lib.la.us/

Vernon Parish Library
1401 Nolan Trace
Leesville, LA 71446
1-800-737-2231
(337) 238-0666 Fax
E-mail thru website
http://www.youseemore.com/
   VernonParish/default.asp
Historic photographs

Webster Parish Library
521 East and West Street
Minden, LA 71055
(318) 371-3080
(318) 371-3081 Fax
bhammett@state.lib.la.us
http://www.webster.lib.la.us/

West Baton Rouge Parish Library
830 North Alexander Avenue
Port Allen, LA 70767
(225) 342-7920
(225) 342-7918 Fax
http://www.youseemore.com/
   WBatonRouge/default.asp

MAINE

Abbott Memorial Library
1 Church Street
Dexter, ME 04930
(207) 924-7292
liz@abbott-library.com
http://www.dextermaine.org/library.
   html

Alice L. Pendleton Library
P. O. Box 77
Islesboro, ME 04848
(207) 734-2218
lgraf@alpl.lib.me.us
http://www.alpl.lib.me.us

Auburn Public Library
49 Spring Street
Auburn, ME 04210
(207) 333-6640
(207) 333-6644 Fax
email@auburnpubliclibrary.org
http://www.auburn.lib.me.us/

Bangor Public Library
145 Harlow Street
Bangor, ME 04401
(207) 947-8336
(207) 945-6694 Fax
bplill@bpl.lib.me.us
http://www.bpl.lib.me.us/
The Bangor Room
African-American resources
Aeronautical collection
Tarratine Club collection
Southern Historical Society collection
New Brunswick Historical Society
   collection
Manuscripts

Blue Hill Public Library
5 Parker Point Road
Blue Hill, ME 04614
(207) 374-5515
(207) 374-5254 Fax
rboulet@bhpl.net
http://www.bluehill.lib.me.us/

**Boothbay Harbor Memorial
Library**
4 Oak Street
Boothbay Harbor, ME 04538
(207) 633-3112
bbhlibrary@bmpl.lib.me.us
http://www.bmpl.lib.me.us/

Camden Public Library
55 Main Street
Camden, ME 04843
(207) 236-3440
(207) 236-6673 Fax
info@librarycamden.org
http://www.librarycamden.org/

Caribou Public Library
30 High Street
Caribou, ME 04736
(207) 493-4214
(207) 493-4654 Fax
ddubois@caribou-public.lib.me.us
http://www.caribou-public.lib.
   me.us/library/home.html

Cary Library
107 Main Street
Houlton, ME 04730
(207) 532-1302
(207) 532-4350 Fax
E-mail thru website
http://www.cary.lib.me.us/

Cumston Public Library
P. O. Box 239
Monmouth, ME 04259
(207) 933-4788
http://www.cumston.lib.me.us/

Curtis Memorial Library
23 Pleasant Street
Brunswick, ME 04011
(207) 725-5242
(207) 725-6313 Fax
info@curtislibrary.com
http://www.curtislibrary.com/

Ellsworth Public Library
20 State Street
Ellsworth, ME 04605
(207) 667-6363
cchurch@ellsworth.lib.me.us
http://www.ellsworth.lib.me.us/

Falmouth Memorial library
5 Lunt Road
Falmouth, ME 04105
(207) 781-2351
library@falmouth.lib.me.us
http://www.falmouth .lib.me.us/

Farmington Public Library
117 Academy Street
Farmington, ME 04938
(207) 778-4312
http://www.farmington.lib.me.us/
Local history

Friend Memorial Public Library
P. O. Box 57
Brooklin, ME 04616
(207) 359-2276
director@friend.lib.me.us
http://www.friendml.org/

Gardiner Public Library
152 Water Street
Gardiner, ME 04345
(207) 582-3312
http://www.gpl.lib.me.us/

Gray Public Library
5 Hancock Street
Gray, ME 04039
(207) 657-4110
(207) 657-4138 Fax
graylib@gray.lib.me.us
http://www.gray.lib.me.us/

Isaac F. Umberhine Public Library
86 Main Street
Richmond, ME 04357
(207) 737-2770
isaac@umberhine.lib.me.us
http://www.umberhine.lib.me.us/

Jackson Memorial Library
P. O. Box 231
Tenants Harbor, ME 04860
(207) 372-8961
E-mail thru website
http://www.jacksonmem.lib.me.us/
   cms/

Kennebunk Free Library
112 Main Street
Kennebunk, ME 04043
(207) 985-2173
(207) 985-4730 Fax
E-mail thru website
http://kennebunklibrary.org/

Lewiston Public Library
200 Lisbon Street
Lewiston, ME 04240
(207) 513-3004
(207) 784-3011
rspeer@ci.lewiston.me.us
http://lplonline.org/

Lithgow Public Library
45 Winthrop Street
Augusta, ME 04330
(207) 626-2415
betsy@lithgow.lib.me.us
http://www.lithgow.lib.me.us/
Main History Collection

Livermore Public Library
P. O. Box 620
Livermore, ME 04253
(207) 897-7173
pbrown@livermore.lib.me.us
http://www.livermore.lib.me.us/
Local history

Maine State Library
64 State House Station
August, ME 04333
(207) 287-5600
(207) 287-5615 Fax
E-mail thru website
http://www.state.me.us/msl/
Government documents
Manuscripts
Avery Collection
Baxter Collection
Thomas Bird Mosher Publications

**Mark and Emily Turner
Memorial Library**
39 Second Street
Presque Isle, ME 04769
(207) 764-2571 or 2572
(207) 768-5756 Fax
sonjaplummer@presqueisle.lib.me.us
http://www.presqueisle.lib.me.us/

McArthur Public Library
270 Main Street
Biddeford, ME 04005
(207) 284-4181
reference@mcarthur.lib.me.us
http://www.mcarthur.lib.me.us/

Milo Free Public Library
4 Pleasant Street
Milo, ME 04463
(207) 943-2612
milo1@milo.lib.me.us
http://www.milo.lib.me.us/

Naples Public Library
P. O. Box 1717
Naples, ME 04055
(207) 693-6841
director@naples.lib.me.us
http://www.naples.lib.me.us/index.htm

New Gloucester Public Library
379 Intervale Road
New Gloucester, ME 04260
(207) 926-4840
srhawkins@maine.rr.com
http://www.newgloucesterlibrary.org/

Old Town Public Library
46 Middle Street
Old Town, ME 04468
(207)827-3972
(207)827-3978 Fax
otpl@old-town.lib.me.us
http://www.old-town.lib.me.us/
   index.asp?Type=BBASIC&SEC={CA
   925F51-9862-4320-AAC4-E0843E3
   365C4}

Orono Public Library
16 Goodridge Drive
Orono, ME 04473
(207) 866-5060
kmarksmolloy@orono.lib.me.us
http://www.orono.lib.me.us/

Patten Free Library
33 Summer Street
Bath, ME 04530
(207) 433-5141
aphillips@patten.lib.me.us
http://www.patten.lib.me.us/
County history

Portland Public Library
5 Monument Square
Portland, ME 04101
(207) 871-1700
reference@portland.lib.me.us
http://www.portlandlibrary.com/
Government documents

Rangeley Public Library
P. O. Box 1150
Rangeley, ME 04970
(207) 864-5529
(207) 864-2523 Fax
info@rangeleylibrary.com
http://rangeleylibrary.com/default.
   asp?Key=1&Cat=1

Rice Public Library
8 Wentworth Street &
2 Walker Street
Kittery, ME 03904
(207) 439-1553
arabella@rice.lib.me.us
http://www.rice.lib.me.us/

Rockport Public Library
P. O. Box 8
Rockport, ME 04856
(207) 236-3642 Phone/Fax
E-mail thru website
http://www.rockport.lib.me.us/

Rumford Public Library
56 Rumford Avenue
Rumford, ME 04276
(207) 364-3661
(207) 364-7296 Fax
creynolds@rumford.lib.me.us
http://www.rumford.lib.me.us/

Scarborough Public Library
48 Gorham Road
Scarborough, ME 04074
(207) 883-4723
(207) 883-9728 Fax
nec@scarborough.lib.me.us
http://www.library.scarborough.
   me.us/#

South Berwick library
37 Portland Street
South Berwick, ME 03908
(207) 384-3308 Phone/Fax
sbpl@south-berwick.lib.me.us
http://www.south-berwick.lib.me.us/

South China Public Library
P. O. Box 417
South China, ME 04358
(207) 445-3094
southchinalibrary.gmail.com
http://www.southchina.lib.me.us/
    Site/Welcome.html

Stratton Public Library
88 Main Street
Stratton, ME 04982
(207) 246-4401
http://www.stratton.lib.me.us/

Thomaston Public Library
60 Main Street
Thomaston, ME 04861
(207) 354-2453
TPL@thomaston.lib.me.us
http://www.thomaston.lib.me.us/

Topsham Public Library
25 Foreside Road
Topsham, ME 04086
(207) 725-1727
director@topshamlibrary.org
http://www.topshamlibrary.org/

Waldoboro Public Library
P. O. Box 768
Waldoboro, ME 04572
(207) 832-4484
wplstaff@waldoboro.lib.me.us
http://www.waldoborolibrary.org/

Waterboro Public Library
P. O. Box 308
East Waterboro, ME 04030
(207) 247-3363
librarian@waterborolibrary.org
http://www.waterborolibrary.org/

Wells Public Library
P. O. Box 699
Wells, ME 04090
(207) 646-8181
(207) 646-5636 Fax
libstaff@wells.lib.me.us
http://www.wells.lib.me.us/

**Whitneyville Public
Library Association**
51 School Street
Whitneyville, ME 04654
(207) 255-8077
journey@maineline.net
http://www.whitneyville.lib.me.us/
Main history
Top-rated children's collection
Art, biography, history, sports &
    science

William Fogg Library
P. O. Box 359
Old Road
Eliot, ME 03903
(207) 439-9437
http://www.william-fogg.lib.me.us/
Fogg Collection

Windham Public Library
217 Windham Center Road
Windham, ME 04062
(207) 892-1908
(207) 892-1915 Fax
igruber@windham.lib.me.us
http://www.windham.lib.me.us/
Main Collection

Winslow Public Library
136 Halifax Street
Winslow, ME 04901
(207) 872-1978
(207) 872-1979 Fax
jlarson@winslow.lib.me.us
http://www.winslow.lib.me.us/

Winter Harbor Public Library
18 Chapel Lane
Winter Harbor, ME 04693
(207) 963-7556
http://www.winterharbor.lib.me.us/

Wiscasset Public Library
21 High Street
Wiscasset, ME 04578
(207) 882-7161
(207) 882-6698 Fax
wpl@wiscasset.lib.me.us
http://www.wiscasset.lib.me.us/
Town histories

York Public Library
15 Long Sands Road
York, ME 03909
(207) 363-2818
(207) 363-7250 Fax
ypl@york.lib.me.us
http://www.york.lib.me.us/

MARYLAND

Allegany County Library System
31 Washington Street
Cumberland, MD 21502
(301) 777-1200
(301) 777-7299 Fax
lmckenney@allconet.org
http://www.youseemore.com/
  Allegany/

Anne Arundel County Public Library
5 Harry S. Truman Parkway
Annapolis, MD 21401
(410) 222-7371
bmorganstern@aacpl.net
http://www.aacpl.net/

Baltimore County Public Library
320 York Road
Towson, MD 21204
(410) 887-6137
lwisotzk@bcpl.net
http://www.bcplonline.org/

Calvert County Public Libraries
850 Costley Way
Prince Frederick, MD 20678
(410) 535-0291 or (301) 855-1862
mhammett@somd.lib.md.us
http://www.calvert.lib.md.us/

Caroline County Public Library
100 Market Street
Denton, MD 21629
(410) 479-1343
(410) 479-1443 Fax
info@carolib.org
http://www.caro.lib.md.us/library/

Carroll County Public Library
1100 Green Valley Road
New Windsor, MD 21776
(410) 386-4500
(410) 386-4509 Fax
http://library.carr.org/

Cecil County Public Library
Elkton Central Library
301 Newark Avenue
Elkton, MD 21921
(410) 996-1055
(410) 996-5604 Fax
ask@ccplnet.org
http://www.cecil.ebranch.info/

Charles County Public Library
2 Garrett Avenue
La Plata, MD 20646
(301) 934-9001 or 870-3520
E-mail thru website
http://www.ccplonline.org/

Dorchester County Public Library
303 Gay Street
Cambridge, MD 21613
(410) 228-7331
(410) 228-6313 Fax
dcpl@dorchesterlibrary.org
http://www.dorchesterlibrary.org/

Eastern Shore Regional Library
122-126 South Division Street
Salisbury, MD 21801
(410) 742-1537
(410) 548-5807 Fax
E-mail thru website
http://www.esrl.lib.md.us/

Enoch Pratt Free Library
400 Cathedral Street
Baltimore, MD 21201
(410) 396-5430
E-mail thru website
http://www.prattlibrary.org/
African-American collection
H. L. Mencken Room
Archives & manuscripts
Prints, drawings & photographs

Frederick County Public Libraries
300 South Seton Avenue, A
Frederick, MD 21701
(301) 600-6329
E-mail thru website
http://www.fcpl.org/index.php
Maryland Room

Harford County Public Library
1221-A Brass Mill Road
Belcamp, MD 21017
(410) 638-3151
caplan@hcplonline.info
http://www.hcplonline.info/

Howard County Library
10375 Little Patuxent Parkway
Columbia, MD 21044
(410) 313-7800
E-mail thru website
http://www.howa.lib.md.us/
Foreign Language Collection
Health Information Collection
American Sign Language resources

Kent County Public Library
408 High Street
Chestertown, MD 21620
(410) 778-3636
(410) 778-6756 Fax
referencedesk@kent.lib.md.us
http://www.kentcountylibrary.org/
   index.php

**Montgomery County
Public Libraries**
2 Metropolitan Court, Suite 4
Gaithersburg, MD 20878
(240) 777-0051
(240) 777-0064 Fax
E-mail thru website
http://www.montgomerycountymd.
   gov/content/libraries/index.asp

**Prince George's County Memorial
Library System**
6532 Adelphi Road
Hyattsville, MD 20782
(301) 699-3500
E-mail thru website
http://www.pgcmls.info/
Maryland Room
Selima Room
Sojourner Room
Tugwell Room

Queen Anne's County Free Library
Centreville Branch
121 South Commerce Street
Centreville, MD 21617
(410) 758-0980
(410) 758-0614 Fax
http://www.quan.lib.md.us/

Ruth Enlow Library of Garrett County
6 North Second Street
Oakland, MD 21550
(301) 334-3996
(301) 334-4152 Fax
info@relib.net
http://www.relib.net/

Somerset County Library System
11767 Beechwood Street
Princess Anne, MD 21853
(410) 651-0852
(410) 651-1388 Fax
gstuckey@some.lib.md.us
http://www.some.lib.md.us/

St. Mary's County Library
23250 Hollywood Road
Leonardtown, MD 20650
(301) 475-2846
(301) 884-4415 Fax
info@stmalib.org
http://www.stmalib.org/

Talbot County Free Library
100 West Dover Street
Easton, MD 21601
(410) 822-1626
(410) 820-8217 Fax
E-mail thru website
http://www.tcfl.org/
Maryland Room

Washington County Free Library
100 South Potomac Street
Hagerstown, MD 21740
(301) 739-3250
ref@washcolibrary.org
http://www.washcolibrary.org/
    index.asp

Wicomico Public Library
122 South Division Street
Salisbury, MD 21801
(410) 749-3612
(410) 548-2968 Fax
askus@wicomico.org
http://www.wicomicolibrary.org/

Worchester County Library
307 North Washington Street
Snow Hills, MD 21863
(410) 632-2600
(410) 632-1159 Fax
mthomas@worc.lib.md.us
http://www.worc.lib.md.us/
Local history

MASSACHUSETTS

Abbot Public Library
235 Pleasant Street
Marblehead, MA 01945
(781) 631-1481
rogers@noblenet.org
http://www.abbotlibrary.org/
The Marblehead Room

Abington Public Library
600 Gliniewicz Way
Abington, MA 02351
(781) 982-2139
(781) 878-7361 Fax
ablib@ocln.org
http://www.abingtonpl.org/

Actor Memorial Library
486 Main Street
Acton, MA 01720
(978) 264-9641
acton@minlib.net
http://www.actonmemoriallibrary.org/
A. F. Davis Collection

Ames Free library
15 Barrows Street
North Easton, MA 02356
(508) 238-2000
E-mail thru website
http://www.amesfreelibrary.org/

Amesbury Public Library
149 Main Street
Amesbury, MA 01913
(978) 388-8148
(978) 388-2662 Fax
mam@mvlc.org
http://www.amesburylibrary.org/

Aquinnah Public Library
1 Church Street
Aquinnah, MA 02535
(508) 645-2314
(508) 645-2188 Fax
aquilib@vineyard.net
http://www.aquinnahlibrary.
   vineyard.net/

Ashland Public Library
66 Front Street
Ashland, MA 01721
(508) 881-0134
http://www.ashlandmass.com/
   ashland-public-library

Athol Public Library
568 Main Street
Athol, MA 01331
(978) 249-9515
(978) 249-7636 Fax
info@athollibrary.org
http://www.athollibrary.org/

Attleboro Public Library
74 North Main Street
Attleboro, MA 02703
(508) 222-0157
wstitt@sailsinc.org
http://www.sailsinc.org/attleboro/
   apl.asp

Ayer Library
26 East Main Street
Ayer, MA 01432
(978) 772-8250
(978) 772-8251 Fax
http://www.ayerlibrary.org/

Bedford Free Public Library
7 Mudge Way
Bedford, MA 01730
(781) 275-9440
(781) 275-3590 Fax
bedford@minlib.net
http://www.bedfordlibrary.net/
The Bedford Collection
The Nickerson Collection

Bellingham Public Library
100 Blackstone Street
Bellingham, MA 02019
(508) 966-1660
(508) 966-3189 Fax
library@bellinghamlibrary.org
http://www.bellinghamlibrary.org/

Belmont Public Library
P. O. Box 125
Belmont, MA 02478
(617) 489-2000 or 993-2850
belmont@minlib.net
http://www.belmont.lib.ma.us/
Claflin Room

Billerica Public Library
15 Concord Road
Billerica, MA 01821
(978) 671-0948
bflaherty@mvlc.org
http://74.220.219.60/~billeri1/

Boston Public Library
700 Boylston Street
Boston, MA 02116
(617) 536-5400 or 859-2270
ask@bpl.org
http://www.bpl.org/

Bridgewater Public Library
15 South Street
Bridgewater, MA 02324
(508) 697-3331
(508) 279-1467 Fax
bwpl@sailsinc.org
http://www.
    bridgewaterpubliclibrary.org/

Burlington Public Library
22 Sears Street
Burlington, MA 01803
(781) 270-1690
(781) 229-0406 Fax
lhodgson@burlmass.org
http://burlingtonpubliclibrary.org/

Cambridge Public Library
449 Broadway
Cambridge, MA 02139
(617) 349-4032
(617) 349-4028
sflannery@minlib.net
http://www.ci.cambridge.ma.us/~CPL/
http://www.ci.cambridge.ma.us/~CPL/
Manuel Rogers Sr. Collection
Bengali Collection
Black Studies Collection

Chelmsford Public Library
25 Boston Road
Chelmsford, MA 01824
(978) 256-5521
bherrmann@mvlc.org
http://www.chelmsfordlibrary.org/

Chelsea Public Library
569 Broadway
Chelsea, MA 02150
(617) 466-4350
(617) 466-4359 Fax
coclibrary@chelseama.gov
http://www.ci.chelsea.ma.us/Public_
 Documents/ChelseaMA_Library/
 index

Cotuit Library
P. O. Box 648
Cotuit, MA 02635
(508) 428-8141
(508) 428-4636 Fax
E-mail thru website
http://www.library.cotuit.ma.us/

East Longmeadow Public Library
60 Center Square
East Longmeadow, MA 01028
(413) 525-5400, ext. 153
speterson@eastlongmeadowma.gov
http://www.eastlongmeadow.org/
 Library/index.html

Edgartown Public Library
P. O. Box 5249
Edgartown, MA 02539
(508) 627-4221
(508) 627-9534 Fax
E-mail thru website
http://www.edgartownlibrary.org/

Falmouth Public Library
300 Main Street
Falmouth, MA 02540
(508) 457-2555
info@falmouthpubliclibrary.org
http://www.falmouthpubliclibrary.org/
Katharine Lee Bates Collection
Local history

Hamilton-Wenham Public Library
14 Union Street
South Hamilton, MA 01982
(978) 468-5577
jdempsey@mvlc.org
http://www.hwlibrary.org/

Haverhill Library
99 Main Street
Haverhill, MA 01830
(978) 373-1586
(978) 373-8466 Fax
cverny@mvlc.org
http://www.haverhillpl.org/
Whittier Collection
Vital Records Collection
Haverhill History Collection

Jacob Edwards Library
236 Main Street
Southbridge, MA 01550
(508) 764-5426
(508) 764-5428 Fax
mmorriss@cwmars.org
http://www.jacobedwardslibrary.org/

Jones Library
43 Amity Street
Amherst, MA 01002
(413) 259-3090
(413) 256-4096 Fax
info@joneslibrary.org
http://www.joneslibrary.org/
Digital Amherst

Marlborough Public Library
35 West Main Street
Marlborough, MA 01752
(508) 624-6900
(508) 485-1494 Fax
sgenovese@cwmars.org
http://www.marlborough-ma.gov/
    Gen/MarlboroughMA_PubLibrary/
    index

Memorial Hall Library
Elm Square
Andover, MA 01810
(978) 623-8400
(978) 623-8407 Fax
rdesk@mhl.org
http://www.mhl.org/

Milford Town Library
80 Spruce Street
Milford, MA 01757
(508) 473-2145
sedmonds@cwmars.org
http://www.milfordtownlibrary.org/

Millicent Library
P. O. Box 30
Fairhaven, MA 02719
(508) 992-5342
(508) 993-7288 Fax
clongworth@sailsinc.org
http://www.millicentlibrary.org/
Local history collection

Milton Public Library
476 Canton Avenue
Milton, MA 02186
(617) 698-5757
miref@ocln.org
http://www.miltonlibrary.org/

Norfolk Public Library
139 Main Street
Norfolk, MA 02056
(508) 528-3380
(508) 528-6417 Fax
jspinney@virtualnorfolk.org
http://library.virtualnorfolk.org/
    public_documents/index

North Adams Public Library
74 Church Street
North Adams, MA 01247
(413) 662-3133
(413) 662-3039 Fax
napl@bcn.net
http://www.naplibrary.com/

Palmer Public Library
1455 North Main Street
Palmer, MA 01069
(413) 283-3330
nmenard@palmer.lib.ma.us
http://www.palmer.lib.ma.us/

Pollard Memorial Library
401 Merrimack Street
Lowell, MA 01852
(978) 970-4120
(978) 970-4117
vwoodley@lowellma.gov
http://www.pollardml.org/

Provincetown Public Library
356 Commercial Street
Provincetown, MA 02657
(508) 487-7094
http://www.ptownlib.com/

Salisbury Public Library
17 Elm Street
Salisbury, MA 01952
(978) 465-5071
librarian@salisburyma.gov
http://www.salisburylibrary.org/

Sargent Memorial Library
427 Massachusetts Avenue
Boxborough, MA 01719
(978) 263-4680
(978) 263-1275 Fax
mstrapko@cwmars.org
http://www.boxlib.org/

South Hadley Public Library
27 Bardwell Street
South Hadley, MA 01075
(413) 538-5045
(413) 539-9250 Fax
jrodio@cwmars.org
http://www.shadleylib.org/

Springfield Library
220 State Street
Springfield, MA 01103
(413) 263-6828
ebader@springfieldlibrary.org
http://www.springfieldlibrary.org/

State Library of Massachusetts
24 Beacon Street
State House, Room 341
Boston, MA 02133
(617) 727-2590
(617) 727-9730 Fax
patrick.mahoney@state.ma.us
http://www.mass.gov/?pageID=afag
encylanding&L=4&L0=Home&L1=
Research+%26+Technology&L2=O
   versight+Agencies&L3=The+Sta
   te+Library+of+Massachusetts&si
   d=Eoaf
Photographs, prints, and pictures
Rare books
Historic maps and atlases
Legislative papers
Historical newspapers

Walpole Public Library
65 Common Street
Walpole, MA 02081
(508) 660-7340
(508) 660-2714 Fax
jerryr@walpole.ma.us
http://www.walpole.ma.us/library.htm

Waltham Public Library
735 Main Street
Waltham, MA 02451
(781) 314-3425
ktranquada@city.waltham.ma.us
   http://www.waltham.lib.ma.us/

Westborough Public Library
55 West Main Street
Westborough, MA 01581
(508) 366-3050
http://www.westboroughlib.org/
The Westborough Room

Westfield Athenaeum
6 Elm Street
Westfield, MA 01085
(413) 568-7833
(413) 568-0988
cpennington@westath.org
http://www.westath.org/

Worcester Public Library
3 Salem Square
Worcester, MA 01608
(508) 799-1655
lgangone@cwmars.org
http://www.worcpublib.org/
U.S. government documents collection

MICHIGAN

Alcona County Library
P. O. Box 348
Harrisville, MI 48740
(989) 724-6796
(989) 724-6173 Fax
E-mail thru website
http://www.alcona.lib.mi.us/

Allen Park Public Library
8100 Allen Road
Allen Park, MI 48101
(313) 381-2425
sblakney@cityofallenpark.org
http://www.allen-park.lib.mi.us/

Alma Public Library
351 N Court
Alma, MI 48801
(989) 463-3966
(989) 466-5901 Fax
ill@alma.lib.mi.us
http://www.youseemore.com/alma/
    default.asp

Ann Arbor District Library
343 South 5th Avenue
Ann Arbor, MI 48104
(734) 327-4263
josie@aadl.org
http://www.aadl.org/

Bad Axe Area Public Library
200 South Hanselman
Bad Axe, MI 48413
(989) 269-8538
(989) 269-2411 Fax
mherrington@badaxelibrary.org
http://main.badaxelibrary.org/bapl/

Baldwin Public Library
300 West Merrill Street
Birmingham, MI 48009
(248) 647-7339
m.custer@baldwinlib.org
http://www.baldwinlib.org/

Bloomfield Township Public Library
1099 Lone Pine Road
Bloomfield Hills, MI 48302
(248) 642-5800
E-mail thru website
http://www.btpl.org/

Brighton District Library
100 Library Drive
Brighton, MI 48116
(810) 229-6571
(810) 229-8924 Fax
E-mail thru website
http://brightonlibrary.info/

Canton Public Library
1200 South Canton Center Road
Canton, MI 48188
(734) 397-0999
davise@cantonpl.org
http://www.cantonpl.org/

Cass District Library
319 M-62 N
Cassopolis, MI 49031
1-800-595-4186
(269) 445-8795 Fax
cass@cass.lib.mi.us
http://www.cass.lib.mi.us/

Chelsea District Library
221 South Main Street
Chelsea, MI 48118
(734) 475-8732
(734) 475-6190 Fax
E-mail thru website
http://www.chelsea.lib.mi.us/

Chesterfield Township Library
50560 Patricia Avenue
Chesterfield, MI 48051
(586) 598-4900
(586) 598-7900 Fax
cheslib@libcoop.net
http://www.libcoop.net/chesterfield/

Detroit Public Library
5201 Woodward Avenue
Detroit, MI 48202
(313) 833-1000
nskowro@detroitpubliclibrary.org
http://www.detroit.lib.mi.us/
Burton Historical Collection
Hackley Collection
Lincoln (digital) Collection
Harvey C. Jackson (digital) Collection

Ecorse Public Library
4184 West Jefferson
Ecorse, MI 48229
(313) 389-2030
dhoward@ecorse.lib.mi.us
http://www.ecorse.lib.mi.us/
African-American History Collection

Escanaba Public Library
400 Ludington Street
Escanaba, MI 49829
(906) 789-7323
epl@uproc.lib.mi.us
http://www.uproc.lib.mi.us/epl/

Farmington Community Library
32737 West 12 Mile Road
Farmington Hills, MI 48334
(248) 553-0300
(248) 553-3228 Fax
E-mail thru website
http://www.farmlib.org/
The Heritage Collection

Flint Public Library
1026 East Kearsley Street
Flint, MI 48502
(810) 232-7111
(810) 249-2633 Fax
askus@fpl.info
http://www.flint.lib.mi.us/

Franklin Public Library
32455 Franklin Road
Franklin, MI 48025
(248) 851-2254
(248) 851-5846 Fax
E-mail thru website
http://www.franklin.lib.mi.us/
Graphic novel collection for teens

Fred C. Fischer Library
167 Fourth Street
Belleville, MI 48111
(734) 699-3291
http://www.belleville.lib.mi.us/

Garden City Public Library
31735 Maplewood Street
Garden City, MI 48135
(734) 793-1830
(734) 793-1831 Fax
http://garden-city.lib.mi.us/

Grace A. Dow Memorial Library
1710 West St. Andrews
Midland, MI 48640
(989) 837-3430
E-mail thru website
http://www.midland-mi.org/
  gracedowlibrary/

Grand Rapids Public Library
111 Library Street NE
Grand Rapids, MI 49503
(616) 988-5400
E-mail thru website
http://www.grapids.lib.mi.us/

Hamburg Township Library
P. O. Box 247
Hamburg, MI 48139
(810) 231-1771
(810) 231-1520 Fax
hamb@tin.lib.mi.us
http://www.hamburglibrary.org/

Hamtramck Public Library
Albert J. Zak Memorial
2360 Caniff
Hamtramck, MI 48212
(313) 365-7050
tamarasochacka@comcast.net
http://www.hamtramck.lib.mi.us/

Hazel Park Memorial Library
123 East Nine Mile Road
Hazel Park, MI 48030
(248) 546-4095
(248) 546-4083 Fax
hzpkill@hazel-park.lib.mi.us
http://www.hazel-park.lib.mi.us/

Howell Carnegie District Library
314 West Grand River
Howell, MI 48843
(517) 546-0720
(517) 546-1494 Fax
kopja@howelllibrary.org
http://www.howelllibrary.org/

Inkster Public Library
Leanna Hicks Public Library
2005 Inkster Road
Inkster, MI 48141
(313) 563-2822
(313) 274-5130 Fax
sstreet@inkster.lib.mi.us
http://www.inkster.lib.mi.us/
Extensive African-American collection

Jackson District Library
244 West Michigan Avenue
Jackson, MI 49201
(517) 788-4087
E-mail thru website
http://www.myjdl.com/

Kalamazoo Public Library
315 South Rose Street
Kalamazoo, MI 49007
(269) 342-9837
(269) 553-7999 Fax
E-mail thru website
http://www.kpl.gov/

Kent District Library
814 West River Center Drive NE
Comstock Park, MI 49321
(616) 784-2007
msmart@kdl.org
http://www.kdl.org/

Lakeland Library Cooperative
4138 Three-Mile Road NW
Grand Rapids, MI 49534
(616) 559-5253
(616) 559-4329 Fax
webmaster@llcoop.org
http://www.lakeland.lib.mi.us/

Lapeer County Information Depot
201 Village West Drive
Lapeer, MI 48446
(810) 664-9521
kate@lib.lapeer.org
http://www.lapeer.lib.mi.us/

Lenawee County Library
4459 West US 223
Adrian, MI 49221
(517) 263-1011
(517) 263-7109 Fax
http://www.lenawee.lib.mi.us/

Library Network
13331 Reeck Road
Southgate, MI 48195
(734) 281-3830
(734) 281-1905 Fax
http://tln.lib.mi.us/

Library of Michigan
P. O. Box 30007
Lansing, MI 48909
(517) 373-1580
(517) 373-4480 Fax
librarian@michigan.gov
http://www.michigan.gov/
   hal/0,1607,7-160-
17445_19270---,00.html
Michigan newspapers
Rare Book Room
Statistical data

Lincoln Park Public Library
1381 Southfield Road
Lincoln Park, MI 48146
(313) 381-0374
(313) 381-2205 Fax
tpowers@lincoln-park.lib.mi.us
http://www.lincoln-park.lib.mi.us/

Livonia Public Library
32777 Five Mile Road
Livonia, MI 48154
(734) 466-2452
(734) 458-6011 Fax
E-mail thru website
http://www.livonia.lib.mi.us/
Government documents
Livonia history
Michigan Collection
Peace Collection

MacDonald Public Library
36480 Main Street
New Baltimore, MI 48047
(586) 725-0273
(586) 725-8360 Fax
goikea@libcoop.net
http://www.macomb.lib.mi.us/
   newbaltimore/

Melvindale Public Library
18650 Allen Road
Melvindale, MI 48122
(313) 429-1090
(313) 388-0432 Fax
kieltyka@melvindale.lib.mi.us
http://www.melvindale.lib.mi.us/

Milford Township Library
330 Family Drive
Milford, MI 48381
(248) 684-0845
thatch@milfordlibrary.info
http://www.milford.lib.mi.us/
Civil War Collection

Monroe County Library System
840 South Roessler Street
Monroe, MI 48161
1-800-462-2050
(734) 241-4722 Fax
nancy.colpaert@monroe.lib.mi.us
http://monroe.lib.mi.us/

Northland Library Cooperative
316 East Chisholm
Alpena, MI 49707
(989) 356-1622
(810) 232-6639 Fax
http://nlc.lib.mi.us/

Northville District Library
212 West Cady Street
Northville, MI 48167
(248) 349-3020
E-mail thru website
http://www.northville.lib.mi.us/

Novi Public Library
45245 West 10 Mile Road
Novi, MI 48375
(248) 349-0720
jfarkas@novilibrary.org
http://novi.lib.mi.us/

Orion Township Public Library
825 Joslyn Road
Lake Orion, MI 48362
(248) 693-3000
lsickles@orionlibrary.org
http://www.orion.lib.mi.us/

Otsego County Library
700 South Otsego Avenue
Gaylord, MI 49735
(989) 732-5841
(989) 732-9401 Fax
ocl@otsego.org
http://www.otsego.lib.mi.us/

Paw Paw District Library
609 West Michigan Avenue
Paw Paw, MI 49079
(269) 657-3800
(269) 657-2603 Fax
ppdl49079@yahoo.com
http://www.pawpaw.lib.mi.us/

Plymouth District Library
223 South Main Street
Plymouth, MI 48170
(734) 453-0750
(734) 453-0733 Fax
info@plymouthlibrary.org
http://plymouthlibrary.org/

Pontiac Public Library
60 East Pike Street
Pontiac, MI 48342
(248) 758-3942
(248) 758-3990 Fax
smccoy@pontiac.mi.us
http://www.pontiac.lib.mi.us/

Presque Isle District Library
18132 Lake Esau Highway
Presque Isle, MI 449777
(989) 595-5051
(989) 595-3146 Fax
PIDLDir@i2k.net
http://www.pidl.org/

Rawson Memorial Library
6495 Pine Street
Cass City, MI 48726
(989) 872-2856
(989) 872-4073 Fax
kvanauken@rawson.lib.mi.us
http://www.rawson.lib.mi.us/

River Rouge Public Library
221 Burke Street
River Rouge, MI 48218
(313) 843-2040
(313) 842-4716 Fax
E-mail thru website
http://www.river-rouge.lib.mi.us/
Archives of newspapers River Rouge
    Herald, Telegram, and River Rouge
    Ghostwriter

Rochester Hills Public Library
500 Olde Towne
Rochester, MI 48307
(248) 656-2900
E-mail thru website
http://www.rhpl.org/

Romulus Public Library
11121 Wayne Road
Romulus, MI 48174
(734) 942-7589
(734) 941-3575 Fax
sadelano@tln.lib.mi.us
http://www.romulus.lib.mi.us/
Parent/Teacher Collection
Michigan Collection

Saginaw Public Libraries
Public Libraries of Saginaw
505 Janes Avenue
Saginaw, MI 48607
(989) 755-0904
(989) 755-9828 Fax
kbutler@saginawlibrary.org
http://www.saginawlibrary.org/

Salem-South Lyn District Library
9800 Pontiac Trail
South Lyon, MI 48178
(248) 437-6431
(248) 437-6593 Fax
dhannon@ssldl.info
http://www.south-lyon.lib.mi.us/

Saline District Library
555 North Maple Road
Saline, MI 48176
(734) 429-5450
(734) 944-0600 Fax
leslee@saline.lib.mi.us
http://saline.lib.mi.us/
Saline History Room

Southfield Public library
26300 Evergreen Road
Southfield, MI 48076
(248) 796-4200
adultref@southfieldlibrary.org
http://www.sfldlib.org/

**Southgate Veterans
Memorial Library**
14680 Dix-Toledo Road
Southgate, MI 48195
(734) 258-3002
(734) 284-9477 Fax
http://www.southgate.lib.mi.us/

**Southwest Michigan
Library Cooperative**
7 West Van Buren Street
Battle Creek, MI 49017
(269) 968-8166
rhulsey@willard.lib.mi.us
http://www.smlc.lib.mi.us/

Sterling Heights Public Library
40255 Dodge Park Road
Sterling Heights, MI 48313
(586) 446-2665
shpl@libcoop.net
http://www.shpl.net/
Oral History Collection (re Sterling
    Heights)
Helen Williams Collection
Newbery and Caldecott Reference
    Collection

Suburban Library Cooperative
44750 Delco Boulevard
Sterling Heights, MI 48313
(586) 685-5750
(586) 685-3010 Fax
hupps@libcoop.net
http://www.libcoop.net/

Taylor Community Library
12303 Pardee Road0
Taylor, MI 48180
(734) 287-4840
ltbaum@tin.lib.mi.us
http://www.taylor.lib.mi.us/

Tecumseh District Library
215 North Ottawa Street
Tecumseh, MI 49286
(517) 423-2238
(517) 423-5519 Fax
questions@tecumseh.lib.mi.us
http://www.tecumseh.lib.mi.us/
Clara Waldron Historical Room

Traverse Area District Library
610 Woodmere Avenue
Traverse City, MI 49686
(231) 932-8500
libadmin@tadl.tcnet.org
http://www.tadl.org/

Trenton Veterans Memorial Library
2790 Westfield Road
Trenton, MI 48183
(734) 676-9777
E-mail thru website
http://www.trenton.lib.mi.us/

**Washtenaw County Library for
the Blind and Physically Disabled**
343 South 5th Avenue
Ann Arbor, MI 48104
1-888-460-0680
wlbpd@aadl.org
http://www.aadl.org/wlbpd

Waterford Township Public Library
5168 Civic Center Drive
Waterford, MI 48329
(248) 674-4831
(248) 674-1910 Fax
jrogers@waterford.lib.mi.us
http://www.waterford.lib.mi.us/

Wayne Public Library
3737 South Wayne Road
Wayne, MI 48184
(734) 721-7832
(734) 721-0341 Fax
medvecky@wayne.lib.mi.us
http://wayne.lib.mi.us/

West Bloomfield Township
Public Library
4600 Walnut Lake Road
West Bloomfield, MI 48323
(248) 682-2120
(248) 232-2291 Fax
E-mail thru website
http://www.wblib.org/

Willard Library
7 West Van Buren Street
Battle Creek, MI 49017
(269) 968-8166
(269) 968-3284
info@willard.lib.mi.us
http://www.willard.lib.mi.us/rooms/

Woodlands Library Cooperative
415 South Superior Street, Suite A
Albion, MI 49224
(517) 629-9469
jseidl@monroe.lib.mi.us
http://woodlands.lib.mi.us/

MINNESOTA

Adrian Branch Library
P. O. Box 39
Adrian, MN 56110
(507) 483-2541
mvaselaar@plumcreeklibrary.net
http://www.plumcreeklibrary.org/
   Adrian/index.html

Albert Lea Public Library
211 East Clark Street
Albert Lea, MN 56007
(507) 377-4350
(507) 377-4339 Fax
phavener@selco.info
http://www.alplonline.org/

Anoka County Library
707 County Road 10 NE
Blaine, MN 55434
(763) 785-3695
Director@anoka.lib.mn.us
http://www.anoka.lib.mn.us/

Arrowhead Library System
5528 Emerald Avenue
Mount Iron, MN 55768
(218) 741-3840
(218) 748-2171 Fax
als@arrowhead.lib.mn.us

Austin Public Library
323 Fourth Avenue NE
Austin, MN 55912
(507) 433-2391
(507) 433-8787 Fax
aplref@selco.info
http://www.austinpubliclibrary.org/

Bayport Public Library
582 North 4th Street
Bayport, MN 55003
(651) 275-4416
(651) 275-4417 Fax
books@bayportlibrary.org
http://bayportlibrary.org/

Blue Earth County Library
100 East Main Street
Mankato, MN 56001
(507) 304-4001
(507) 304-4013 Fax
E-mail thru website
http://beclibrary.org/

Brownsdale Public Library
P. O. Box 302
Brownsdale, MN 55918
(507) 567-2177
brownlib@wolf.co.net
http://www.smig.net/
   brownsdalelibrary/

Buckham Memorial Library
11 Division Street East
Faribault, MN 55021
(507) 334-2089
(507) 384-0503 Fax
djames@ci.faribault.mn.us
http://www.faribault.org/library

Buhl Public Library
P. O. Box 664
Buhl, MN 55713
(218) 258-3391 Phone/Fax
ssamuels@arrowhead.lib.mn.us
http://www.buhl.lib.mn.us/

Carver County Library System
4 City Hall Plaza
Chaska, MN 55318
(952) 448-9395
(952) 448-9392
mbrechon@co.carver.mn.us
http://www.carverlib.org/

Cloquet Public Library
320 Fourteenth Street
Cloquet, MN 55720
(218) 879-1531
mlukkari@arrowhead.lib.mn.us
http://www.cloquet.lib.mn.us/

Dakota County Public Library
1101 West County Road 42
Burnsville, MN 55306
(952) 891-0300
E-mail thru website
http://www.co.dakota.
    mn.us/LeisureRecreation/
    CountyLibraries/default.htm

Douglas County Library
720 Fillmore
Alexandra, MN 56308
(320) 762-3014
(320) 762-3036 Fax
library@douglascounty.lib.mn.us
http://douglascountylibrary.org/

Duluth Public Library
520 West Superior Street
Duluth, MN 55802
(218) 730-4200
(218) 723-3822 Fax
jsheriff@duluth.lib.mn.us
http://www.duluth.lib.mn.us/
The Duluth Collection
The Minnesota Collection

East Central Regional Library
244 South Birch Street
Cambridge, MN 55008
1-888-234-1293
(763) 689-7389 fax
ecregion@ecrl.lib.mn.us
http://ecrl.lib.mn.us/

Gilbert Public Library
P. O. Box 758
Gilbert, MN 55741
(218) 748-2230
(218) 748-2229 Fax
amyhay@arrowhead.lib.mn.us
http://www.gilbert.lib.mn.us/

Godel Memorial Library
314 East Johnson Avenue
Warren, MN 56762
(218) 745-5465
(218) 745-8807 Fax
warren@nwrlilb.org
http://www.nwrlib.org/godel.htm

Grand Marais Public Library
P. O. Box 280
Grand Marais, MN 55604
(218) 387-1140
gmlib@arrowhead.lib.mn.us
http://www.grandmaraislibrary.org/

Grand Rapids Area Library
140 NE 2nd Street
Grand Rapids, MN 55744
(218) 326-7640
(218) 326-7644 Fax
manderson@arrowhead.lib.mn.us
http://www.arrowhead.lib.mn.us/
  grawww/

Great River Regional Library
1300 West St. Germain Street
St. Cloud, MN 56301
(320) 650-2500
E-mail thru website
http://www.griver.org/

Greenbush Public Library
P. O. Box 9
Greenbush, MN 56726
(218) 782-2218 Phone/Fax
greenbush@nwrlib.org
http://www.nwrlib.org/greenbush.htm

Hallock Public Library
163 Third Street S
Hallock, MN 56728
(218) 843-2401
hallock@nwrlib.org
http://www.nwrlib.org/hallock.htm

Hennepin County Library
12601 Ridgedale Drive
Minnetonka, MN 55305
(952) 847-8500
E-mail thru website
http://www.hclib.org/

Hibbing Public Library
2020 East 5th Avenue
Hibbing, MN 55746
(218) 362-5959
(218) 312-9779 Fax
hibbingpl@arrowhead.lib.mn.us
http://www.hibbing.mn.us/index.
  asp?Type=B_BASIC&SEC={4C1587
  28-884C-42F1-A81C-
  C44EAC59740A}
Bob Dylan Collection

Houston Public Library
202 East Cedar Street
Houston, MN 55943
(507) 896-7323
hpublib@mchsi.com
http://houston.govoffice.com/index.
  asp?Type=B_
  BASIC&SEC={2A7E1584-1902-
  4220-9512-C7C012FFA8DB}

Kitchigami Regional Library System
P. O. Box 84
Pine River, MN 56474
(218) 587-2171
(218) 587-4855 Fax
info@krls.org
http://krls.org/
Native American Authors Collection
Native American Histories
World War II Collection

La Crescent Public Library
321 Main Street
La Crescent, MN 55947
(507) 895-4047
lbeach@selco.info
http://sites.google.com/site/lcrlib/

Lake Agassiz Regional Library
P. O. Box 900
Moorhead, MN 56561
(218) 233-3757
(218) 233-7556 Fax
lakeagassiz@larl.org
http://www.larl.org/

Marshall-Lyon County Library
301 West Lyon Street
Marshall, MN 56258
(507) 537-7003
library@marshalllyonlibrary.org
http://marshalllyonlibrary.org/

Martin County Library System
110 North Park Street
Fairmont, MN 56031
(507) 238-4207
(507) 238-4208 Fax
jjepse@tds.lib.mn.us
http://www.
   martincountylibrarysystem.org/

Metropolitan Library Service Agency
1619 Dayton Avenue, Suite 314
St. Paul, MN 55104
(651) 645-5731
(651) 549-3169 Fax
http://www.melsa.org

Minneapolis Public Library
Hennepin County Library
12601 Ridgedale Drive
Minnetonka, MN 55305
(952) 847-8500
E-mail thru website
http://www.hclib.org/

Montevideo-Chippewa County Public Library
224 South 1st Street
Montevideo, MN 56265
(320) 269-6501
(320) 269-8696 Fax
http://www.montelibrary.org/

Moose Lake Public Library
313 Elm Avenue
Moose Lake, MN 55767
(218) 485-4424
dshaw@arrowhead.lib.mn.us
http://www.moose-lake.lib.mn.us/

New Ulm Public Library
17 North Broadway
New Ulm, MN 56073
(507) 359-8331
(507) 354-3255 Fax
lhlavs@tds.lib.mn.us
http://www.newulmlibrary.org/
German Heritage Collection

Nobles County Library
407 Twelfth Street
Worthington, MN 56187
1-800-954-7160
(507) 372-2982 Fax
rspiller@plumcreeklibrary.net
http://nclibrary.org/

Northfield Library
210 Washington Street
Northfield, MN 55057
(507) 645-6606
lynne.young@ci.northfield.mn.us
http://www.ci.northfield.mn.us/
   library/

Northwest Regional Library
P. O. Box 593
Thief River Falls, MN 56701
(218) 681-1066
(218) 681-4355 Fax
bjauquet@nwrlib.org
http://www.nwrlib.org/

Olivia Public Library
405 South 10th Street
Olivia, MN 56277
(320) 523-1738
sueh@olivia.lib.mn.us
http://olivia.govoffice.
    com/index.asp?Type=B_
    LIST&SEC={F407CB04-3D51-4A76-
    8100-449A399BA6AD}

Owatonna Public Library
P. O. Box 387
Owatonna, MN 55060
(507) 444-2460
(507) 444-2465 Fax
E-mail thru website
http://www.owatonna.lib.mn.us/

Paynesville Public Library
119 Washburne Avenue
Paynesville, MN 56362
(320) 243-7343
http://www.paynesvillearea.com/
    community/library.html

Pelican Rapids Public Library
P. O. Box 371
Pelican Rapids, MN 56572
(218) 863-7055
(218) 863-7056 Fax
E-mail thru website
http://pelicanrapids.lib.mn.us/

Plum Creek Library System
290 South Lake Street
Worthington, MN 56187
(507) 376-5803
(507) 376-9244 Fax
clang@plumcreeklibrary.net
http://www.plumcreeklibrary.org/

Ramsey County Library
4570 North Victoria Street
Shoreview, MN 55126
(651) 486-2300
snemitz@rclreads.org
http://www.ramsey.lib.mn.us/

Red Lake Falls Public Library
P. O. Box 115
Red Lake Falls, MN 56750
(218) 253-2992
redlake@nwrlib.org
http://www.nwrlib.org/rlf.htm

Red Wing Public Library
225 East Avenue
Red Wing, MN 55066
(651) 385-3673
rwpl@selco.lib.mn.us
http://redwing.lib.mn.us/

Redwood Falls Public Library
509 South Lincoln Street
Redwood Falls, MN 56283
(507) 627-8650
(507) 627-5004 Fax
http://www.redwoodfallslibrary.org/

Rochester Public Library
101 Second Street NE
Rochester, MN 55904
(507) 328-2309
E-mail thru website
http://www.rochesterpubliclibrary.org/

Roseau Public Library
121 Center Street E, Suite 100
Roseau, MN 56751
(218) 463-2825 Phone/Fax
roseau@nwrlib.org
http://www.nwrlib.org/roseau.htm

Rushford Public Library
P. O. Box 250
Rushford, MN 55971
(507) 864-7600
(507) 864-7003 Fax
shart@selco.info
http://www.rushford.lib.mn.us/

Scott County Public Library System
13090 Alabama Avenue S
Savage, MN 55378
(952) 707-1760
http://www.scott.lib.mn.us/

Silver Bay Public Library
9 Davis Drive
Silver Bay, MN 55614
(218) 226-4331
illsil@arrowhead.lib.mn.us
http://www.silverbay.com/library.htm

**Southeastern Libraries Cooperating/
Southeast Library System**
2600 Nineteenth Street NW
Rochester, MN 55901
1-800-992-5061
(507) 288-8697 Fax
E-mail thru website
http://www.selco.lib.mn.us/

St. Paul Public Library
90 West 4th
St. Paul, MN 55012
(651) 266-7000
sppl.info@ci.stpaul.mn.us
http://www.sppl.org/

Stillwater Public Library
224 Third Street North
Stillwater, MN 55082
(651) 275-4338
(651) 275-4342 Fax
splinfo@ci.stillwater.mn.us
http://www.stillwaterlibrary.org/

Thief River Falls Public Library
P. O. Box 674
Thief River Falls, MN 56701
(218) 681-4325
(218) 681-4355 Fax
trfcirc@nwrlib.org
http://www.nwrlib.org

Thorson Memorial Library
P. O. Box 1040
Elbow Lake, MN 56531
(218) 685-6850 Phone/Fax
library@runestone.ne
http://www.alexweb.net/library/

Traverse des Sioux Library System
1400 Madison Avenue, Suite 622
Mankato, MN 56001
(507) 625-6169
pbiest@tds.lib.mn.us
http://www.tds.lib.mn.us/

Two Harbors Public Library
320 Waterfront Drive
Two Harbors, MN 55616
(218) 834-3148
(218) 834-6201 Fax
thpl@arrowhead.lib.mn.us
http://www.two-harbors.lib.mn.us/

Van Horn Public Library
115 Southeast 3rd Street
Pine Island, MN 55963
(507) 356-8558
http://pineisland.lib.mn.us/

Viking Library System
204 North Cascade
Fergus Falls, MN 56537
(218) 739-5286
pwerner@viking.lib.mn.us
http://www.viking.lib.mn.us/

Virginia Public Library
215 Fifth Avenue S
Virginia, MN 55792
(218) 748-7525
(218) 748-7527 Fax
E-mail thru website
http://www.virginia.lib.mn.us/

Wabasso Public Library
P. O. Box 190
Wabasso, MN 56293
(507) 342-5279
(507) 342-2329 Fax
http://www.plumcreeklibrary.org/
  wabasso/

Warroad Public Library
202 Main Avenue NE
Warroad, MN 56763
(218) 386-1283 Phone/Fax
warroad@nwrlib.org
http://www.nwrlib.org/warroad.htm

Washington County Public Library
8595 Central Park Place
Woodbury, MN 55125
(651) 275-8500
(651) 275-8509 Fax
E-mail thru website
http://www.co.washington.mn.us/
  info_for_residents/library/

Winona Public Library
P. O. Box 1247
Winona, MN 55987
(507) 452-4582
jstetina@selco.info
http://www.cityofwinona-mn.com/
  se3bin/clientgenie.cgi
Bell Art Room

MISSISSIPPI

Bolivar County Library System
104 South Leflore Avenue
Cleveland, MS 38732
1-888-268-8076
(662) 843-4701 Fax
http://www.bolivar.lib.ms.us/

**Central Mississippi Regional
Library System**
P. O. Box 1749
Brandon, MS 39043
(601) 825-0100
(601) 825-0199 Fax
kthieling@cmrls.lib.ms.us
http://www.cmrls.lib.ms.us/

Columbus-Lowndes Public Library
314 North Seventh Street
Columbus, Ms 39701
(662) 329-5300
(662) 329-5156 Fax
ashands@lowndes.lib.ms.us
http://www.lowndes.lib.ms.us/

Dixie Regional Library System
111 North Main Street
Pontotoc, MS 38863
(662) 489-3960
(662) 489-7777 Fax
jmcneece@dixie.lib.ms.us
http://www.dixie.lib.ms.us/

First Regional Library
370 West Commerce Street
Hernando, MS 38632
(662) 429-4439
(662) 429-8853 Fax
cnathan@firstregional.org
http://www.firstregional.org./

Hancock County Library System
312 Highway 90
Bay St. Louis, MS 39520
(228) 467-5282
pfurr@hancock.lib.ms.us
http://www.hancock.lib.ms.us/

Harrison County Library System
2600 24th Avenue, #6
Gulfport, MS 39501
(228) 868-1383
r.lipscomb@harrison.lib.ms.us
http://www.harrison.lib.ms.us/

Jackson-Hinds Library System
Eudora Welty Library
300 North State Street
Jackson, MS 39201
1-800-968-5803
(601) 968-5806 Fax
reference@jhlibrary.com
http://www.jhlibrary.com/

Laurel-Jones County Library
530 Commerce Street
Laurel, MS 39440
(601) 428-4313
(601) 428-0597 Fax
http://www.laurel.lib.ms.us/

Lee-Itawamba Library System
Lee County Library
219 North Madison Street
Tupelo, MS 38804
(662) 841-9027
(or)
Itawamba Library
210 West Cedar Street
Fulton, MS 38843
(662) 862-4926
circulation@li.lib.ms.us
http://www.li.lib.ms.us/

Long Beach Public Library
209 Jeff Davis Avenue
Long Beach, MS 39560
(228) 863-0711
(228) 863-8511 Fax
jripoll@cableone.net
http://www.longbeach.lib.ms.us/

**Meridian-Lauderdale County
Public Library**
2517 Seventh Street
Meridian, MS 39301
(601) 693-6771
(601) 486-2260 Fax
library@meridian.lib.ms.us
http://www.meridian.lib.ms.us/

Noxubee County Library
103 East King Street
Macon, MS 39341
(662) 726-5461 Phone/Fax
http://www.noxubee.lib.ms.us/
Extensive oral history of Noxubee
 County

Pearl River County Library System
900 Goodyear Boulevard
Picayune, MS 39466
(601) 798-5081
(601) 798-5082 Fax
ltufaro@pearlriver.lib.ms.us
http://www.pearlriver.lib.ms.us/

**Starkville-Oktibbeha County
Public Library System**
326 University Drive
Starkville, MS 39759
(662) 323-2766
(662) 323-9140 Fax
http://www.starkville.lib.ms.us/

**Warren County-Vicksburg
Public Library**
700 Veto Street
Vicksburg, MS 39180
(601) 636-6411
deb@warren.lib.ms.us
http://www.warren.lib.ms.us/
Local History Department

Washington County Library System
341 Main Street
Greenville, MS 38701
(662) 335-2331
(662) 390-4758 Fax
kclanton@washington.lib.ms.us
http://www.washington.lib.ms.us/

**Waynesboro-Wayne County
Library System**
712 Wayne Street
Waynesboro, MS 39367
(601) 735-2268 or 1-866-735-2268
(601) 735-6407 Fax
wlib@wwcls.lib.ms.us
http://www.wwcls.lib.ms.us/

MISSOURI

Brentwood Public Library
8765 Eulalie Avenue
Brentwood, MO 63144
(314) 963-8630
circulation@bplmo.org
http://brentwood.lib.mo.us/

Cape Girardeau Public Library
301 South Broadview
Cape Girardeau, MO 63703
(573) 334-5279
bmartin@capelibrary.org
http://capelibrary.org/

Carnegie Public Library
101 West Clay
   Albany, MO 64402
   (660) 726-5615
   (660) 726-4213 Fax
   librarian@carnegie.lib.mo.us
   mailto:librarian@carnegie.lib.
   mo.us
http://carnegie.lib.mo.us/
Historical Gentry County images

Carthage Public Library
612 South Garrison Avenue
Carthage, MO 64836
(417) 237-7040
(417) 237-7041 Fax
carthage@carthagelibrary.org
http://carthage.lib.mo.us/

Centralia Public Library
210 South Jefferson Street
Centralia, MO 65240
(573) 682-2036
(573) 682-5556 Fax
centraliapl@gmail.com

http://www.centraliapubliclibrary.com/

Christian County Library
1005 North 4th Avenue
Ozark, MO 65721
(417) 581-2432
E-mail thru website
http://christiancounty.lib.mo.us/

Daniel Boone Regional Library
P. O. Box 1267
Columbia, MO 65205
(573) 443-3161
(573) 443-3281 Fax
E-mail thru website
http://www.dbrl.org/

Dunklin County Library
209 North Main
Kennett, MO 63857
(573) 888-3561 or 2261
(573) 888-6393 Fax
jonell@dunklin-co.lib.mo.us
http://dunklin-co.lib.mo.us/
Charles H. Baker Military Collection

Ferguson Municipal Public Library
35 North Florissant Road
Ferguson, Missouri 63135
(314) 521-4820
(314) 521-1275 Fax
http://www.ferguson.lib.mo.us/

Henry County Library
123 East Green Street
Clinton, MO 64735
(660) 885-2612
(660) 885-8953 Fax
http://tacnet.missouri.org/hcl/

Howard County Public Library
201 South Main
Fayette, MO 65248
(660) 248-3348
cmonckto@yahoo.com
http://www.hocopub.lib.mo.us/

Jefferson County Library
5678 State Road PP
High Ridge, MO 63049
(636) 677-8689
(636) 677-1769 Fax
pklipsch@jeffcolib.org
http://www.jeffersoncountylibrary.org/

Joplin Public Library
300 South Main Street
Joplin, MO 64801
(417) 623-7953
(417) 624-5217 Fax
jpl@joplinpubliclibrary.org
http://www.joplinpubliclibrary.org/

**Kansas City Metropolitan Library
and Information Network**
15624 East 24 Highway
Independence, MO 64050
(816) 521-7257
(816) 461-0966 Fax
susanburton@kcmlin.org
http://www.kcmlin.org/

Kansas City Public Library
14 West 10th Street
Kansas City, MO 64105
(816) 701-3400
(816) 701-3401 Fax
E-mail thru website
http://www.kclibrary.org/

Kirkwood Public Library
140 East Jefferson
Kirkwood, MO 63122
(314) 821-5770
wsleight@kirkwoodpubliclibrary.org
http://kpl.lib.mo.us/

Livingston County Library
450 Locust Street
Chillicothe, MO 64601
(660) 646-0547
(660) 646-5504 Fax
librarian@livingstoncountylibrary.org
http://www.livingstoncountylibrary.
   org/

Maplewood Public Library
7550 Lohmeyer Avenue
Maplewood, MO 63143
(314) 781-READ
maplewoodpl@yahoo.com
http://www.maplewood.lib.mo.us/
   index.htm

McDonald County Library
808 Bailey
Pineville, MO 64856
(417) 223-4489
(417) 223-4011 Fax
carecline@yahoo.com
http://www.librarymail.org/

Mercer County Library
601 Grant
Princeton, MO 64673
(660) 748-3725
(660) 748-3723 Fax
http://www.mcl.lib.mo.us/
Local history collection and artifacts

Mid-Continent Public Library
15616 East 24 Highway
Independence, MO 64050
(816) 836-5200
info@mcpl.lib.mo.us
http://www.mcpl.lib.mo.us/

Mississippi County Library District
Clara Drinkwater Newnam Library
105 East Marshall
Charlston, MO 63834
(573) 683-6748
(573) 683-2761 Fax
http://missco.lib.mo.us/

Missouri River Regional Library
P. O. Box 89
Jefferson City, MO 65102
(573) 634-2464
(573) 634-7028 Fax
E-mail thru website
http://www.mrrl.org/

North Kansas City Public Library and High School Media Center
2251 Howell Street
North Kansas City, MO 64116
(816) 221-3360
(816) 221-8298 Fax
E-mail thru website
http://www.northkclibrary.org/

Poplar Bluff Public Library
318 North Main Street
Poplar Bluff, MO 63901
(573) 686-8639
(573) 785-6876 Fax
library@poplarbluff.org
http://poplarbluff.org/library/

Pulaski County Library District
P. O. Box 340
Richland, MO 65556
(573) 765-3642
(573) 765-5395 Fax
http://www.pulaskicounty.lib.mo.us/

Richmond Heights Memorial Library
8001 Dale Avenue
Richmond Heights, MO 63117
(314) 645-6202
(314) 781-3434 Fax
http://rhml.lib.mo.us/

Riverside Regional Library
P. O. Box 389
Jackson, MO 63755
(573) 243-8141
(573) 243-8142 Fax
NHowland@showme.net
http://www.riversideregionallibrary.org/

Rock Hill Public Library
9741 Manchester Road
Rock Hill, MO 63119
(314) 962-4723
http://www.rockhill.lib.mo.us/

Rolla Public Library
900 Pine Street
Rolla, MO 65401
(573) 364-2604
(573) 341-5768 Fax
http://rollapubliclibrary.org/rolla/
    default.asp

Saint Joseph Public Library
502 North Woodbine Road
Saint Joseph, MO 64506
(816) 236-2136
http://www.sjpl.lib.mo.us/
Lozo-Needles historical photo collection

Sikeston Public Library
121 East North Street
Sikeston, MO 63801
(573) 471-4140
reifert@sikeston.lib.mo.us
http://www.sikeston.lib.mo.us/

Springfield-Greene County Library District
P. O. Box 760
Springfield, MO 65801
(417) 883-5366, ext. 5
(417) 889-2547 Fax
lisas@thelibrary.org
http://thelibrary.springfield.
   missouri.org/

St. Charles City-County Public Library
P. O. Box 529
St. Peters, MO   63376
(636) 441-2300
(636) 441-3132 Fax
csandstedt@stchlibrary.org
http://www.youranswerplace.org/
Bizelli-Flaming Local History Collection

St. Clair County Library
115 Chestnut Street
Osceola, MO 64776
(417) 646-2214
(417) 646-8643 Fax
stclaircountylibrary@gmail.com
http://mostclair.lib.mo.us/

St. Louis Public Library
1301 Olive Street
St. Louis, MO 63103
(314) 241-2288
(314) 539-0393 Fax
webref@slpl.org
http://www.slpl.org/index.asp

Texas County Library
117 West Walnut
Houston, MO 65483
(417) 967-2258
(417) 967-2262 Fax
hlibrary@train.missouri.org
http://train.missouri.org/library/
   index.htm

Trails Regional Library
432 North Holden
Warrensburg, MO 64093
(660) 747-1699
(660) 747-5774 Fax
hicklink@trl.lib.mo.us
http://trl.lib.mo.us/

University City Public Library
6701 Delmar Boulevard
University City, MO 63130
(314) 727-3150
lballard@ucpl.lib.mo.us
http://www.ucpl.lib.mo.us/

Valley Park Community Library
320 Benton Street
Valley Park, MO 63088
(636) 225-5608
(636) 825-0079 Fax
bmorris@valleyparklibrary.org
http://www.valleyparklibrary.org/
   valleypark/

Webster Groves Public Library
301 East Lockwood Avenue
Webster Groves, MO 63119
(314) 961-3784
http://wgpl.lib.mo.us/

MONTANA

**Anaconda-Montana
Hezrst Free Library**
401 Main Street
Anaconda, MT 59711
(406) 563-6932
jfinn@mtlib.org
http://www.anacondamt.org/library.
   htm

Belgrade Community Library
106 North Broadway
Belgrade, MT 59714
(406) 388-4346
http://www.belgradelibrary.org/

Bozeman Public Library
626 E. Main Street
Bozeman, MT 59715
(406) 582-2400
(406) 582-2424 Fax
E-mail thru website
http://www.bozemanlibrary.org/

Chouteau County Library
1518 Main Street
Fort Benton, MT
(406)622-5222
(406)622-5294 Fax
http://chouteaucountylibrary.
   googlepages.com/

Flathead County Library System
247 1st Avenue E
Kalispell, MT 59901
(406) 758.5820
(406) 758-5868 Fax
kcrowley@flathead.mt.gov
http://www.flatheadcountylibrary.org/

Glacier County Library
21 First Avenue SE
Cut Bank, MT 59427
(406) 873-4572
(406) 873-4845 Fax
glibrary@northerntel.net
http://www.glaciercountymt.org/
   library/

Great Falls Public Library
301 Second Avenue North
Great Falls, MT 59401
(406) 453-0349
jheckel@greatfallslibrary.org
http://www.greatfallslibrary.org/

Jocko Valley Public Library
P. O. Box 158
Arlee, MT 59821
(406) 726-3572
(406) 726-3572 Fax
arl3572@blackfoot.net
http://www.blackfoot.net/~arl3572/

Kohrs Memorial Library
501 Missouri Avenue
Deer Lodge, MT 59722
1-888-872-2622
(406) 846-2622 Phone/Fax
wkkohrs@yahoo.com
http://kohrslibrary.org/

Lewis & Clark Library
120 S. Last Chance Gulch
Helena, MT 59601
(406) 447-1690
http://www.lewisandclarklibrary.
   org/

Lewistown Public Library
701 West Main
Lewistown, MT 59457
(406) 538-212
bridgett@lewistownlibrary.org

Lincoln County Public Libraries
220 West 6th Street
Libby, MT 59923
(406) 293-2778
(406) 293-4235 Fax
library@lincolncountylibraries.com
http://www.lincolncountylibraries.com

Madison Valley Public Library
P. O. Box 178
Ennis, MT 59729
(406) 682-7244
(406) 682-7669 Fax
ennislib@3rivers.net
http://www.3rivers.net/~ennislib/

Miles City Public Library
1 South 10th Street
Miles City, MT 59301
(406) 234-1496
(406) 234-2095 Fax
mcpl@midrivers.com
http://milescitypubliclibrary.org/
L. A. Huffman Collection
Historic Montana Room

Mineral County Library Association
105 North Main Street
Keyser, WV 26726
(304) 788-3222
http://www.youseemore.com/mineral/

Missoula Public Library
301 East Main
Missoula MT 59802
(406) 721-2665
(406) 728-5900 Fax
mslaplib@missoula.lib.mt.us
http://www.missoulapubliclibrary.org/

Montana State Library
P. O. Box 201800
Helena, MT 59620
(406) 444-3115
dstaffeldt@mt.gov
http://msl.state.mt.us/

Parmly Billings Library
510 N. Broadway
Billings, MT 59101
(406) 657-8258
cochranb@ci.billings.mt.us
http://ci.billings.mt.us/index.
   asp?NID=258

Wedsworth Memorial Library
13 North Front Street
Cascade, MT 59421
(406) 468-2848
wedsworth@3riversdbs.net
http://www.cascademontana.com/
   wedsworth/
Complete set of Lewis & Clark
   Journals

NEBRASKA

Ainsworth Public Library
P. O. Box 207
Ainsworth, NE 69210
(402) 387-2032
(402) 387-0209 Fax
aplibrary@threeriver.net
http://www.ainsworthlibrary.com/

Alice M. Farr Library
1603 "L" Street
Aurora, NE 68818
(402) 694-2272
afl@hamilton.net
http://www.cityofaurora.org/
   default.aspx?pageid=54

Alliance Public Library
1750 Sweetwater Avenue
Alliance, NE 69301
(308) 762-1387
http://alliancelibrary.org:8080/
   webopac/main?siteid=1

Beatrice Public Library
100 North 16th Street
Beatrice, NE 68310
(402) 223-3584
lriedesel@beatrice.lib.ne.us
http://www.beatrice.ne.gov/library/

Columbus Public Library
2504 Fourteenth Street
Columbus, NE 68601
(402) 564-7116
(402) 563-3378 Fax
jowens@columbus.ne.us
http://www.columbuslibrary.info/

Grand Island Public Library
Edith Abbott Memorial Library
211 North Washington Street
Grand Island, NE 68801
(308) 385-5333
(308) 385-5339 Fax
http://www.gi.lib.ne.us/

Hartington Public Library
106 South Broadway, Box 458
Hartington, NE 68739
(402) 254-6245 Phone/Fax
citylibrary@hartel.net
http://www.hartingtonpublibrary.org/

Hastings Public Library
P. O. Box 849
Hastings, NE 68902
(402) 461-2346
rstaff@hastings.lib.ne.us
http://www.hastings.lib.ne.us/

Holdrege Area Public Library
604 East Avenue
Holdrege, NE 68949
(308) 995-6556
info@holdregelibrary.org
http://www.holdregelibrary.org/

John A. Stahl Library
330 North Colfax
West Point, NE 68788
(402) 372-3831
wplibrary@cableone.net
http://www.wplibrary.com/

Kearney Public Library and Information Center
2020 First Avenue
Kearney, NE 68847
(308) 233-3281 or 3282
(308) 233-3291 Fax
mwilliams@kearneygov.org
http://cityofkearney.org/index.
   asp?NID=542

Keene Memorial Library
1030 North Broad Street
Fremont, NE 68025
(402) 727-2694
(402) 727-2693 Fax
stephens@keene.lib.ne.us
http://www.fremontne.gov/index.
   aspx?NID=26

Kimball Public Library
208 South Walnut Street
Kimball, NE 69145
(308) 235-4523
http://www.ci.kimball.ne.us/city/
   library.htm
Area history collection
Western Nebraska Observer on
   microfilm

Lincoln City Libraries
136 South 14th Street
Lincoln, NE 68508
(402) 441-8575
s.Connell@lincolnlibraries.org
http://www.lcl.lib.ne.us/

Mead Public Library
P. O. Box 203
Mead, NE 68041
(402) 624-6605
meadpl@microlnk.com
http://www.meadnebraska.org/library/

Morton-James Public Library
923 First Corso
Nebraska City, NE 68410
(402) 873-5609
mlibrary@neb.rr.com
http://www.morton-
   jamespubliclibrary.com/

Norfolk Public Library
308 Prospect Avenue
Norfolk, NE 68701
(402) 844-2100
jhilkema@ci.norfolk.ne.us
http://www.ci.norfolk.ne.us/library/

North Platte Public Library
120 West 4th Street
North Platte, NE 69101
(308) 535-8036
(308) 535-8296 Fax
library@ci.north-platte.ne.us
http://www.ci.north-platte.ne.us/
   library/

Omaha Public Library
215 South 15th Street
Omaha, NE 68102
(402) 444-4833 or 4844
gsorensen@omahapubliclibrary.org
http://www.omaha.lib.ne.us/

Papillion Public Library
Sump Memorial Library
222 North Jefferson Street
Papillion, NE 68046
(402) 597-2040
(402) 339-8019 Fax
robin.clark@sumplibrary.info
http://www.papillion.ne.us/library/
   library.htm

Randolph Public Library
Lied Randolph Public Library
P. O. Box 307
Randolph, NE 68771
(402) 337-0046
librarian@rlibrary.org
http://www.rlibrary.org/

Rock County Library
P. O. Box 465
Bassett, NE 68714
(402) 684-3800
(402) 684-3930 Fax
rockcolib@huntel.net
http://www.huntel.net/rockcolib/

Scottsbluff Public Library
1809 Third Avenue
Scottsbluff, NE 69361
(308) 630-6250
http://www.scottsbluff.org/lib/
1925-Present federal documents

Seward Memorial Library
233 South 5th Street
Seward, NE 68434
(402) 643-3318
info@sewardlibrary.org
http://www.sewardlibrary.org/
Collection of novelty cake pans

Sidney Public Library
1112 Twelfth Avenue
Sidney, NE 69162
(308) 254-3110
spl@sidneypubliclibrary.org
http://www.sidneypubliclibrary.org/
Tatjana B. Seda Heritage Room
1873-Present issues of Sidney Sun
   and Telegraph newspapers on
   microfilm

St. Edward Public Library
P. O. Box 249
St. Edward, NE 68660
(402) 678-2204 Phone/Fax
sepl@gpcom.net
http://www.megavision.net/sepl/

Sump Memorial Library
222 North Jefferson Street
Papillion, NE 68046
(402) 597-2040
(402) 339-8019 Fax
robin.clark@sumplibrary.info
http://www.papillion.ne.us/library/
   library.htm

NEVADA

Boulder City Library
701 Adams Boulevard
Boulder City, NV 89005
(702) 293-1281
(702) 293-0239 Fax
http://www.bclibrary.org

Carson City Library
900 N. Roop Street
Carson City, NV 89701
(775) 887-2244
cclb@ci.carson-city.nv.us
http://www.carsoncitylibrary.org/

Douglas County Public Library
P. O. Box 337
Minden, NV 89423
(775) 782-9841
(775) 782-5754 Fax
http://douglas.lib.nv.us/

Elko County Library
720 Court Street
Elko, NV 89801
(775) 738-3066
(775) 738-8262 Fax
jmhammon@clan.lib.nv.us
http://www.elkocountylibrary.org/
   elko.htm

Henderson Libraries
280 S. Green Valley Parkway
Henderson, NV 89012
(702) 492-7252
reference@hdpl.org
http://www.mypubliclibrary.com/

**Las Vegas–Clark
County Library Dist.**
833 Las Vegas Boulevard, North
Las Vegas, Nevada 89101
(702) 734-READ
E-mail thru website
http://www.lvccld.org/
African-American collection

Pahrump Community Library
701 East Street
Pahrump, NV 89048
(775) 727-5930
(775) 727-6209 Fax
director@pahrumplibrary.com
www.pahrumplibrary.com

Washoe County Library
301 South Center Street
P. O. Box 2151
Reno, NV 89505
(775) 327-8300
(775) 327-8393 Fax
library@washoecounty.us
http://libwww.washoecounty.us/

NEW HAMPSHIRE

Aaron Cutler Memorial Library
269 Charles Bancroft Highway
Litchfield, NH 03052
(603) 424-4044
cutler_library@comcast.net
http://www.cutlerlibrary.blogspot.com/

Amherst Town Library
14 Main Street
Amherst, NH 03031
(603) 673-2288
(603) 672-6063 Fax
library@amherst.lib.nh.us
http://www.amherst.lib.nh.us/

Bedford Public Library
3 Meetinghouse Road
Bedford, NH 03110
(603) 472-2300
(603) 472-2978 Fax
msenatro@bedford.lib.nh.us
http://www.bedford.lib.nh.us/

Derry Public Library
64 East Broadway
Derry, NH 03038
(603) 432-6140
derrylib@derrypl.org
http://www.derry.lib.nh.us/

Dover Public Library
73 Locust Street
Dover, NH 03820
(603) 516-6050
(603) 516-6053 Fax
d.lafrance@dover.nh.gov
http://www.dover.lib.nh.us/

Durham Public Library
7 Mill Road, Unit H
Durham, NH 03824
(603) 868-6699
(603) 868-9944 Fax
durhampl@gmail.com
http://www.durhampubliclibrary.org/

Exeter Public Library
4 Chestnut Street
Exeter, NH 03833
(603) 772-3101
(603) 772-7548 Fax
ref@exeterpl.org
http://www.exeterpl.org/

Hollis Social Library
P. O. Box 659
Hollis, NH 03049
(603) 465-7721
Director@hollis.lib.nh.us
http://www.hollis.nh.us/library/

Hooksett Public Library
1701-B Hooksett Road
Hooksett, NH 03106
(603) 485-6092
(603) 485-6193 Fax
hplbooks@hooksettlibrary.org
http://www.hooksett.lib.nh.us/

Howe Library
13 South Street
Hanover, NH 03755
(603) 643-4120
reference@thehowe.org
http://www.thehowe.org/

Keene Public Library
60 Winter Street
Keene, NH 03431
(603) 352-0157
(866) 743-0446 Toll-free fax
E-mail thru website
http://www.ci.keene.nh.us/library/

Kelley Library
234 Main Street
Salem, NH 03079
(603) 898-7064
kelleylb@salem.lib.nh.us
http://www.salem.lib.nh.us/

Lane Memorial Library
2 Academy Avenue
Hampton, NH 03842
(603) 926-3368
(603) 926-1348 Fax
library@hampton.lib.nh.us

Leach Library
268-B Mammoth Road
Londonderry, NH 03053
(603) 432-1132
(603) 437-6610 Fax
bostertag-holtkamp@
   londonderrynh.org
http://www.londonderrynh.org/
   library/library.htm

Manchester City Library
405 Pine Street
Manchester, NH 03103
(603) 624-6550
E-mail thru website
http://216.204.202.157/
   website/Default.
   aspx?alias=216.204.202.157/
   website/library

Merrimack Public Library
470 Daniel Webster Highway
Merrimack, NH 03054
(603) 424-5021
(603) 424-7312 Fax
mmkpl@merrimack.lib.nh.us
http://www.merrimack.lib.nh.us/

New Hampshire State Library
20 Park Street
Concord, NH 03301
(603) 271-2393
janet.eklund@dcr.nh.gov
http://www.nh.gov/nhsl/

Pelham Public Library
24 Village Green
Pelham, NH 03076
(603) 635-7581
(603) 635-6952 Fax
librarydirector@pelhamweb.com
http://www.pelhamweb.com/library/

Portsmouth Public Library
175 Parrott Avenue
Portsmouth, NH 03801
(603) 427-1540
(603) 433-0981 Fax
info@lib.cityofportsmouth.com
http://www.cityofportsmouth.com/
   library/index.htm
Henry Clay Barnabee Collection
World War II records
Local history collection
Art collection

Richards Free Library
58 North Main Street
Newport, NH 03773
(603) 863-3430
(603) 863-3022 Fax
rfl@newport.lib.nh.us
http://www.newport.lib.nh.us/

Wadleigh Memorial Library
49 Nashua Street
Milford, NH 03055
(603) 673-2408
(603) 672-6064 Fax
director@wadleigh.lib.nh.us
http://www.wadleigh.lib.nh.us/

NEW JERSEY

Atlantic City Free Public Library
1 North Tennessee Avenue
Atlantic City, NJ 08221
(609) 345-2269
E-mail thru website
http://acfpl.org/

Atlantic County Library System
40 Farragut Avenue
Mays Landing, NJ 08330
(609) 625-2776
(609) 625-8143 Fax
contactus@aclsvs.org
http://www.atlanticlibrary.org/
Egg Harbor City and the German-
   American Experience (digitized)
1850-1930 immigration records
   (digitized)
Civil War-era records (digitized)
Sheet music collection

Bayonne Free Public Library
697 Avenue C
Bayonne, NJ 07002
(201) 858-6970
library@bayonnelibrary.org
http://www.bayonnelibrary.org/

**Belleville Public Library and
Information Center**
221 Washington Avenue
Belleville, NJ 07109
(973) 450-3434
(973) 759-6731 Fax
clarue@bellepl.org
http://www.bellepl.org/
Historic photographs
Newspaper archive

**Bergen County Cooperative
Library System**
810 Main Street
Hackensack, NJ 07601
(201) 489-1283
(201) 489-4215 Fax
ruth@bccls.org
http://www.bccls.org/

Berkeley Heights Public Library
290 Plainfield Avenue
Berkeley Heights, NJ 07922
(908) 464-9333
(908) 464-7098 Fax
sbakos@bhplnj.org
http://www.youseemore.com/
   BerkeleyHeights/

Bernards Township Library
32 South Maple Avenue
Basking Ridge, NJ 07920
(908) 204-3031
(908) 766-1580 Fax
ameany@bernards.org
http://www.bernardslibrary.org/

Bernardsville Public Library
1 Anderson Hill Road
Bernardsville, NJ 07924
(908) 766-0118
(908) 766-2464 Fax
librarian@bernardsvillelibrary.org
http://www.bernardsvillelibrary.org/

Brielle Public Library
610 South Street
Brielle, NJ 08730
(732) 528-9381
(732) 223-0346 Fax
rbidnick@co.monmouth.nj.us
http://www.dreamseeker.org/njbiz/
  bpl/

Burlington County Library System
5 Pioneer Boulevard
Westampton, NJ 08060
(609) 267-9660
(609) 267-4091
E-mail thru website
http://www.bcls.lib.nj.us/

Butler Public Library
1 Ace Road
Butler, NJ 07405
(973) 838-3262
Kulsum.Quadri@butlerlibrary.org
http://www.butlerlibrary.org/

Camden County Library System
M. Allen Vogelson Regional Branch
Library
203 Laurel Road
Voorhees, NJ 08043
(856) 772-1636
(856) 772-6105 Fax
E-mail thru website
http://www.camden.lib.nj.us/

Cape May County Library
DN2030, 4 Moore Road
Cape May Court House, NJ 08210
(609) 463-6350
(609) 465-3895 Fax
Director@cmclibrary.org
http://www.cmclibrary.org/

Cherry Hill Free Public Library
1100 Kings Highway North
Cherry Hill, NJ 08034
(856) 667-0300
(856) 667-9503 Fax
info@chplnj.org
http://www.cherryhill.lib.nj.us/
  rooms/portal/page/Sirsi_HOME

Chester Library
250 West Main Street
Chester, NJ 07930
(908) 879-7612
(908) 879-8695 Fax
susan.persak@chesterlib.org
http://chester-library.gti.net/

Clarence Dillon Public Library
2336 Lamington Road
Bedminster, NJ 07921
(908) 234-2325
E-mail thru website
http://www.youseemore.com/
  ClarenceDillon/default.asp

Clark Public Library
303 Westfield Avenue
Clark, NJ 07056
(732) 388-5999
(732) 388-7866 Fax
director@clarklibrary.org
http://www.youseemore.com/
  ClarkPL/default.asp

Clifton Public Library
Clifton Memorial Library
292 Piaget Avenue
Clifton, NJ 07011
(973) 772-5500
zembicki@cliftonpl.org
http://www.cliftonpl.org/

Cranford Library
224 Walnut Avenue
Cranford, NJ 07016
(908) 709-7272
(908) 709-1658 Fax
library@cranfordnj.org
http://www.cranford.com/library/

Cumberland County Library
800 East Commerce Street
Bridgeton, NJ 08302
(856) 453-2210
(856) 451-1940 Fax
http://www.clueslibs.org/

Denville Public Library
121 Diamond Spring Road
Denville, NJ 07834
(973) 627-6555
http://www.denvillelibrary.org/

Dover Free Public Library
32 East Clinton Street
Dover, NJ 07801
(973) 366-0172
(973) 366-0175 Fax
E-mail thru website
http://www.dfpl.org/

East Hanover Library
415 Ridgedale Avenue
East Hanover, NJ 07936
(973) 428-3075
gayle.carlson@easthanoverlibrary.com
http://www.easthanoverlibrary.com/

Edison Public Library
340 Plainfield Avenue
Edison, NJ 08817
(732) 287-2298
http://www.lmxac.org/edisonlib/

Elizabeth Public Library
11 South Broad Street
Elizabeth, NJ 07202
(908) 354-6060
eplreference@elizpl.org
http://www.njpublib.org/

Englewood Public Library
31 Engle Street
Englewood, NJ 07631
(201) 568-2215
jacobsen@bccls.org

Fairfield Free Public Library
261 Hollywood Avenue
Fairfield, NJ 07004
(973) 227-3575
(973) 227-7305 Fax
ffpl@ffpl.org
http://www.ffpl.org/

Flemington Free Public Library
118 Main Street
Flemington, NJ 08822
(908) 782-5733
flemingtonlibrary@gmail.com
http://www.flemingtonpubliclibrary.
 org/

Fort Lee Public Library
320 Main Street
Fort Lee, NJ 07024
(201) 592-3615
ftlecirc@bccls.org
http://fortlee.bccls.org/
Silent films made in Ft. Lee, along
 with stills
Historical film magazine on microfilm

Franklin Lakes Public Library
470 DeKorte Drive
Franklin Lakes, NJ 07417
(201) 891-2224
http://www.franklinlakeslibrary.org/

Free Public Library of Monroe Township
306 South Main Street
Williamstown, NJ 08080
(856) 629-1212
mtlibrary@buyrite.com
http://www.monroetownshiplibrary.org/
Cinema literary collection
New Jerseyana

Gloucester County Library System
389 Wolfert Station Road
Mullica Hill, NJ 08062
(856) 223-6000
(856) 223-6039 Fax
gloucester@gcls.org
http://www.gcls.org/default.php

Haddon Heights Public Library
P. O. Box 240
Haddon Heights, NJ 08035
(856) 547-7132
(856) 547-2867 Fax
bob@haddonheightslibrary.com
http://www.haddonheights.lib.nj.us/
New Jersey history

Hunterdon County Library
314 State Highway 12, Building 3
Flemington, NJ 08822
(908) 788-1444
(908) 806-4862 Fax
library@hclibrary.us
http://www.hclibrary.us/

Keansburg Waterfront Public Library
55 Shore Boulevard
Keansburg, NJ 07734
(732) 787-0636
(732) 787-0631 Fax
[website closed]

Library Company of Burlington
23 West Union Street
Burlington, NJ 08016
(609) 386-1273 Phone/Fax
Lib@burlingtonnj.us
http://www.burlingtonnj.us/LCoB.html
Note: In continuous operation since 1757

Linden Free Public Library
31 East Henry Street
Linden, NJ 07036
(908) 298-3830
http://www.lindenpl.org/

Long Hill Township Public Library
917 Valley Road
Gillette, NJ 07933
(908) 647-2088
(908) 647-2098 Fax
director@longhilllibrary.org
http://longhill.mainlib.org/

Margaret E. Heggan Free Public Library
208 East Holly Avenue
Hurffville, NJ 08080
(856) 589-3334
(856) 582-2042 Fax
info@hegganlibrary.org
http://www.hegganlibrary.org/

Margate Public Library
8100 Atlantic Avenue
Margate, NJ 08402
(609) 822-4700
http://www.margatelibrary.org/

Mercer County Library System
2751 Brunswick Pike
Lawrenceville, NJ 08648
(609) 989-6807
director@mcl.org
http://webserver.mcl.org/
State resources

Millburn Free Public Library
200 Glen Avenue
Millburn, NJ 07041
(973) 376-1006
(973) 376-0104 Fax
patricia@millburn.lib.nj.us
http://www.millburn.lib.nj.us/

Monmouth County Library
125 Symmes Drive
Manalapan, NJ 07726
(732) 431-7220
http://www.monmouthcountylib.org/
Monmouth County Historical Room
Municipal Government Information
   Center

Montclair Public Library
50 South Fullerton Avenue
Montclair, NJ 07042
(973) 744-0500
(973) 744-5268 Fax
webmaster@montlib.com
http://montlib.com/

Morris County Library
30 East Hanover Avenue
Whippany, NJ 07981
(973) 285-6934
mocolib1@gti.net
http://www.gti.net/mocolib1/MCL.
   html

Mount Arlington Public Library
333 Howard Boulevard
Mount Arlington, NJ 07856
(973) 398-1516
http://www.gti.net/mountarlington/

Mountainside Public Library
Constitution Plaza
Mountainside, NJ 07092
(908) 233-115
(908) 232-7311 Fax
E-mail thru website
http://www.mountainsidelibrary.org/
Harry and Wende Devlin Collection

Newark Public Library
P. O. Box 630
Newark, NJ 07101
(973) 733-7784
wgrey@npl.org
http://www.npl.org/
Charles F. Cummings New Jersey
   Information Center
James Brown African-American Room
The Autograph Collection

North Haledon
Free Public Library
129 Overlook Avenue
North Haledon, NJ 07508
(973) 427-6213
http://www.northhaledonlibrary.org/

Ocean City Free Public Library
1735 Simpson Avenue
Ocean City, NJ 08226
(609) 399-2434
(609) 398-8944 Fax
cmaloney_ocfpl@hotmail.com
http://www.oceancitylibrary.org/

Paramus Public Library
E116 Century Road
Paramus, NJ 07652
(201) 599-1300
paracirc@bccls.org
http://paramus.bccls.org/

Parsippany-Troy Hills Public Library System
449 Halsey Road
Parsippany, NJ 07054
(973) 887-5150
E-mail thru website
http://www.parsippanylibrary.org/

Paterson Free Public Library
250 Broadway
Paterson, NJ 07501
(973) 321-1223
bowmand@patersonpl.org
http://www.patersonpl.org/

Pennsuken Free Public Library
5605 Crescent Boulevard
Pennsauken, NJ 08110
(856) 665-5959
(856) 486-0142 Fax
E-mail thru website
http://www.pennsaukenlibrary.org/

Piscataway Public Library
John F. Kennedy Library
500 Hoes Lane
Piscataway, NJ 08854
(732) 463-1633
E-mail thru website
http://www.piscatawaylibrary.org/

Princeton Public Library
65 Witherspoon Street
Princeton, NJ 08542
(609) 924-9529
LBurger@princetonlibrary.org
http://www.princeton.lib.nj.us/

Ramsey Free Public Library
30 Wyckoff Avenue
Ramsey, NJ 07446
(201) 327-1445
ramscirc@bccls.org
http://www.ramseylibrary.org/

Ridgewood Public Library
125 North Maple Avenue
Ridgewood, NJ 07450
(201) 670-5600
ngreene@ridgewoodlibrary.org
http://www.ridgewoodlibrary.org/

Roxbury Public Library
103 Main Street
Succasunna, NJ 07876
(973) 584-2400
comments@RoxburyLibrary.org
http://www.roxburylibrary.org/

Scotch Plains Public Library
1927 Bartle Avenue
Scotch Plains, NJ 07076
(908) 322-5007
Library@ScotLib.org
http://www.scotlib.org/

Somerset County Library System
P. O. Box 6700
Bridgewater, NJ 08807
(908) 526-4016
E-mail thru website
http://www.somerset.lib.nj.us/

South Brunswick Public Library
110 Kingston Lane
Monmouth Junction, NJ 08852
(732) 329-4000
ccarbone@sbpl.info
http://www.sbpl.info/

Sussex County Library System
125 Morris Turnpike
Newton, NJ 07860
(973) 948-3660
(973) 948-2071 Fax
pollakoff@sussexcountylibrary.org
http://www.sussexcountylibrary.org/
Regional collections

Teaneck Public Library
840 Teaneck Road
Teaneck, NJ 07666
(201) 837-4171
(201) 837-0410 Fax
mccue@bccls.org
http://www.teaneck.org/
Collection of folktales from around
   the world
Friedrich Collection – scholarly
   history of children's literature

Trenton Free Public Library
120 Academy Street
Trenton, NJ 08608
(609) 392-7188
kbrayl@trentonlib.org
http://www.trentonlib.org/

Vineland Public Library
1058 East Landis Avenue
Vineland, NJ 08360
(856) 794-4244
http://www.vineland.lib.nj.us/

Wayne Public Library
461 Valley Road
Wayne, NJ 07470
(973) 694-4272
(973) 692-0907 or 0637   Fax
E-mail thru website
http://www.waynepubliclibrary.org/

West Deptford Free Public Library
420 Crown Point Road
Thorofare, NJ 08086
(856) 845-5593
admin@westdeptford.lib.nj.us
http://www.westdeptford.lib.nj.us/

West Orange Public Library
46 Mount Pleasant Avenue
West Orange, NJ 07052
(973) 736-0198
admin@westorangelibrary.org
http://www.wopl.lib.nj.us/

Westwood Public Library
49 Park Avenue
Westwood, NJ 07675
(201) 664-0583
westwood@bccls.org
http://www.marthaurbiel.
   com-a.googlepages.com/
   westwoodlibrarywebsite

Whippanong Library
1000 Route 10 W
Whippany, NJ 07981
(973) 428-2460
general@whippanong.org
http://www.whippanong.org/

Woodbridge Public Library
1 George Frederick Plaza
Woodbridge, NJ 07095
(732) 634-4450
(732) 634-1569 Fax
E-mail thru website
http://www.woodbridge.lib.nj.us/

NEW MEXICO

Alamogordo Public Library
920 Oregon Avenue
Alamogordo, NM 88310
(575) 439-4140
bmeagher@ci.alamogordo.nm.us
http://ci.alamogordo.nm.us/coa/
    communityservices/library.htm

**Albuquerque-Bernalillo County
Library System**
501 Copper Avenue NW
Albuquerque, NM 87102
(505) 768-5170
jclarke@cabq.gov
http://www.cabq.gov/library/

Artesia Public Library
306 West Richardson
Artesia, NM 88210
(505) 746-4252
apublib@pvtnetworks.net
http://www.pvtnetworks.net/~apublib/
New Mexico and Southwest
    collections

Belen Public Library
333 Becker Street
Belen, NM 87002
(505) 864-7522
http://www.youseemore.com/belen/

Capitan Public Library
P. O. Box 1169
Capitan, NM 88316
(575) 354-3035
(575) 354-3223 Fax
capitanlibrary@gmail.com
http://www.capitanlibrary.org/

Carlsbad Public Library
101 South Halagueno Street
Carlsbad, NM 88220
(575) 885-6776
cplref@elinlib.org
http://www.cityofcarlsbadnm.com/
    community_development/library/

Clovis-Carver Public Library
701 North Main Street
Clovis, NM 88101
(575) 769-7840
(575) 769-7842 Fax
library@cityofclovis.org
http://www.library.cityofclovis.org/
Southwestern collection
Hispanic collection

El Rito Library
P. O. Box 5
El Rito, NM 87530
(575) 581-4608
elritopubliclibrary@yahoo.com
http://www.elritolibrary.org/

Española Public Library
Richard Lucero Center
313 North Paseo de Oñate
Española, NM 87532
(505) 747-6087
(505) 753-5543 Fax
http://www.youseemore.com/
    espanola/

Farmington Public Library
2101 Farmington Avenue
Farmington, NM 87401
(505) 599-1270
E-mail thru website
http://www.infoway.org/

Hobbs Public Library
509 North Shipp
Hobbs, NM 88240
(575) 397-9328
reference@hobbspubliclibrary.org
http://www.hobbspubliclibrary.org/

Los Lunas Public Library
P. O. Box 1209
Los Lunas, NM 87031
(505) 839-3850
(505) 352-3582 Fax
shetterc@loslunasnm.gov
http://www.loslunasnm.gov/index.
   aspx?NID=103

Lovington Public Library
115 South Main Street
Lovington, NM 88260
(505) 396-3144
lpl@elin.lib.nm.us
http://lovingtonpublib.leaco.net/

Marshall Memorial Library
110 South Diamond Street
Deming, NM 88030
(505) 546-9202
(505) 546-9649 Fax
demingpl@cityofdeming.org
http://www.youseemore.com/
   Marshall/

Octavia Fellin Public Library
115 West Hill Avenue
Gallup, NM 87301
(505) 863-1291
libsuper@ci.gallup.nm.us
http://ofpl.ci.gallup.nm.us/
Southwestern Collection
Art collection

Rio Rancho Public Library
P. O. Box 15670
Rio Rancho, NM 87124
(505) 891-5013
(505) 892-4782 Fax
wcicola@ci.rio-rancho.nm.us
http://www.ci.rio-rancho.nm.us/
   index.aspx?NID=70

Roswell Public Library
301 North Pennsylvania Avenue
Roswell, NM 88201
(575) 622-7101
rplref@roswellpubliclibrary.org
http://www.roswellpubliclibrary.org/
Roswell Daily Record from 1903

Ruidoso Public Library
107 Kansas City Road
Ruidoso, NM 88345
(575) 258-3704
BeverlyMcFarland@ruidoso-nm.gov
http://www.youseemore.com/
   ruidosopl/
New Mexico History Collection

Sante Fe Public Library
145 Washington Street
Santa Fe, NM 87501
(505) 955-6780
library@santafenm.gov
http://www.santafelibrary.org/

Taos Public Library
402 Camino de la Placita
Taos, NM 87571
(575) 758-3063
librarian@taosgov.com
http://www.taoslibrary.org/

Thomas Branigan Memorial Library
200 East Picacho Avenue
Las Cruces, NM 88001
(575) 528-4000
(575) 528-4030 Fax
kteaze@las-cruces.org
http://library.las-cruces.org/

Tucumcari Library System
602 South 2nd Street
Tucumcari, NM 88401
(505) 461-0295
(505) 461-0297 Fax
mmolinas@cityoftucumcari.com
http://www.youseemore.com/
    tucumcari/

Woolworth Community Library
P. O. Box 1249
Jal, NM 88252
(575) 395-3268
(575) 395-2138 Fax
jpittam@leaco.net
http://www.woolworth.org/

NEW YORK

Adams Center Free Library
18267 State Route 177
Adams Center, NY 13606
(315) 583-5501
(315) 583-6247 Fax
E-mail thru website
http://www.adamscenterfreelibrary.
    org/

Adams Free Library
2 North Main Street
Adams, NY 13605
(315) 232-2265 Phone/Fax
E-mail thru website
http://www.adamsfreelibrary.org/

Albany Public Library
161 Washington Avenue
Albany, NY 12210
(518) 427-4300
(518) 449-3386 Fax
aplweb@uhls.lib.ny.us
http://www.albanypubliclibrary.org/

Amenia Free Library
P. O. Box 27
Amenia, NY 12501
(845) 373-8273 Phone/Fax
amenialib@nescape.net
http://amenia.lib.ny.us/

Amsterdam Free Library
28 Church Street
Amsterdam, NY 12010
(518) 842-1080
(518) 842-1169 Fax
http://www.amsterdamfreelibrary.com/
The Recorder 1988-present on
    microfilm

Ardsley Public Library
9 American Legion Drive
Ardsley, NY 10502
(914) 693-6636
(914) 693-6837 Fax
http://www.ardsleylibrary.org/

Avon Free Library
143 Genesee Street
Avon, NY 14414
(585) 226-8461
(585) 226-6615 Fax
http://avonfreelibrary.blogspot.com/

Baldwinsville Public Library
33 East Genesee Street
Baldwinsville, NY 13027
(315) 635-5631
(315) 635-6760 Fax
info@bville.lib.ny.us
http://www.bville.lib.ny.us/
Local History Room
Microfilm of Baldwinsville
    newspapers from mid-1800s
New York State documents

Bancroft Public Library
P. O. Box 515
Salem, NY 12865
(518) 854-7463
pculver@slibrary.org
http://www.slibrary.org/
Cemetery archives

Beekman Library
11 Town Center Boulevard
Beekman, NY [zipcode unknown]
(845) 724-3414
http://www.beekmanlibrary.org

Bell Memorial Library
P. O. Box 725
Nunda, NY 14517
(585) 468-2266 Phone/Fax
pgalbraith@pls-net.org
http://nunda.pls-net.org/

Blodgett Memorial Library
37 Broad Street
Fishkill, NY 12524
(845) 896-9215
(845) 896-9243 Fax
blodmem@optonline.net
http://blodgett.fishkill.lib.ny.us/

Branchport Free Library
Modeste Bedient Memorial Library
3699 Route 54-A
Branchport, NY 14418
(315) 595-2899
http://www.branchportlibrary.org/

Brentwood Public Library
34 Second Avenue
Brentwood, NY 11717
(631) 273-7883
brenref@suffolk.lib.ny.us
http://brentwood.suffolk.lib.ny.us/

Brewster Public Library
79 Main Street
Brewster, NY 10509
(845) 279-6421
(845) 279-0043 Fax
brewsterlibrary@yahoo.com
http://www.brewsterlibrary.org/
Local History Collection
Brewster Standard newspaper from
    1870 to 1982

Briarcliff Manor Public Library
1 Library Road
Briarcliff Manor, NY 10510
(914) 941-7072
(914) 941-7091 Fax
gmahoney@wlsmail.org
http://www.briarcliffmanorlibrary.org/

Brighton Memorial Library
2300 Elmwood Avenue
Rochester, NY 14618
(585) 784-5300
E-mail thru website
http://www.brightonlibrary.org/

Bronxville Public Library
201 Pondfield Road
Bronxville, NY 10708
(914) 337-7680
(914) 337-0332 Fax
Brolibrary@westchesterlibraries.org
http://villageofbronxville.com/
    sub1d.htm
Local History Room

Brooklyn Public Library
Grand Army Plaza
Brooklyn, NY 11238
(718) 230-2100
E-mail thru website
http://www.brooklynpubliclibrary.org/
The Brooklyn Collection

Broome County Public Library
185 Court Street
Binghamton, NY 13901
(607) 778-6400
bcpl@bclibrary.info
http://www.bclibrary.info/

Brunswick Community Library
605 Brunswick Road
Troy, NY 12180
(518) 279-4023
director@brunswicklibrary.org
http://www.brunswicklibrary.org/

**Buffalo and Erie County
Public Library**
1 Lafayette Square
Buffalo, NY 14203
(716) 858-8900
(716) 858-6211 Fax
E-mail thru website
http://www.buffalolib.org/
The Mark Twain Room
The Grosvenor Room

C. W. Clark Memorial Library
160 North Main Street
Oriskany Falls, NY 13425
(315) 821-7850
cwclarklibrary@midyork.org
http://www.midyork.org/
   OriskanyFalls/

Cairo Public Library
P. O. Box 720
Cairo, NY 12413
(518) 622-9864
(518) 622-9874 Fax
cairolibrary@mhcable.com
http://cairo.lib.ny.us/

Canajoharie Library and Art Gallery
2 Erie Boulevard
Canajoharie, NY 13317
(518) 673-2314
(518) 673-5243 Fax
llafera@sals.edu
http://www.clag.org/

Canastota Public Library
102 West Center Street
Canastota, NY 13032
(315) 697-7030
(315) 697-8653 Fax
lmetzger@midyork.org
http://www.canastotalibrary.org/

Chappaqua Library
195 South Greeley Avenue
Chappaqua, NY 10514
(914) 238-4779
(914) 238-3597 Fax
thornton@wlsmail.org
http://www.chappaqualibrary.org/

Chatham Public Library
11 Woodbridge Avenue
Chatham, NY 12037
(518) 392-3666
(518) 392-1546 Fax
chathampubliclibrary@chatham.
   k12.ny.us
http://chatham.lib.ny.us/

Chatauqua-Cattarauqua Library System
106 West 5th Street
Jamestown, NY 14701
(716) 484-7135
(716) 483-6880 Fax
cway@cclslib.org
http://www.cclslib.org/

Claverack Library
629 Route 23-B, Box 417
Claverack, NY 12513
(518) 851-7120 Phone/Fax
claveracklibrary@yahoo.com
http://claverack.lib.ny.us/

Clayville Library Association
P. O. Box 282
Clayville, NY 13322
(315) 839-5893
(315) 839-5070 Fax
http://www.clayvillelibrary.org/

Clifton Park-Halfmoon Public Library
475 Moe Road
Clifton Park, NY 12065
(518) 371-8622
(518) 371-3799 Fax
director@sals.edu
http://www.cphlibrary.org/

Clinton Community Library
P. O. Box 6
Clinton Corners, NY 12514
(845) 266-5530
(845) 266-5748 Fax
library@cl.epals.com
http://clinton.lib.ny.us/
Comprehensive children's collection

Clinton Essex Franklin Library System
33 Oak Street
Plattsburgh, NY 12901
(518) 563-5190
(518) 563-0421 Fax
info2@cefls.org
http://www.cefls.org

Cold Spring Harbor Library
95 Harbor Road
Cold Spring Harbor, NY 11724
(631) 692-6820
(631) 692-6827 Fax
cshrib@suffolk.lib.ny.us
http://cshlibrary.suffolk.lib.ny.us/

Commack Public Library
18 Hauppauge Road
Commack, NY 11725
(631) 499-0888
lpastore@suffolk.lib.ny.us
http://commack.suffolk.lib.ny.us/

Community Free Library
86 Public Square
Holley, NY 14470
(585) 638-6987
(585) 638-7436 Fax
sshaw@nioga.org
http://www.holleylibrary.org/

Connetquot Public Library
760 Ocean Avenue
Bohemia, NY 11716
(631) 567-5079
cnqt_comments@yahoo.com
http://www.connetquot.lib.ny.us/

Copiague Memorial Public Library
50 Deauville Boulevard
Copiague, NY 11726
(631) 691-1111
(631) 691-5098 Fax
wehaveitall@copiaguelibrary.org
http://ww2.copiaguelibrary.org/
  default.htm

Crandall Public Library
251 Glen Street
Glens Falls, NY 12801
(518) 792-6508
(518) 792-5251 Fax
mcdonald@crandalllibrary.org
http://www.crandalllibrary.org/

Croton Free Library
171 Cleveland Drive
Croton-on-Hudson, NY 10520
(914) 271-6612
http://www.crotonfreelibrary.org/

**Cutchogue-New Suffolk
Free Library**
P. O. Box 935
Cutchogue, NY 11935
(631) 734-6360
(631) 734-7010 Fax
cutclib@suffolk.lib.ny.us
http://www.cutchoguelibrary.org/

D. R. Evarts Library
80 Second Street
Athens, NY 12015
(518) 945-1417
(518) 945-1725 Fax
athens@mhcable.com
http://evarts.athens.lib.ny.us/

Dansville Public Library
200 Main Street
Dansville, NY 14437
(585) 335-6720
director@dansville.lib.ny.us
http://dansville.lib.ny.us/

David A. Howe Public Library
155 North Main Street
Wellsville, NY 14895
(585) 593-3410
(585) 593-4176 Fax
wellsville@stls.org
http://www.davidahowelibrary.org/

Deposit Free Library
159 Front Street
Deposit, NY 13754
(607) 467-2577
(607) 467-5669 Fax
DE_ILL@4cty.org
http://www.depositchamber.com/
  Library.html

Desmond-Fish Library
Alice Curtis Desmond and Hamilton Fish Library
P. O. Box 265
Garrison, NY 10524
(845) 424-3020
dflstaff@highlands.com
http://dfl.highlands.com/
Extensive electronic media collection

DeWitt Community Library
3649 Erie Boulevard East
Shopping Town Mall
DeWitt, NY 13214
(315) 446-3578
info@dewittcommunitylibrary.org
http://www.dewlib.org/

Dobbs Ferry Public Library
55 Main Street
Dobbs Ferry, NY 10522
(914) 693-6614
(914) 693-4671 Fax
dobref@westchesterlibraries.org
http://www.dobbsferrylibrary.org/

Dover Plains Library
1797 Route 22
Wingdale, NY 12594
(845) 832-6605
(845) 832-6616 Fax
library@doverlib.org
http://dover.lib.ny.us/

**East Greenbush
Community Library**
10 Community Way
East Greenbush, NY 12061
(518) 477-7476
(518) 477-6692 Fax
egmlibrary@gmail.com
http://www.eastgreenbushlibrary.org/

East Hampton Library
159 Main Street
East Hampton, NY 11937
(631) 324-0222
(631) 329-5947 Fax
ehamlib@suffolk.lib.ny.us
http://www.easthamptonlibrary.org/
Extensive Long Island Collection
Thomas Moran Biographical Art
   Collection

East Meadow Public Library
1886 Front Street
East Meadow, NY 11554
(516) 794-2570
(516) 794-2949 Fax
E-mail thru website
http://www.eastmeadow.info/

Eastchester Public Library
11 Oakridge Place
Eastchester, NY 10709
(914) 793-5055
(914) 793-7862 Fax
http://www.eastchesterlibrary.org/

Emma S. Clark Memorial Library
120 Main Street
Setauket, NY 11733
(631) 941-4080
reference@emmaclark.org
http://www.emmaclark.org/

Fair Haven Public Library
P. O. Box 602
Fair Haven, NY 13064
(315) 947-5851
fairhave@twcny.rr.com
http://www.fairhavenlibrary.org

Fairport Public Library
1 Village Landing
Fairport, NY 14450
(585) 223-9091
E-mail thru website
http://www.fairportlibrary.org/

Fayetteville Free Library
300 Orchard Street
Fayetteville, NY 13066
(313) 637-6374
(313) 637-2306 Fax
sconsidine@fayettevillefreelibrary.org
http://www.fayettevillefreelibrary.org/
Motto sheet music collection
Local history

Field Library
4 Nelson Avenue
Peekskill, NY 10566
(914) 737-1212
(914) 737-0714 Fax
scanaan@wlsmail.org
http://www.peekskill.org/
Local history collection
The Lincoln Collection
Down Syndrome collection

Finger Lakes Library System
119 East Green Street
Ithaca, NY 14850
1-800-909-3557
(607) 273-3618 Fax
http://www.flls.org/

Flower Memorial Library
Roswell P. Flower Memorial Library
229 Washington Street
Watertown, NY 13601
(315) 785-7705
(315) 788-2584 Fax
http://www.flowermemoriallibrary.org/

Floyd Memorial Library
539 First Street
Greenport, NY 11944
(631) 477-0660
(631) 477-2647 Fax
flydlib@suffolk.lib.ny.us
http://floydmemoriallibrary.
   northfork.net/

Four County Library System
304 Clubhouse Road
Vestal, NY 13850
(607) 723-8236
(607) 723-1722 Fax
pbrown@4cls.org
http://www.4cls.org/

Franklin Free Library
P. O. Box 947
Franklin, NY 13775
(607) 829-2941
(607) 829-5017 fax
FR.ILL@4cls.org
http://www.franklinfreelibrary.org/

Galway Public Library
P. O. Box 207
Galway, NY 12074
(518) 882-6385
apoulin@sals.edu
http://www.galwaypubliclibrary.org/

Gates Public Library
1605 Buffalo Road
Rochester, NY 14624
(585) 247-6446
(585) 426-5733 Fax
http://www.gateslibrary.org/

Geneva Free Library
244 Main Street
Geneva, NY 14456
(315) 789-5303
(315) 789-9835 Fax
mnyerges@PLS-Net.org
http://genevapubliclibrary.net/

Germantown Library
P. O. Box 468
Germantown, NY 12526
(518) 537-5800
(518) 537-5928 Fax
germantownlibrary@valstar.net
http://germantownlibrary.org/

Gilbertsville Free Library
P. O. Box 332
Gilbertsville, NY 13776
(607) 783-2832
librarian@stny.rr.com
http://www.gilbertsville.com/
   Library.htm
Local history collection
Women in history collection

Gold Coast Public Library
50 Railroad Avenue
Glen Head, NY 11545
(516) 759-8300 or 8308
goldcoast1@optonline.net
http://www.goldcoastlibrary.org/

Goshen Public Library
203 Main Street
Goshen, NY 10924
(845) 294-6606
(845) 294-7158 Fax
http://goshenpubliclibrary.org/

Great Neck Library
159 Bayview Avenue
Great Neck, NY 11023
(516) 466-8055
(516) 829-8297 Fax
comments@greatnecklibrary.org
http://www.greatnecklibrary.org/

Greenburgh Public Library
300 Tarrytown Road
Elmsford, NY 10523
(914) 721-8200
(914) 721-8201 Fax
director@greenburghlibrary.org
http://www.greenburghlibrary.org/
   scripts/index.cfm

Greenville Public Library
P. O. Box 8
Greenville, NY 12083
(518) 966-8205
(518) 966-4822 Fax
bflach@francomm.com
http://greenville.lib.ny.us/

Greenwood Lake Public Library
79 Waterstone Road
Greenwood Lake, NY 10925
(845) 477-8377
(845) 477-8397 Fax
joan@gwllibrary.org
http://www.gwllibrary.org/

Grinnell Library
2642 East Main Street
Wappingers Falls, NY 12590
(845) 297-3428
(845) 297-1506 Fax
gldirector@gmail.com
http://www.grinnell.wappingers.lib.
   ny.us/

Guernsey Memorial Library
3 Court Street
Norwich, NY 13815
(607) 334-4034
(607) 336-3901 Fax
guernsey@4cls.org
http://www.4cls.org/webpages/
    members/norwich/NORWICH.
    html

Haines Falls Free Library
52 North Lake Road
Haines Falls, NY 12436
(518) 589-5707
(518) 589-0311 Fax
hainesfalllibrary@hvc.rr.com
http://hainesfalls.lib.ny.us/

Hastings-on-Hudson Public Library
7 Maple Avenue
Hastings-on-Hudson, NY 10706
(914) 478-3307
(914) 478-4813 Fax
has@westchesterlibraries.org
http://www.hastingslibrary.org

**Haverstraw King's Daughters
Public Library**
10 West Ramapo Road
Garnerville, NY 10923
(845) 786-3800
(845) 786-3791 Fax
E-mail thru website
http://www.hkdpl.org/

Heermance Memorial Library
1 Ely Street
Coxsackie, NY 12051
(518) 731-8084
(518) 731-8264 Fax
director@hml.lib.ny.us
http://www.hml.lib.ny.us/

Hendrick Hudson Free Library
185 Kings Ferry Road
Montrose, NY 10548
(914) 739-5654
director@henhudlibrary.org
http://www.henhudfreelibrary.org/

Henrietta Public Library
455 Calkins Road
Rochester, NY 14623
(585) 334-3401
pbemhar@libraryweb.org
http://www.hpl.org/

Highland Public Library
30 Church Street
Highland, NY 12528
(845) 691-2275
(845) 691-6302 Fax
jkelsall@highlandlibrary.org
http://www.highlandlibrary.org/

Hillside Public Library
155 Lakeville Road
New Hyde Park, NY 11040
(516) 355-7850
hillsidelibrary@yahoo.com
http://www.nassaulibrary.org/hillside/

Hiram Halle Memorial Library
271 Westchester Avenue
Pound Ridge, NY 10576
(914) 764-5085
(914) 764-5319 Fax
hhml@wlsmail.org
http://www.poundridgelibrary.org/

Howard Public Library
3607 County Route 70-A
Hornell, NY 14843
(607) 566-2412
(607) 566-3679 Fax
nelsonl@stls.org
http://www.howardpubliclibrary.com/

Hudson Area Association Library
400 State Street
Hudson, NY 12534
(518) 828-1792
(518) 822-0567 Fax
hudsonarealibrary@gmail.com
http://hudson.lib.ny.us/

Hunter Public Library
P. O. Box 376
Hunter, NY 12442
(518) 263-4655 Phone/Fax
hunter@francomm.com
http://hunter.lib.ny.us/

Huntington Memorial Library
62 Chestnut Street
Oneonta, NY 13820
(607) 432-1980
on.sarah@4cls.org
http://www.hmloneonta.org/

Hurley Library
P. O. Box 660
Hurley, NY 12443
(845) 338-2092 Phone/Fax
hurleydirector@hvc.rr.com
http://hurley.lib.ny.us/

Hyde Park Free Library
2 Main Street
Hyde Park, NY 12538
(845) 229-7791
(845) 229-6521 Fax
hyplib@yahoo.com
http://hydeparklibrary.org/

Irvington Public Library
12 South Astor Street
Irvington-on-Hudson, NY 10533
(914) 591-7840
irvref@wlsmail.org
http://www.irvingtonlibrary.org/

**James Prendergast
Library Association**
509 Cherry Street
Jamestown, NY 14701
(716) 484-7135
cway@cclslib.org
http://www.prendergastlibrary.org/

Jervis Public Library
613 North Washington Street
Rome, NY 13440
(315) 336-4570
E-mail thru website
http://www.jervislibrary.org/
Local history

John C. Hart Memorial Library
1130 Main Street
Shrub Oak, NY 10588
(914) 245-5262
pbarresi@wlsmail.org
http://www.yorktownlibrary.org/

Julia L. Butterfield
Memorial Library
10 Morris Avenue
Cold Spring, NY 10516
(845) 265-3040
butterfd@gmail.com
http://www.butterfieldlibrary.org/

Katonah Village Library
26 Bedford Road
Katonah, NY 10536
(914) 232-3508
katref@wlsmail.org
http://www.katonahlibrary.org/
Art collection
Collection of plays and books about
    them

Kent Public Library
17 Sybil's Crossing
Kent Lakes, NY 10512
(845) 225-8585
(845) 225-8549 Fax
library@kentlibrary.org
http://www.kentlibrary.org/

Kinderhook Memorial Library
P. O. Box 293
Kinderhook, NY 12106
(518) 758-6192
oklibrary@berk.com
http://oklibrary.org/

Kingston Library
55 Franklin Street
Kingston, NY 12401
(845) 331-0507
(845) 331-7981 Fax
director@kingstonlibrary.org
http://www.kingstonlibrary.org/

Kirkland Town Library
55-1/2 College Street
Clinton, NY 13323
(315) 853-2038
(315) 853-1785 Fax
clinton@midyork.org
http://www.kirklandtownlibrary.org/

LaGrange Association Library
488 Freedom Plains Road, Route 55
Poughkeepsie, NY 12603
(845) 452-3141
(845) 452-1974 Fax
lagrangelib@hotmail.com
http://laglib.org/

Lake Placid Public Library
2471 Main Street
Lake Placid, NY 12946
(518) 523-3200
librarian@lakeplacidlibrary.org
http://www.lakeplacidlibrary.org/

Larchmont Public Library
121 Larchmont Avenue
Larchmont, NY 10538
(914) 834-2281
(914) 834-0351 Fax
larchmontlibrary@hotmail.com
http://www.larchmontlibrary.org/

Lewiston Public Library
305 South 8th Street
Lewiston, NY 14092
(716) 754-4720
(716) 754-7386 Fax
http://www.lewistonpubliclibrary.org/

Lisle Free Library
P. O. Box 305
Lisle, NY 13797
(607) 692-3115
li.ill@4cls.org
http://www.4cls.org/webpages/
    members/lisle/index.html

Liverpool Public Library
310 Tulip Street
Liverpool, NY 13088
(315) 457-0310
(315) 453-7867 Fax
info@lpl.org
http://www.lpl.org/

Livingston Free Library
P. O. Box 105
Livingston, NY 12541
(518) 851-2270 Phone/Fax
livlib@netscape.net
http://livingston.lib.ny.us/

Lockport Public Library
P. O. Box 475
Lockport, NY 14095
(716) 433-5935
E-mail thru website
http://www.lockportlibrary.org/
Local history collection

Macsherry Library
112 Walton Street
Alexandria Bay, NY 13607
(315) 482-2241
http://www.macsherrylibrary.org/

Mahopac Public Library
668 Route 6
Mahopac, NY 10541
(845) 628-2009
(845) 628-0672 Fax
library@mahopaclibrary.org
http://www.mahopaclibrary.org/

Mamaroneck Public Library
102 Mamaroneck Avenue
Mamaroneck, NY 10543
(914) 698-1250
themamaronecklibrary@gmail.com
http://www.mamaronecklibrary.org/

Manlius Library
1 Arkie Albanese Avenue
Manlius, NY 13104
(315) 682-6400
manliuslibrary@yahoo.com
http://www.manliuslib.org/

Marlboro Free Library
P. O. Box 780
Marlboro, NY 12542
(845) 236-7272
(845) 236-7635 Fax
http://www.marlborolibrary.org/

Mary L. Wilcox Memorial Library
2630 Main Street
Whitney Point, NY 13862
(607) 692-3159
http://www.4cls.org/WhitneyPoint/
    MWmemoriallibrary.htm

Mastics-Moriches-Shirley Community Library
407 William Floyd Parkway
Shirley, NY 11967
(631) 399-1511
(631) 281-4442 Fax
E-mail thru website
http://www.communitylibrary.org/

Maxwell Memorial Library
14 Genesee Street
Camillus, NY 13031
(315) 672-3661
maxmemlib@yahoo.com
http://www.
    maxwellmemoriallibrary.org/

Middle Country Public Library
101 Eastwood Boulevard
Centereach, NY 11720
(631) 585-9393
(631) 585-5035 Fax
webmaster@mcpl.lib.ny.us
http://www.mcpl.lib.ny.us/

Middletown Thrall Library
11-19 Depot Street
Middletown, NY 10940
(845) 341-5454
thrall7@warwick.net
http://www.thrall.org/

Mid-Hudson Library System
103 Market Street
Poughkeepsie, NY 12601
(845) 471-6060
(845) 454-5940 Fax
webaccount@midhudson.org
http://midhudson.org/

Mid-York Library System
1600 Lincoln Avenue
Utica, NY 13502
(315) 735-8328
(315) 735-0943 Fax
http://www.midyork.org

Millbrook Free Library
3 Friendly Lane
Millbrook, NY 12545
(845) 677-3611
(845) 677-5127 Fax
millbrook.library@verizon.net
http://millbrooklibrary.org/

Moffat Library of Washingtonville
6 West Main Street
Washingtonville, NY 10992
(845) 496-5483
(845) 496-6854 Fax
moffat@rcls.org
http://www.moffatlibrary.org/

Monroe County Library System
115 South Avenue
Rochester, NY 14604
(585) 428-7300
E-mail thru website
http://www3.libraryweb.org/
    home2.aspx

Monroe Free Library
44 Millpond Parkway
Monroe, NY 10950
(845) 783-4411
http://monroefreelibrary.org/2009/
    index.php#

Moore Memorial Library
59 Genesee Street
Greene, NY 13778
(607) 656-9349
gr.mary@4cls.org
http://www.4cls.org/greene/greene.
  html

Morton Memorial Library
22 Elm Street
Pine Hill, NY 12465
(845) 254-4222 Phone/Fax
charlisweiss@yahoo.com
http://morton.pinehill.lib.ny.us/

Mount Kisco Public Library
55 Maple Avenue
Mt. Kisco, NY 10549
(914) 666-8041
(914) 666-3899 Fax
sriley@wlsmail.org
http://www.mountkiscolibrary.org/

Mount Pleasant Public Library
350 Bedford Road
Pleasantville, NY 10570
(914) 769-0548
director@mountpleasantlibrary.org
http://www.mountpleasantlibrary.org/

Mount Vernon Public Library
28 South 1st Avenue
Mount Vernon, NY 10550
(914) 668-1840
(914) 668-1018 Fax
http://www.
  mountvernonpubliclibrary.org/
Haynes Collection
Local history room
Government documents

Naples Library
118 South Main Street
Naples, NY 14512
(585) 374-2757
bwarner@pls-net.org
http://www.naples.pls-net.org/

Nassau Library System
900 Jerusalem Avenue
Uniondale, NY 11553
(516) 292-8920
(516) 481-4777 Fax
thresher@nassaulibrary.org
http://www.nassaulibrary.org/

New City Library
220 North Main Street
New City, NY 10956
(845) 634-4997 or 4962
(845) 634-0173 Fax
vrutter@rcls.org
http://www.newcitylibrary.org/

New Hartford Public Library
2 Library Lane
New Hartford, NY 13413
(315) 733-1535
http://www.
  newhartfordpubliclibrary.org/

New Hyde Park Village Library
[now consolidated with Hillside
Public Library]

New Lebanon Library
550 State Route 20
New Lebanon, NY 12125
(518) 794-8844
leb@taconic.net
http://newlebanon.lib.ny.us/

New Rochelle Public Library
1 Library Plaza
New Rochelle, NY 10801
(914) 632-7878
(914) 632-0262 Fax
tgeoffino@nrpl.org
http://www.nrpl.org/

New York Mills Public Library
Mid-York Library System
1600 Lincoln Avenue
Utica, NY 13502
(315) 735-8328
(315) 735-0943 Fax
E-mail thru website
http://www.nymills.com/

New York Public Library
Stephen A. Schwarzman Building
5th Avenue and 42nd Street
New York, NY 10018
(212) 930-0800
E-mail thru website
http://www.nypl.org/
Spencer Collection
Photography Collection
Pforzheimer Collection
Manuscripts & Archives Collection
Arents Collection

New York State Library
Cultural Education Center
Empire State Plaza
Albany, NY 12230
(518) 474-5930
(518) 474-5786 Fax
circ@mail.nysed.gov
http://www.nysl.nysed.gov/
Historical manuscripts
Sheet music collection
Photograph collections

Newburgh Free Library
124 Grand Street
Newburgh, NY 12550
(845) 563-3600
(845) 563-3602 Fax
mverdi@rcls.org
http://www.newburghlibrary.org/
Local history

Niagara Falls Public Library
Earl W. Brydges Building
1425 Main Street
Niagara Falls, NY 14305
(716) 286-4911
http://www.niagarafallspubliclib.org/

Nioga Library System
6575 Wheeler Road
Lockport, NY 14094
(716) 434-6167
(716) 434-8231 Fax
E-mail thru website
http://catalog.nioga.org/rooms/
    portal/page/Sirsi_HOME

North Castle Public Library
19 Whippoorwill Road East
Armonk, NY 10504
(914) 273-3887
cansnes@wlsmail.org
http://www.northcastlelibrary.org/
    library_2007/HTML/index.htm

North Chatham Free Library
Main Street, Route 203
North Chatham, NY 12132
(518) 766-3211 Phone/Fax
nclibrary@taconic.net
http://northchatham.lib.ny.us/

North Salem Free Library
Ruth Keeler Memorial Library
276 Titicus Road
North Salem, NY 10560
(914) 669-5161
(914) 669-5173 Fax
keelerlibrary@yahoo.com
http://www.northsalemlibrary.org/

NorthEast-Millerton Library
P. O. Box 786
Millerton, NY 12546
(518) 789-3340
(518) 789-6802 Fax
nemlib@fairpoint.net
http://nemillertonlibrary.org/

Northern Onondaga Public Library
8686 Knowledge Lane
Cicero, NY 13039
(315) 699-2534
http://www.nopl.org/

**Northport-East Northport
Public Library**
151 Laurel Avenue
Northport, NY 11768
(631) 261-6930
E-mail thru website
http://www.nenpl.org/

Nyack Library
59 South Broadway
Nyack, NY 10960
(845) 358-3370
(845) 358-6429 Fax
reference@nyacklibrary.org
http://nyacklibrary.org/

Oceanside Library
30 Davison Avenue
Oceanside, NY 11572
(516) 766-2360
ocl@oceansidelibrary.com
http://www.oceansidelibrary.com/#

Ogden Farmer's Library
269 Ogden Center Road
Spencerport, NY 14559
(585) 617-6181
(585) 352-3406 Fax
library@ogdenny.com
http://www.ogdenny.com/
   TownGovernment/
Departments/Library//
Local History Collection

Olean Public Library
134 North 2nd Street
Olean, NY 14760
(716) 372-0200
(716) 372-8651 Fax
info@oleanlibrary.org
http://www.oleanlibrary.org/

Olive Free Library Association
4033 Route 28-A
West Shokan, NY 12494
(845) 657-2482
(845) 657-2664 Fax
olivefreelibrary@hvc.rr.com
http://olive.westshokan.lib.ny.us/

Onondaga County Public Library
Robert P. Kinchen Central Library
The Galleries of Syracuse
447 South Salina Street
Syracuse, NY 13202
(315) 435-1800
edaily@onlib.org
http://www.onlib.org/
McGrath sacred choral music
Local history
Government documents

Onondaga Free Library
4840 West Seneca Turnpike
Syracuse, NY 13215
(315) 492-1727
(315) 492-1323 Fax
onondagafree@yahoo.com
http://www.oflibrary.org/

Oswego Public Library
120 East Second Street
Oswego, NY 13126
(315) 341-5867
oswegopl@northnet.org
http://www.oswegopubliclibrary.org/

Paine Memorial Free Library
2 Gilliland Lane
Willsboro, NY 12996
(518) 963-4478
http://www.willsborony.com/
   painememoriallibrary/

Patterson Library
P. O. Box 418
Patterson, NY 12563
(845) 878-6121
phaar@pattersonlibrary.org
http://www.pattersonlibrary.org/

Pawling Free Library
11 Broad Street
Pawling, NY 12564
(845) 855-3444
(845) 855-8138 Fax
director@pawlinglibrary.org
http://www.pawlinglibrary.org/

Pearl River Public Library
80 Franklin Avenue
Pearl River, NY 10965
(845) 735-4084
(845) 735-4041 Fax
prlibrary1@earthlink.net
http://www.pearlriverlibrary.org/

Pelham Public Library
530 Colonial Avenue
Pelham, NY 10803
(914) 738-1234
contactus@pelhamlibrary.org
http://www.pelhamlibrary.org/

Penfield Public Library
1985 Baird Road
Penfield, NY 14526
(585) 340-8720
(585) 340-8748 Fax
E-mail thru website
http://www.libraryweb.org/penfield/

Penn Yan Public Library
214 Main Street
Penn Yan, NY 14527
(315) 536-6114
(315) 536-0131 Fax
lhovergaard@pypl.org
http://www.pypl.org/

Philmont Public Library
P. O. Box 816
Philmont, NY 12565
(518) 672-5010 Phone/Fax
library@philmont.org
http://www.philmont.org/library/
   index.html

Phoenicia Library
48 Main Street
Phoenicia, NY 12464
(845) 688-7811
phoenicialibrary@gmail.com
http://phoenicia.lib.ny.us/

Pine Plains Free Library
P. O. Box 325
Pine Plains, NY 12567
(518) 398-1927
(518) 398-6085 Fax
pinelib@fairpoint.net
http://pineplains.lib.ny.us/

Pioneer Library System
2557 State Route 21
Canandaigua, NY 14424
(585) 394-8260
(585) 394-1935 Fax
info@pls-net.org
http://www.pls-net.org/

Plattekill Public Library
2047 Route 32
Modena, NY 12548
(845) 883-7286
plattekill_lib@hotmail.com
http://plattekill.lib.ny.us/
Regional collection

Plattsburgh Public Library
19 Oak Street
Plattsburgh, NY 12901
(518) 563-0921
(518) 563-1681 Fax
parrottej@cityofplattsburgh-ny.gov
http://www.plattsburghlib.org/
Extensive local history collection

Pleasant Valley Free Library
P. O. Box 633
Pleasant Valley, N 12569
(845) 635-8460
(845) 635-9556 Fax
danielapulice@hotmail.com
http://www.pleasantvalleylibrary.org/

Poestenkill Library
P. O. Box 305
Poestenkill, NY 12140
(518) 283-3721
(518) 283-5618 Fax
poes1@uhls.lib.ny.us
http://www.poestenkilllibrary.org/

**Port Chester-Rye Brook Public
Library**
1 Haseco Avenue
Port Chester, NY 10573
(914) 939-6710
http://www.portchesterlibrary.org/

Port Washington Public Library
1 Library Drive
Port Washington, NY 11050
(516) 883-4400
library@pwpl.org
http://www.pwpl.org/
Local history digital archives

**Poughkeepsie Public Library
District**
Adriance Memorial Library
93 Market Street
Poughkeepsie, NY 12601
(845) 485-3445
(845) 485-3789 Fax
tlawrence@poklib.org
http://www.poklib.org/

Pulteney Free Library
P. O. Box 215
Pulteney, NY 14874
(607) 868-3652
PTL_Barb@STLS.org
http://www.pulteney.org/

Purchase Free Library
3093 Purchase Street
Purchase, NY 10577
(914) 948-0550
http://www.purchasefreelibrary.org

Putnam Valley Free Library
30 Oscawana Lake Road
Putnam Valley, NY 10579
(845) 528-3242
(845) 528-3297 Fax
http://www.putnamvalleylibrary.org/

Queens Library
89-11 Merrick Boulevard
Jamaica, NY 11432
(718) 990-0704
(718) 291-2695 Fax
joanne.king@queenslibrary.org
http://www.queenslibrary.org/#
 Jazz collections
Long Island history collection

Ramapo Catskill Library System
619 Route 17M
Middletown, NY 10940
(845) 343-1131
(845) 343-1205 Fax
E-mail thru website
http://www.rcls.org/

Red Creek Library
4595 Route 21N
Canandaigua, NY 14424
(716) 394-8260
(716) 394-1935 Fax
http://www.redcreekny.net/library.htm

Red Hook Public Library
7444 South Broadway
Red Hook, NY 12571
(845) 758-3241
(831) 304-3241 Fax
RPublicLibrary@hvc.rr.com
http://redhook.lib.ny.us/

Reed Memorial Library
1733 Route 6
Carmel, NY 10512
(845) 225-2439
(845) 225-1436 Fax
jbuck@carmellibrary.org
http://reed.carmel.lib.ny.us/

Richmond Memorial Library
19 Ross Street
Batavia, NY 14020
(585) 343-9550
(585) 344-4651 Fax
btvdir@nioga.org
http://www.batavialibrary.org/
Local history collection

Riverhead Free Library
330 Court Street
Riverhead, NY 11901
(631) 727-3228
(631) 727-4762 Fax
ljacobs@suffolk.lib.ny.us
http://river.suffolk.lib.ny.us/

**Roeliff Jansen
Community Library**
2609 Route 23
Hillsdale, NY 12529
(518) 325-4101
http://www.roejanlibrary.org/

Rosendale Library
P. O. Box 482
Rosendale, NY 12472
(845) 658-9013
(845) 658-3752 Fax
rosendalelibrary@hvi.net
http://www.rosendalelibrary.org/
Local History Collection

Round Lake Public Library
P. O. Box 665
Round Lake, NY 12151
(518) 899-2285
(518) 899-0006 Fax
roundlake@sals.edu
http://roundlake.sals.edu/

Rye Free Reading Room
1061 Boston Post Road
Rye, NY 10580
(914) 967-0480
khadeler@ryelibrary.org
http://www.ryelibrary.org/

Sachem Public Library
150 Holbrook Road
Holbrook, NY 11741
(631) 588-5024
sachlib@suffolk.lib.ny.us
http://sachem.suffolk.lib.ny.us/
E. Bassford Hawkins arrowhead
    collection
Historical newspapers

Salamanca Public Library
155 Wildwood Avenue
Salamanca, NY 14779
(716) 945-1890
(716) 945-2741 Fax
tsharbaugh@salmun.com
http://www.salmun.com/dept/
    library/library.htm

Salina Free Library
100 Belmont Street
Mattydale, NY 13211
(315) 454-4524
(315) 454-3466 Fax
info@salinalibrary.org
http://www.salinalibrary.org/

Sarah Hull Hallock Free Library
56-58 Main Street
Milton, NY 12547
(845) 795-2200
(845) 795-1005 Fax
miltonlibrary@hvc.rr.com
http://hallock.milton.lib.ny.us/

Saratoga Springs Public Library
49 Henry Street
Saratoga Springs, NY 12866
(518) 584-7860
(518) 584-7866 Fax
E-mail thru website
http://www.sspl.org/
Local history room

Saugerties Public Library
91 Washington Avenue
Saugerties, NY 12477
(845) 246-4317
(845) 246-0858 Fax
jserrano@saugertiespubliclibrary.org
http://saugertiespubliclibrary.org/

Scarsdale Public Library
54 Olmsted Road
Scarsdale, NY 10583
(914) 722-1300
SCAasstdirector@wlsmail.org
http://www.scarsdalelibrary.org/
   about/index.html
Historic American newspapers
Local history, with photographs

Schenectady County Public Library
99 Clinton Street
Schenectady, NY 12305
(518) 388-4500
scpl@scpl.org
http://www.scpl.org/
Local history collections

Seneca Falls Library
47 Cayuga Street
Seneca Falls, NY 13148
(315) 568-8265
(315) 568-1606 Fax
http://www.senecafallslibrary.org/

Seymour Public Library
176-178 Genesee Street
Auburn, NY 13021
(315) 252-2571
seymourlibrary@seymourlibrary.org
http://www.seymourlibrary.org/
History Room

Sidney Memorial Public Library
8 River Street
Sidney, NY 13838
(607) 563-1200
(607) 563-7675 Fax
si.robin@4cls.org
http://www.4cls.org/sidney/smpl.htm

Skene Memorial Library
1017 Main Street
Fleischmanns, NY 12430
(845) 254-4581
librarian@skenelib.org
http://www.skenelib.org/
Regional collection

Smith Memorial Library
21 Miller Avenue
Chautauqua, NY 14722
(716) 357-6296
(716) 357-3657 Fax
lkinnear@ciweb.org
http://www.ciweb.org/library/

Smithtown Library
1 North Country Road
Smithtown, NY 11787
(631) 265-2072
http://www.smithlib.org/

Somers Library
P. O. Box 443
Somers, NY 10589
(914) 232-5717
somers@wlsmail.org
http://www.somerslibrary.org/

South Salem Library
Lewisboro Library
P. O. Box 477
South Salem, NY 10590
(914) 763-3857
lewisborolibrary@gmail.com
http://www.southsalemlibrary.org/
http://www.lewisborolibrary.org/

Southern Adirondack Library System
22 Whitney Place
Saratoga Springs, NY 12866
(518) 584-7300
(518) 587-5589 Fax
sdallas@sals.edu
http://www.sals.edu/

Southern Tier Library System
9424 Scott Road
Painted Post, NY 14870
(607) 962-3141
(607) 962-5356 Fax
stls@stls.org
http://www.stls.org/

Southold Free Library
P. O. Box 697
Southold, NY 11971
(631) 765-2077
(631) 765-2197 Fax
cmmacarth@optonline.net
http://sohd.suffolk.lib.ny.us/

Southworth Library
24 West Main Street
Dryden, NY 13053
(607) 844-4782
(607) 844-5310 Fax
southworth@twcny.rr.com
http://southworthlibrary.org/
Copies of every issue of Rumsey's
    Companion, Dryden's first
    newspaper
An original manuscript of Abraham
    Lincoln's
Original copies of the Centennial
    History of Dryden, 1797-1897

Staatsburg Library Society
70 Old Post Road
Staatsburg, NY 12580
(845) 889-4683
(845) 889-8414 Fax
staatslibrary@yahoo.com
http://staatsburg.lib.ny.us/

Stanford Free Library
14 Creamery Road
Stanfordville, NY 12581
(845) 868-1341
(845) 868-7482 Fax
stanfordlibrary@optonline.net
http://stanfordlibrary.org/

Steele Memorial Library
Chemung County Library District
101 East Church Street
Elmira, NY 14901
(607) 733-8611
(607) 733-9176 Fax
E-mail thru website
http://www.steele.lib.ny.us/

Stone Ridge Public Library
P. O. Box 188
Stone Ridge, NY 12484
(845) 687-7023
(845) 687-0094 Fax (Shared. Call first)
stoneridgelibrary@hvc.rr.com
http://www.stoneridgelibrary.org/

Sullivan Free Library
P. O. Box 337
Bridgeport, NY 13030
(315) 633-2253
(315) 633-2945 Fax
bridgeport@midyork.org
http://www.sullivanfreelibrary.org/

Tivoli Free Library
P. O. Box 400
Tivoli, NY 12583
(845) 757-3771
tivlib@webjogger.net
http://www.tivolilibrary.org/

Tompkins County Public Library
101 East Green Street
Ithaca, NY 14850
(607) 272-4557
(607) 272-8111 Fax
jsteiner@tcpl.org
http://www.tcpl.org/

Town of Chester Public Library
P. O. Box 451
Chestertown, NY 12817
(518) 494-5384
library@chesterlibrary.org
http://www.chesterlib.adirondack.
   ny.us/
Oral history collection

Town of Esopus Library
P. O. Box 1167
Port Ewen, NY 12466
(845) 338-5580
(845) 338-5583 Fax
esopuslibrary@hvc.rr.com
http://www.esopuslibrary.org/

Tuckahoe Public Library
71 Columbus Avenue
Tuckahoe, NY 10707
(914) 961-2121
(914) 961-3832 Fax
dcoppola@wlsmail.org
http://www.tuckahoelibrary.org/

Tully Free Library
12 State Street
Tully, NY 13159
(315) 696-8606
(315) 696-8120 Fax
ltickner@ocpl.lib.ny.us
http://www.tullylibrary.org/

Upper Hudson Library System
28 Essex Street
Albany, NY 12206
(518) 437-9880
(518) 437-9884 Fax
diane@uhls.lib.ny.us
http://www.uhls.org/new/

Utica Public Library
303 Genesee Street
Utica, NY 13501
(315) 735-2279
E-mail thru website
http://www.uticapubliclibrary.org/#

Valatie Free Library
P. O. Box 336
Valatie, NY 12184
(518) 758-9321
ValatieLibrary@fairpoint.net
http://valatielibrary.org/

Valley Cottage Library
110 Route 303
Valley Cottage, NY 10989
(845) 268-7700
vclref@rcls.org
http://www.vclib.org/#

Village Library of Morris
Box 126
Morris, NY 13808
(607) 263-2080
http://www.4cls.org/OTSEGO.HTML

Warner Library
121 North Broadway
Tarrytown, NY 10591
(914) 631-7734
(914) 631-2324 Fax
pcohn@wlsmail.org
http://www.warnerlibrary.org/

Wayland Free Library
101 West Naples Street
Wayland, NY 14572
(585) 728-5380
(585) 728-5002 Fax
deutschk@stls.org
http://www.gunlockelibrary.org/

Webster Public Library
980 Ridge Road
Webster, NY 14580
(585) 872-7075
tbennett@mcls.rochester.lib.ny.us
http://www.websterlibrary.org/

Weedsport Public Library
2795 East Brutus Street
Weedsport, NY 13166
(315) 834-6222
claustin@twcny.rr.com
http://www.flls.org/weedsport/

West Hurley Library
42 Clover Street
West Hurley, NY 12491
(845) 679-6405
(845) 679-2144 Fax
mailbox@westhurleylibrary.org
http://westhurleylibrary.org/

West Nyack Free Library
65 Strawtown Road
West Nyack, NY 10994
(845) 358-6081
(845) 358-4071 Fax
staff@westnyacklib.org
http://www.westnyacklib.org/

Westbury Public Library
445 Jefferson Street
Westbury, NY 11590
(516) 333-0176
(516) 333-1752 Fax
contactus@westburylibrary.org
http://www.westburylibrary.org/

Westchester Library System
540 White Plains Road, Suite 200
Tarrytown, NY 10591
(914) 674-3600
(914) 674-4185 Fax
E-mail thru website
http://www.westchesterlibraries.org/

White Plains Public Library
100 Martine Avenue
White Plains, NY 10601
(914) 422-1400
(914) 422-1462 Fax
E-mail thru website
http://www.whiteplainslibrary.org/

William K. Sanford Town Library
629 Albany Shaker Road
Loudonville, NY 12211
(518) 458-9274
wkslibry@uhls.lib.ny.us
http://www.colonie.org/library/

Wood Library
134 North Main Street
Canandaigua, NY 14424
(585) 394-1381
WoodLibrary@OWWL.org
http://www.woodlibrary.org/

Woodstock Library
5 Library Lane
Woodstock, NY 12498
(845) 679-2213
(845) 679-7149 Fax
http://woodstock.org/

Woodward Memorial Library
7 Wolcott Street
LeRoy, NY 14482
(585) 768-8300
(585) 768-4768 Fax
wmlib@nioga.org
http://www.
    woodwardmemoriallibrary.org/

Yonkers Public Library
1 Larkin Center
Yonkers, NY 10701
(914) 337-1500
http://www.ypl.org/

Your Home Public Library
107 Main Street
Johnson City, NY 13790
(607) 797-4816
JC.Steve@4cls.org
http://www.yhpl.org/

NORTH CAROLINA

Alamance County Public Libraries
May Memorial Library
342 South Spring Street
Burlington, NC 27215
(336) 229-3588
(336) 229-3592 Fax
http://www.alamancelibraries.org/

Albemarle Regional Library
P. O. Box 68
Winton, NC 27986
(252) 358-7832
http://www.albemarle-regional.lib.
  nc.us/
Paul Ronal Jenkins Photograph
  Collection
World War II collection

Appalachian Regional Library
[no address or phone number
given]
E-mail thru website
http://www.arlibrary.org/

Braswell Memorial Library
727 North Grace Street
Rocky Mount, NC 27804
(252) 442-1951
E-mail thru website
http://www.braswell-library.org/

Burke County Public Library
204 South King Street
Morganton, NC 28655
(828) 437-5638
(828) 433-1914 Fax
admin@bcpls.org
http://www.bcpls.org/

Catawba County Library System
115 West C Street
Newton, NC 28658
(828) 465-8664
lreed@catawbacountync.gov
http://www.catawbacountync.gov/
  library/

Catskill Public Library
1 Franklin Street
Catskill, NY 12414
(518) 943-4230
(518) 943-1439 Fax
cpldirector@mhcable.com
http://catskill.lib.ny.us/

Chapel Hill Public Library
100 Library Drive
Chapel Hill, NC 27514
(919) 968-2777
library@townofchapelhill.org
http://chapelhillpubliclibrary.org/

**Charlotte and Mecklenburg
County Public Library**
310 North Tryon Street
Charlotte, NC 28202
(704) 416-0100
E-mail thru website
http://www.plcmc.lib.nc.us/

Chatham County Libraries
P. O. Box 1809
Pittsboro, NC 27312
(919) 542-8200
(919) 542-8272 Fax
mail@chathamlibraries.org
http://www.chathamnc.org/Index.
   aspx?page=126
Local history collection

**Cumberland County
Public Library**
300 Maiden Lane
Fayetteville, NC 28301
(910) 483-7727, ext. 210
ris@cumberland.lib.nc.us
http://www.cumberland.lib.nc.us/
North Carolina collection

Forsyth County Public Library
660 West Fifth Street
Winston-Salem, NC 27101
(336) 703-3011
(336) 727-2549 Fax
E-mail thru website
http://www.forsyth.cc/library/

Gaston-Lincoln Regional Library
1555 East Garrison Boulevard
Gastonia, NC 28054
(704) 868-2164
(704) 853-0609 Fax
celler@co.gaston.nc.us
http://www.glrl.lib.nc.us/
McConnell Art Collection
Newspaper collection
North Carolina collections

Greensboro Public Library
P. O. Box 3178
Greensboro, NC 27402
(336) 373-2471
E-mail thru website
http://www.greensboro-nc.gov/
   departments/library

Haywood County Public Library
678 South Haywood Street
Waynesville, NC 28786
(828) 452-5169
rbusko@haywoodnc.net
http://www.haywoodlibrary.org/

Henderson County Public Library
301 North Washington Street
Hendersonville, NC 28739
(828) 697-4725
E-mail thru website
http://www.henderson.lib.nc.us/#
The Baker-Barber [NC history]
   Collection
The Stillwell [architecture] Collection

Hickory Library
375 Third Street NE
Hickory, NC 28601
(828) 304-0500
(828) 304-0023 Fax
msizemore@ci.hickory.nc.us
http://www.hickorygov.com/
   department/?fDD=12-0

High Point Public Library
901 North Main Street
High Point, NC 27262
(336) 883-3660
(336) 883-3636 Fax
E-mail thru website
http://www.highpointpubliclibrary.
   com/

McDowell County Public Library
90 West Court Street
Marion, NC 28752
(828) 652-3858
(828) 652-2098 Fax
mcdowellcountypubliclibrary@
  yahoo.com
http://www.mcdowellpubliclibrary.
  org/index.php

Pettigrew Regional Library
201 East 3rd Street
Plymouth, NC 27962
(252) 793-2875
(252) 793-2818 Fax
headquarters@pettigrewlibraries.org
http://www.pettigrewlibraries.org/
North Carolina postcard collection

Rockingham County Public Library
527 Boone Road
Eden, NC 27288
(336) 627-1106
(336) 623-1258 Fax
jstephens@rcpl.org
http://www.rcpl.org/

Rowan Public Library
210 West Fisher Street
Salisbury, NC 28144
(704) 216-8228
(704) 216-8237 Fax
info@rowancountync.gov
http://www.rowancountync.gov/
  GOVERNMENT/Departments/
  PublicLibrary/tabid/145/Default.
  aspx

Edith M. Clark History Room

Transylvania County Library
212 South Gaston Street
Brevard, NC 28712
(828) 884-3151
anna.yount@transylvaniacounty.org
http://transylvania.lib.nc.us/

Union County Public Library
316 East Windsor Street
Monroe, NC 28112
(704) 283-8184
E-mail thru website
http://www.union.lib.nc.us/
Historical collections

Wake County Public Libraries
Cameron Village Regional Library
1930 Clark Avenue
Raleigh, NC 27605
(919) 856-6710
askalibrarian@co.wake.nc.us
http://www.wakegov.com/libraries/
  default.htm

Wilson County Public Library
249 Nash Street W
Wilson, NC 27893
(252) 237-5355
gneedham@wilson-co.com
http://wilsoncountypubliclibrary.
  sirsi.net/rooms/portal/page/
  Sirsi_HOME
Local History Room

NORTH DAKOTA

Adams County Library
103 Sixth Street N
Hettinger, ND 58639
(701) 567-2741 Phone/Fax
http://www.adamscountylibrary.org/

Alfred Dickey Public Library
105 Third Avenue SE
Jamestown, ND 58401
(701) 252-2990
Ask@ADPL.org
http://www.adpl.org/

Beulah Public Library
116 North Central Avenue
Beulah, ND 58523
(701) 873-2884
http://www.beulahlibrary.
   org/#LOCATION

**Bismarck Veterans Memorial
Public Library**
515 North 5th Street
Bismarck, ND 58501
(701) 355-1480
(701) 221-3729 Fax
ask-a-librarian@mail.infolynx.org
http://www.bismarcklibrary.org/

Dickinson Area Public Library
139 Third Street W
Dickinson, ND 58601
1-800-422-0541
(701) 456-7702 Fax
Dickinson.Library@sendit.nodak.edu
http://www.dickinsonlibrary.com/

Fargo Public Library
102 Third Street N
Fargo, ND 58102
(701) 241-1472
askreference@cityoffargo.com
http://www.cityoffargo.com/
   CityInfo/Departments/Library/
North Dakota Collection
Daily Argus   1881-1891
Fargo Forum   1891-Present
New York Times   1960-Present

Grand Forks Public Library
2110 Library Circle
Grand Forks, ND 58201
(701) 772-8116
(701) 772-1379 Fax
gfplreference@hotmail.com
http://www.grandforksgov.com/
   library/index.html

Hazen Public Library
P. O. Box 471
Hazen, ND 58545
(701) 748-2977
(701) 748-2988 Fax
hazenpl@mail.infolynx.org
http://www.hazenlibrary.org/

Lake Region Public Library
423 Seventh Street NE
Devils Lake, ND 58301
(701) 662-2220
(701) 662-2281 Fax
lakeregion.pl@sendit.nodak.edu
http://www.ci.devils-lake.nd.us/
   departments/library.html

McLean-Mercer Regional Library
P. O. Box 505
Riverdale, ND 58565
(701) 654-7652
(701) 654-7526 Fax
mmrlib@westriv.com
http://www.mmrlibrary.org/

Minot Public Library
516 Second Avenue SW
Minot, ND 58701
(701) 852-1045
(701) 852-2595 Fax
mholbach@srt.com
http://www.minotlibrary.org/

Morton Mandan Public Library
609 West Main Street
Mandan, ND 58554
(701) 667-5365
mortonmandanlibrary@
    mailinfolynx.org
http://www.mortonmandanlibrary.org/

North Dakota State Library
604 East Boulevard Avenue,
Dept. 250
Bismarck, ND 58505
1-800-472-2104
(701) 328-2040 Fax
statelib@nd.gov
http://www.library.nd.gov/#
State documents
Grand Forks Herald 3/28/1882 –
    3/31/93
Bismarck Tribune 6/30/1885-Present
Fargo Forum 11/17/1891-Present

Oakes Public Library
804 Main Street
Oakes, ND 58474
(701) 742-2466 or 3234
(701) 742-3234
pahl@oakes.k12.nd.us
http://oakesnd.com/library.php

Stutsman County Library
910 Fifth Street SE
Jamestown, ND 58401
(701) 252-1531
stutsman@daktel.com
http://www.co.stutsman.nd.us/
    cntylibrary.html

Ward County Public Library
405 Third Avenue SE
Minot, ND 58701
1-800-932-8932
library@co.ward.nd.us
http://www.co.ward.nd.us/library/

OHIO

Akron-Summit County Public Library
60 South High Street
Akron, OH 44326
(330) 643-9000
djenning@akronlibrary.org
http://www.ascpl.lib.oh.us/

Archbold Community Library
205 Stryker Street
Archbold, OH 43502
(419) 446-2783
(419) 446-2142 Fax
E-mail thru website
http://www.youseemore.com/
   archbold/default.asp
Local History Collection

Ashland Public Library
224 Claremont Avenue
Ashland, OH 44805
(419) 289-8188
(419) 281-8552 Fax
pjordan@ashland.lib.oh.us
http://www.ashland.lib.oh.us/

Astabula County District Library
335 West 44th Street
Astabula, OH 44004
(440) 997-9341
(440) 998-1198 Fax
tokarcwi@polin.org
http://www.ashtabula.lib.oh.us/

Bellevue Public Library
224 East Main Street
Bellevue, OH 44811
(419) 483-4769
(419) 483-0158 Fax
http://www.bellevue.lib.oh.us/

Briggs Lawrence County Public Library
321 South 4th Street
Ironton, OH 45638
(740) 532-1124
aut@briggslibrary.org
http://www.briggslibrary.com/

Bristol Public Library
Box 220
Bristolville, OH 44402
(330) 889-3651
(330) 889-9794 Fax
E-mail thru website
http://www.youseemore.com/
   bristolpl/

Carnegie Public Library
127 South North Street
Washington Courthouse, OH 43160
(740) 335-2540
(740) 335-2928 Fax
girtonpo@oplin.org
http://www.cplwcho.org/

**Carnegie Public Library
of East Liverpool**
219 East 4th Street
East Liverpool, OH 43920
(330) 385-2048
(330) 385-7600 Fax
eastliv@oplin.org
http://www.carnegie.lib.oh.us/

Carroll County District Library
70 Second Street NE
Carrollton, OH 44615
(330) 627-2613
(330) 627-2523 Fax
E-mail thru website
http://www.carroll.lib.oh.us/

Champaign County Library
1060 Scioto Street
Urbana, OH   43078
(937) 653-3811
(937) 653-5679 Fax
champref@oplin.org
http://www.champaign.lib.oh.us/
Champaign County Children's Home
   records 1892-1910
Champaign County Probate Court
   guardianship records 1892-1907

**Cincinnati and Hamilton
County Public Library**
800 Vine Street
Cincinnati, OH 45202
(513) 369-6900
E-mail thru website
http://www.cincinnatilibrary.org/

Clark County Public Library
201 South Fountain Avenue
Springfield, OH 45506
(937) 328-6903
library@ccpl.lib.oh.us
http://www.ccpl.lib.oh.us/

Clermont County Public Library
326 Broadway Street
Batavia, OH 45103
(513) 732-2736
(513) 732-3177 Fax
E-mail thru website
http://www.clermont.lib.oh.us/

**Cleveland Heights-University
Heights Public Library**
2345 Lee Road
Cleveland Heights, OH 44118
(216) 932-3600
nlevin@heightslibrary.org
http://www.chuhpl.lib.oh.us/

Cleveland Public Library
325 Superior Avenue NE
Cleveland, OH 44114
(216) 623-2800
Holly.Carroll@cpl.org
http://www.cpl.org/

Columbus Metropolitan Library
96 South Grant Avenue
Columbus, OH 43215
(614) 645-2275
E-mail thru website
http://www.columbuslibrary.org/

Conneaut Public Library
304 Buffalo Street
Conneaut, OH 44030
(440) 593-1608
E-mail thru website
http://www.conneaut.lib.oh.us/

Dayton Metro Library
215 East 3rd Street
Dayton, OH 45402
(937) 463-2665
http://www.daytonmetrolibrary.org/

Defiance Public Library
320 Fort Street
Defiance, OH 43512
(419) 782-1456
(419) 782-6235 Fax
E-mail thru website
http://www.defiance.lib.oh.us/

Dover Public Library
525 North Walnut Street
Dover, OH 44622
(330) 343-6123
cooleyda@oplin.org
http://www.doverlibrary.org/

Elyria Public Library
320 Washington Avenue
Elyria, OH 44035
(440) 323-5747
epl@elyrialibrary.org
http://www.elyria.lib.oh.us/
Extensive foreign film collection

Euclid Public Library
631 East 222nd Street
Euclid, OH 44123
(216) 261-5300
(216) 261-0575 Fax
dperdzock@euclidlibrary.org
http://www.euclid.lib.oh.us/Home.aspx

Fairfield County District Library
210 North Broad Street
Lancaster, OH 43130
(740) 653-2745
E-mail thru website
http://www.fairfield.lib.oh.us/

**Findlay-Hancock
County Public Library**
206 Broadway
Findlay, OH 45840
(419) 422-1712
(419) 422-0638 Fax
winkleje@findlaylibrary.org
http://www.findlay.lib.oh.us/
Local history collection

**Franklin-Springboro
Public Libraries**
44 East 4th Street
Franklin, OH 45005
(937) 746-2665
(937) 746-2847 Fax
http://www.franklin.lib.oh.us/

Garnet A. Wilson Public Library
207 North Market Street
Waverly, OH 45690
(740) 947-4921
(740) 947-2918 Fax
dirgaw@0plin.org
http://www.pike.lib.oh.us/

Geauga County Public Library
12701 Ravenwood Drive
Chardon, OH 44024
(440) 286-6811
(440) 286-7419 Fax
geaugapl@oplin.org
http://www.geauga.lib.oh.us/

Granville Public Library
217 East Broadway
Granville, OH 43023
(740) 587-0196
(740) 587-0197 Fax
ncrobson@npls.org
http://www.granvillelibrary.org/

Greene County Public Library
P. O. Box 520
Xenia, OH 45385
(937) 352-4000
(937) 372-4673 Fax
comments@gcpl.lib.oh.us
http://www.greenelibrary.info/

Harris-Elmore Public Library
Box 45
Elmore, OH 43416
(419) 855-3380
(419) 855-7012 Fax
http://library.norweld.lib.oh.us/
    Harris-Elmore/
Grace Luebke Local History Room

**Henderson Memorial
Public Library**
54 East Jefferson Street
Jefferson, OH 44047
(440) 576-3761
(440) 576-8402 Fax
hmpl@oplin.org
http://www.henderson.lib.oh.us/

Hubbard Public Library
436 West Liberty Street
Hubbard, OH 44425
(330) 534-3512
(330) 534-7836 Fax
http://www.hubbard.lib.oh.us/

Lakewood Public Library
15425 Detroit Avenue
Lakewood, OH 44107
(216) 226-8275
(216) 521-4327 Fax
lpl@lkwdpl.org
http://www.lkwdpl.org/

**Leetonia Community
Public Library**
24 Walnut Street
Leetonia, OH 44431
(330) 427-6635
(330) 427-2378 Fax
smithand@oplin.org
http://www.leetonia.lib.oh.us/

Lima Public Library
650 West Market Street
Lima, OH 45801
(419) 228-5113
reference@limalibrary.com
http://www.youseemore.com/lima/
    default.asp

Logan County Public Library
220 North Main Street
Bellefontaine, OH 43311
(937) 599-4189
(937) 599-5503 Fax
lcdlref@oplin.org
http://www.loganco.lib.oh.us/

Lorain Public Library
351 Sixth Street
Lorain, OH 44052
(440) 244-1192
(440) 244-1733 Fax
http://www.lorain.lib.oh.us/

**Mansfield/Richland County
Public Library**
43 West 3rd Street
Mansfield, OH 44902
(419) 521-3100
director@mrcpl.org
http://www.mrcpl.org/

Martins Ferry Public Library
P. O. Box 130
Martins Ferry, OH 43935
(740) 633-0314
(740) 633-0935 Fax
myersyv@oplin.org
http://www.mfpl.org/

Marvin Memorial Library
29 West Whitney Avenue
Shelby, OH 44875
(419) 347-5576
(419) 347-7285 Fax
bavinan@oplin.org
http://www.shelbymm.lib.oh.us/

McKinely Memorial Library
40 North Main Street
Niles, OH 44446
(330) 652-1704
(330) 652-5788 Fax
mckinley@mcklib.org
http://www.mckinley.lib.oh.us/

Medina County District Library
210 South Broadway
Medina, OH 44256
(330) 725-0588
(330) 725-2053 Fax
E-mail thru website
http://www.medina.lib.oh.us/

**Meigs County District
Public Library**
216 West Main Street
Pomeroy, OH 45769
(740) 992-5813
(740) 992-6140 Fax
E-mail thru website
http://www.youseemore.com/Meigs/

Mentor Public Library
8215 Mentor Avenue
Mentor, OH 44060
(440) 255-8811
lynn.hawkins@mentorpl.org
http://www.mentor.lib.oh.us/

Minerva Public Library
677 Lynnwood Drive
Minerva, OH 44657
(330) 868-4101
(330) 868-4267 Fax
dillieto@oplin.org
http://www.minerva.lib.oh.us/

Morley Library
184 Phelps Street
Painesville, OH 44077
(440) 352-3383
http://www.morley.lib.oh.us/

New Madison Public Library
Licking County Library
101 West Main Street
Newark, OH 43055
(740) 349-5500
E-mail thru website
http://www.newarklibrary.info/

NOLA Regional Library System
Northeast Ohio Regional
Library System
4445 Mahoning Avenue NW
Warren, OH 44483
(330) 847-7744
(330) 847-7704 Fax
bill.martino@neo-rls.org
http://www.nolanet.org/

Northwest Library District
NORWELD Regional Library System
181-1/2 South Main Street
Bowling Green, OH 43402
1-800-848-0144
(419) 353-8310 Fax
agray@wcnet.org
http://www.norweld.lib.oh.us/

Orrville Public Library
230 North Main Street
Orrville, OH 44667
(330) 683-1065
(330) 683-1984 Fax
askus@orrville.lib.oh.us
http://www.orrville.lib.oh.us/

**Pickaway County District
Public Library**
1160 North Court Street
Circleville, OH 43113
(740) 477-1644
(740) 474-2855 Fax
E-mail thru website
http://www.pickawaylib.org/

Portage County District Library
10482 South Street
Garrettsville, OH 44231
1-800-500-5179
http://www.portagecounty.lib.oh.us/

Portsmouth Public Library
1220 Gaillia Street
Portsmouth, OH 45662
(740) 354-5688
E-mail thru website
http://www.portsmouth.lib.oh.us/

Preble County District Library
450 South Barron Street
Eaton, OH 45320
(937) 456-4250
(937) 456-6092 Fax
pcdllibrary@oplin.org
http://www.pcdl.lib.oh.us/

**Public Library of Mount Vernon
and Knox County**
201 North Mulberry Street
Mount Vernon, OH 43050
(740) 392-2665
(740) 397-3866 Fax
library@knox.net
http://www.knox.net/

**Public Library of Youngstown
and Mahoning County**
305 Wick Avenue
Youngstown, OH 44503
(330) 744-8636
(330) 744-2258 Fax
csears@libraryvisit.org
http://www.ymc.lib.oh.us/

Rocky River Public Library
1600 Hampton Road
Rocky River, OH 44116
(440) 333-7610
(440) 331-4920 Fax
j.lonsak@rrpl.org
http://www.rrpl.org/

Rodman Public Library
215 East Broadway Street
Alliance, OH 44601
(330) 821-2665
(330) 821-5053 Fax
http://www.rodmanlibrary.com/
Local history collections

Sandusky Library
114 West Adams Street
Sandusky, OH 44870
(419) 625-3834
(419) 625-4574 Fax
http://www.sandusky.lib.oh.us/

Shaker Heights Public Library
16500 Van Aken Boulevard
Shaker Heights, OH 44120
(216) 991-2030
dickinson@shakerlibrary.org
http://www.shpl.lib.oh.us/

Stark County District Library
715 Market Avenue N
Canton, OH 44702
(330) 452-0665
(330) 452-0403 Fax
mbaker@starklibrary.org
http://www.starklibrary.org/

**Steubenville and Jefferson
County Public Library**
Public Library of Steubenville and
Jefferson County
407 South 4th Street
Steubenville, OH 43952
(740) 282-9782
(740) 282-2919 Fax
alanh@oplin.org
http://www.steubenville.lib.oh.us/

Tiffin-Seneca Public Library
77 Jefferson Street
Tiffin, OH 44883
(419) 447-3751
(419) 447-3045 Fax
tiffin@oplin.org
http://www.tiffinsen.lib.oh.us/
Historical newspaper collection

**Toledo-Lucas County
Public Library**
325 North Michigan Street
Toledo, OH 43604
(419) 259-5207
(419) 255-1334 Fax
Dorcel.Dowdell@toledolibrary.org
http://www.library.toledo.oh.us/
Images collection 1870s-Present
Block Card Collection

Twinsburg Public Library
10050 Ravenna Road
Twinsburg, OH 44087
(330) 425-4268
(330) 425-3622 Fax
leonardla@twinsburglibrary.org
http://www.twinsburglibrary.org/
  newweb/

Upper Arlington Public Library
2800 Tremont Road
Upper Arlington, OH 43221
(614) 486-9621
E-mail thru website
http://www.ualibrary.org/

Wadsworth Public Library
132 Broad Street
Wadsworth, OH 44281
(330) 334-5761
(330) 334-6605 Fax
E-mail thru website
http://www.wadsworth.lib.oh.us/

**Warren-Trumbull County
Public Library**
444 Mahoning Avenue NW
Warren, OH 44483
(330) 399-8807
E-mail thru website
http://www.wtcpl.org/site/c.
  iqLSI0OyGnF/b.3842493/k.A055/
  WTCPL_Welcome.htm
Local history center

**Washington County
Public Library**
615 Fifth Street
Marietta, OH 45750
(740) 373-1057
justin.mayo@wcplib.lib.oh.us
http://www.wcplib.lib.oh.us/

**Washington-Centerville
Public Library**
111 West Spring Valley Road
Centerville, OH 45458
(937) 433-8091
(937) 433-1366 Fax
libadmin@wcpl.lib.oh.us
http://www.wclibrary.info

Wayne County Public Library
220 West Liberty Street
Wooster, OH 44691
(330) 262-0916
(330) 262-2905 Fax
glubelski@wcpl.info
http://www.wayne.lib.oh.us/

Westerville Public Library
126 South State Street
Westerville, OH 43081
(614) 882-7277
barlowd@westervillelibrary.org
http://www.wpl.lib.oh.us/

Westlake Porter Public Library
27333 Center Ridge Road
Westlake, OH 44145
(440) 871-2600
http://www.westlakelibrary.org/

Wickliffe Public Library
1713 Lincoln Road
Wickliffe, OH 44092
(440) 944-6010 or 516-7323
(440) 944-7264 Fax
http://www.wickliffe.lib.oh.us/

Willoughby-Eastlake Public Library
263 East 305th Street
Willowick, OH 44095
(440) 943-2203
(440) 943-2383 Fax
kathy.dugan@welibrary.info
http://www.wepl.lib.oh.us/#

Wood County District
Public Library
251 North Main Street
Bowling Green, OH 43402
(419) 352-5104
(419) 354-0405 Fax
woodref@oplin.org
http://wcdpl.lib.oh.us/
Oral histories
Local history, including scrapbooks

Worthington Public Library
820 High Street
Worthington, OH 43085
(614) 807-2600
meribah@worthingtonlibraries.org
http://www.worthingtonlibraries.org/

OKLAHOMA

Ada Public Library
124 South Rennie
Ada, OK 74820
1-888-607-4532
(580) 436-0534 Fax
staff@ada.lib.ok.us
http://www.ada.lib.ok.us/
Over 20 filmstrips

Altus Public Library
421 North Hudson
Altus, OK 73521
1-888-302-9053
(580) 477-3626 Fax
spls@spls.lib.ok.us
http://www.spls.lib.ok.us/index.html

Anadarko Community Library
215 West Broadway
Anadarko, OK 73055
1-888-607-1747
(405) 247-2024 Fax
http://www.anadarkopl.okpls.org/

Ardmore Public Library
320 E Street NW
Ardmore, OK 73401
(580) 223-8290
(580) 221-3240 Fax
lhaggerty@ardmorelibrary.org
http://www.ardmorepublic.lib.ok.us/
McGalliard Historical Collection of
    photographs and documents

Bartlesville Public Library
600 South Johnstone
Bartlesville, OK 74003
(918) 338-4161
bpl@bartlesville.lib.ok.us
http://www.bartlesville.lib.ok.us

Buckley Public Library
408 Dewey Avenue
Poteau, OK 74953
(918) 647-3833 or 4444
(918) 647-8910 Fax
library@buckley.lib.ok.us
http://www.buckley.lib.ok.us

**Chickasaw Regional
Library System**
601 Railway Express
Ardmore, OK 73401
1-888-520-8103
(580) 223-3280 Fax
crlsref@oltn.odl.state.ok.us
http://www.regional-sys.lib.ok.us/

Choctaw County Library
703 East Jackson
Hugo, OK 74743
(580) 326-5591
(580) 326-7388 Fax
hugolib@oklibrary.net
http://www.hugo.lib.ok.us/

Duncan Public Library
2211 North Highway 81
Duncan, OK 73533
(580) 255-0636
(580) 255-6136 Fax
abrown@duncan.lib.ok.us
http://www.youseemore.com/duncan/

**Eastern Oklahoma District
Library System**
814 West Okmulgee Street
Muskogee, OK 74401
(918) 683-2846
(918) 682-9466 Fax
muskpublib@eok.lib.ok.us
http://www.eodls.lib.ok.us/index.html

Guymon Public Library
206 Northwest 5th Street
Guymon, OK 73942
1-866-821-4258
(580) 338-2659 Fax
guymonpublib@guymon.lib.ok.us
http://www.guymon.lib.ok.us/

Henryetta Public Library
518 West Main Street
Henryetta, OK 74437
(918) 652-7377
(918) 652-2796 Fax
hplib@henryettalibrary.org
http://www.henryettalibrary.org/

Latimer County Public Library
301 West Ada
Wilburton, OK 74578
(918) 465-3751
(918) 465-4287 Fax
bambeck@sepl.lib.ok.us
http://www.latimer.lib.ok.us/

Lawton Public Library
110 Southwest 4th Street
Lawton, OK 73501
(580) 581-3450
dsnider@cityof.lawton.ok.us
http://www.cityof.lawton.ok.us/
  library/

Mabel C. Fry Library
1200 Lakeshore Drive
Yukon, OK 73099
(405) 354-8232
(405) 350-7928 Fax
skilmer@yukon.lib.ok.us
http://www.yukon.lib.ok.us/

McAlester Public Library
401 North 2nd Street
McAlester, OK 74501
(918) 426-0930
(918) 423-5731 Fax
seplwebmaster@gmail.com
http://www.mcalester.lib.ok.us/
Historical photos
Newspapers, some of which are:
South McAlester Capital   1894-1906
McAlester Weekly Tribune   1912-1914
New State Tribune   1912
McAlester Messenger   1904-1905
McAlester News   1907-1908
Oklahoma Star   1874-1876
Oklahoma Star Vindicator   1877-1879
South McAlester Republican 1904-1906
South McAlester Review   1899

Metropolitan Library System
[no address given]
(405) 606-3725
director@metrolibrary.org
http://www.mls.lib.ok.us/

Miami Public Library
200 North Main
Miami, OK 74354
(918) 541-2292
http://www.miami.lib.ok.us/

Mounds Public Library
Julia Crowder McClellan
Memorial Library
15 West 14th Street
Mounds, OK 74047
(918) 827-3949 Phone/Fax
mounds_library@mound.lib.ok.us
http://www.mounds.okpls.org/

**National Cowboy & Western
Heritage Museum and Library**
1700 Northeast 63rd Street
Oklahoma City, OK 73111
(405) 478-2250
info@nationalcowboymuseum.org
http://www.
    nationalcowboymuseum.org/
    research/r_index.html

Okmulgee Public Library
218 South Okmulgee
Okmulgee, OK 74447
(918) 756-1448
http://www.okmulgeelibrary.org/

Pioneer Library System
225 North Webster
Norman, OK 73069
(405) 701-2600
(405) 701-2608 Fax
E-mail thru website
http://www.pioneer.lib.ok.us/

**Public Library of Enid and
Garfield County**
120 West Maine
Enid, OK 73701
1-888-261-4904
(580) 233-2948 Fax
mmears@enid.org
http://www.enid.org/library/

**Southeastern Public
Library System**
401 North 2nd
McAlester, OK 74501
1-800-562-9520
(918) 426-0543 Fax
whanway@sepl.lib.ok.us
http://www.sepl.lib.ok.us/

Southern Prairie Library System
421 North Hudson
Altus, OK 73521
1-888-302-9053
(580) 477-3626 Fax
spls@spls.lib.ok.us
http://spls.lib.ok.us/

Spiro Public Library
208 South Main Street
Spiro, OK 74959
1-800-261-3520
(918) 962-5320 Fax
stokes@sepl.lib.ok.us
http://www.spiro.lib.ok.us/

Stillwater Public Library
1107 South Duck
Stillwater, OK 74074
(405) 372-3633
(405) 624-0552 Fax
lreynolds@stillwater.org
http://www.stillwater.lib.ok.us/
Local government documents

Thomas-Wilhite Memorial Library
101 East Thomas Street
Perkins, OK 74059
(405) 547-5185
(405) 547-1040 Fax
perkinslibrary@cityofperkins.net
http://cityofperkins.net/index.
  php?page=Library

Tulsa City-County Library
400 Civic Center
Tulsa, OK 74103
(918) 596-7977
(918) 596-7895 Fax
E-mail thru website
http://www.tulsalibrary.org/

Wagoner Public Library
302 North Main Street
Wagoner, OK 74467
(918) 485-2126
(918) 485-0179 Fax
http://www.wagoner.lib.ok.us/

Watonga Public Library
301 North Prouty
Watonga, OK 73772
(580) 623-7748
(580) 623-7747 Fax
bookwoman@watonga.lib.ok.us
http://www.watongapl.okpls.org/

Western Plain Library System
501 South 28th Street
Clinton, OK 73601
(580) 323-0974
1-888-363-9958
(580) 323-1190 Fax
jane.janzen@wplibs.com
http://www.wplibs.com/

OREGON

Albany Public Library
333 Broadalbin Street SW
Albany, OR 97321
(541) 917-7500
E-mail thru website
http://library.ci.albany.or.us

Canby Public Library
292 N. Holly
Canby, OR 97013
(503) 266-3394
hoferh@ci.canby.or.us
http://www.ci.canby.or.us/
   Canbylibrary/library.htm

Cedar Mill Community Library
12505 NW Cornell Road
Portland, OR 97229
(503) 644-0043
(503) 644-3964 Fax
AskUsCML@wccls.org
http://www.cedarmill.plinkit.org

**Chetco Community
Public Library**
405 Alder Street
Brookings, OR 97415
(541) 469-7738
http://www.chetcolibrary.org/

**Clackamas Corner (reference)
Library**
11750 SE 82nd Ave., Suite D
Happy Valley, OR, 97086
(503) 722-6222
tcref@lincc.lib.or.us
http://library.co.clackamas.or.us/lib

Coos Bay Public Library
525 Anderson Ave.
Coos Bay, OR, 97420
(541) 269-1101
http://bay.cooslibraries.org/

**Corvallis-Benton County
Public Library**
645 NW Monroe Ave
Corvallis OR 97330
(541) 766-6793
E-mail thru website
http://www.thebestlibrary.net/joomla/

Cottage Grove Public Library
700 E. Gibbs Ave
Cottage Grove, OR 97424
(541) 942-3828
E-mail thru website
http://www.cottagegrove.plinkit.org/

Crook County Library
175 NW Meadow Lakes Dr.
Prineville, OR 97754
(541) 447-7978
(541) 447-1308 Fax
E-mail thru website
http://www.crooklib.org

Dallas Public Library
950 Main St.
Dallas, OR 97338
(503) 623-2633
(503) 623-7357 Fax
Donna.Zehner@ci.dallas.or.us
http://www.ci.dallas.or.us/index.
   asp?nid=102
Collection includes regional info

Deschutes Public Library
507 N.W. Wall Street
Bend, OR 97701
(541) 312-1021
(541) 389-2982 Fax
toddd@dpls.us
http://www.dpls.lib.or.us/

Driftwood Public Library
801 SW Hwy 101, #201
Lincoln City, OR 97367
(541) 996-2277
librarian@driftwoodlib.org
http://www.driftwoodlib.org/
[Presently closed for renovations]

Estacada Public Library
825 NW Wade
Estacada, OR 97023
(503) 630-8273
(503) 630-8282 Fax
bethm@lincc.org
http://www.estacada.lib.or.us/
[Temporarily closed due to flood
   damage]

Eugene Public Library
100 West 10th Ave.
Eugene, Oregon 97401
(541) 682-5450
LibraryAskUs@ci.eugene.or.us
http://www.eugene-or.gov/library

Gladstone Public Library
135 E. Dartmouth
Gladstone, OR 97027
(503) 656-2411
glref@lincc.lib.or.us
http://www.gladstone.lib.or.us/

Hermiston Public Library
235 E. Gladys Avenue
Hermiston, OR 97838
(541) 567-2882
library@hermiston.or.us
http://www.hermistonlibrary.us/

Hillsboro Public Library
2850 NE Brookwood Parkway,
Hillsboro, OR 97124
(503) 615-6500
mikesm@ci.hillsboro.or.us
http://www.hillsboro.plinkit.org/

Independence Public Library
175 Monmouth St.
Independence, OR 97351
(503) 838-1811
(503) 838-4486 Fax
robinp@ccrls.org
http://www.ccrls.org/independence/

Junction City Public Library
726 Greenwood Street
Junction City, OR 97448
(541) 998-8942
http://www.ci.junction-city.or.us/
   library/

La Grande Public Library
2006 Fourth Street
La Grande, OR 97850
(541) 962-1339
(541) 962-1335
http://www.ci.la-grande.or.us/dept_
   library.cfm

Lake Oswego Public Library
706 4th Street
Lake Oswego, OR 97034
(503) 636-7628
E-mail thru website
http://www.ci.oswego.or.us/library/

McMinnville Public Library
225 NW Adams Street
McMinnville, OR 97128
(503) 435-5562
libref@ci.mcminnville.or.us
http://www.maclibrary.org/

Langlois Library
P. O. Box 277
Langlois, OR 97450
(541) 348-2066
(541) 348-2066 Fax
langlois@currycountylibraries.org
http://www.polibrary.org/
   homepage_langlois.htm

Ledding Library of Milwaukie
10660 SE 21st Avenue
Milwaukie, OR 97222
503-786-7580
http://www.milwaukie.lib.or.us/

Molalla Public Library
P.O. Box 1289
201 E 5th Street
Molalla, OR 97038
(503) 829-2593
(503) 759-3486 Fax
moref@lincc.lib.or.us
http://www.molalla.lib.or.us/

Monmouth Public Library
168 S. Ecols Street
Monmouth, OR 97361
(503) 838-1932
(503) 838-3899 Fax
Library@ci.monmouth.or.us http://
   www.ccrls.org/monmouth/

Multnomah County Library
801 SW 10th Avenue
Portland, OR 97205
(503) 988-5123
E-mail thru website
http://www.multcolib.org/
Collections in Chinese, Vietnam &
   Russian
John Wilson collections include
   natural history, Pacific NW, Native
   American literature
Government Documents Room
Sterling Room For Writers

Newport Public Library
35 NW Nye St.
Newport, OR 97365
(541) 265-2153
reference@newportlibrary.org
http://www.newportlibrary.org/

Oregon City Public Library
362 Warner Milne Road
Oregon City OR 97045
(503) 657-8269
http://www.oregoncity.lib.or.us

Oregon Historical Society
1200 SW Park Avenue
Portland, OR 97205
(503) 306-5198 24-hour
orhist@ohs.org
http://www.ohs.org/
Research library

Oregon State Library
250 Winter St. NE
Salem, OR 97301
(503) 378-4243
(503) 585-8059 Fax
reference@library.state.or.us
http://oregon.gov/OSL/
Provides books for blind

Port Orford Library
P.O. Box 130
Port Orford, OR 97465
(541) 332-5622
(541) 332-2140 Fax
polibrary@currycountylibraries.org
http://www.polibrary.org/
    homepage_pol.htm

Sandy Public Library
38980 Proctor Blvd.
Sandy, Oregon 97055
(503)-668-5537
bethks@lincc.lib.or.us
http://www.cityofsandy.com/index.
    asp?Type=B_BASIC&SEC={B12694
    E1-88CD-4C67-8B9F-
    5DF3D767FA51}

Seaside Public Library
1131 Broadway
Seaside, OR 97138
(503)738-6742
http://www.seasidelibrary.org/

Springfield Public Library
225 Fifth Street
Springfield, Oregon 97477
(541) 726-3766
(541) 726-3747 Fax
library@ci.springfield.or.us
http://www.ci.springfield.or.us/
    library/

Tigard Public Library
13500 SW Hall Blvd.,
Tigard, OR 97223
(503) 684-6537
(503) 598-7515 Fax
E-mail/feedback thru website
http://www.tigard-or.gov/library/

Toledo Public Library
173 NW 7th Street
Toledo, Oregon 97391
(541)336-3132
http://www.cityoftoledo.org/library.
    htm

Wallowa County Library
207 NW Logan
Enterprise, OR 97828
(541) 426-3969
wclib@eoni.com
http://www.co.wallowa.or.us/library/

West Linn Public Library
1595 Burns Street
West Linn, OR 97068
(503) 656-7853
wlrefpage@lincc.lib.or.us
http://westlinnoregon.gov/library/
    library-home/

Wilsonville Public Library
8200 SW Wilsonville Road
Wilsonville, OR 97070
(503) 682-2744
(503) 682-8685 Fax
wvref@lincc.org
http://www.wilsonville.lib.or.us/

Woodburn Public Library
280 Garfield Street
Woodburn, OR 97071
503-982-5263
anna.stavinoha@ci.woodburn.or.us
    http://woodburnlibrary.org/

PENNSYLVANIA

Adams County Library System
140 Baltimore Street
Gettysburg, PA 17325
(717) 334-5716
(717) 334-7992 Fax
robinl@adamslibrary.org
http://www.adamslibrary.org/

**Andrew Carnegie Free Library &
Music Hall**
300 Beechwood Avenue
Carnegie, PA 15106
(412) 276-3456
(412) 276-9472 Fax
http://www.carnegiecarnegie.com/

B. F. Jones Memorial library
Aliquippa District Library Center
663 Frankliln Avenue
Aliquippa, PA 15001
(724) 375-2900
(724) 375-3274 Fax
http://www.aliquippa.lib.pa.us/

Beaver County Library System
109 Pleasant Drive, Suite 101
Aliquippa, PA 15001
(724) 378-6227
Mecolombo@beavercountypa.gov
http://www.beaverlibraries.org/

Berks County Public Libraries
100 South 5th Street
Reading, PA 19602
(610) 655-6350
(610) 478-9035 Fax
rplref@reading.lib.pa.us
http://www.berks.lib.pa.us

Bethlehem Area Public Library
11 West Church Street
Bethlehem, PA 18018
(610) 867-3761
info@bapl.org
http://www.bapl.org/
Large collection of Spanish materials

Bradford Area Public Library
67 West Washington Street
Bradford, PA 16701
(814) 362-6527
bapublib@atlanticbb.net
http://www.bradfordlibrary.org/

Carnegie Library of Pittsburgh
4400 Forbes Avenue
Pittsburgh, PA 15213
(412) 622-3114
info@carnegielibrary.org
http://www.clpgh.org/
William R. Oliver Special [historical]
   Collections

Chester County Library System
450 Exton Square Parkway
Exton, PA 19341
(610) 280-2600
(610) 280-2688 Fax
mdube@ccls.org
http://www.ccls.org/

Citizens Library
55 South College Street
Washington, PA 15301
(724) 222-2400
(724) 225-7303 Fax
citlib@citlib.org
http://www.citlib.org/
Observer-Reporter since 1808
Local history collection

Columbia Public Library
24 South 6th Street
Columbia, PA 17512
(717) 684-2255
(717) 684-5920 Fax
lgreybill@columbia.lib.pa.us
http://www.columbia.lib.pa.us/
   columbia/site/default.asp

Cumberland County Library System
19 S. West Street
Carlisle, PA 17013
(717) 240-6175
(717) 240-7770 Fax
librarywebmaster@ccpa.net
http://www.ccpa.net/index.
   asp?NID=35

Dauphin County Library System
101 Walnut Street
Harrisburg, PA 17101
(717) 234-4961
COntactW9bDCLS@dcls.org
http://dcls.org/

Delaware County Library System
Upper Darby and Sellers Memorial Library
76 South State Road
Upper Darby, PA 19082
(610) 789-4440
(484) 461-9026 Fax
upperdarby@delco.lib.pa.us
http://www.delcolibraries.org/

Ephrata Public Library
550 South Reading Road
Ephrata PA 17522
(717) 738-9291
(717) 721-3003 Fax
http://www.ephratapubliclibrary.org/

Erie County Library System
160 East Front Street
Erie, PA 16507
(814) 451-6900
(814) 451-6969 Fax
reference@erielibrary.org
http://www.ecls.lib.pa.us/

Free Library of Philadelphia
1901 Vine Street
Philadelphia, PA 19103
(215) 686-5322
E-mail thru website
http://www.library.phila.gov/

Haverford Township Free Library
1601 Darby Road
Havertown, PA 19083
(610) 446-3082
(610) 853-3090 Fax
library@haverfordlibrary.org
http://www.haverfordlibrary.org/

Herr Memorial Library
500 Market Street
Mifflinburg, PA 17844
(570) 966-0831
(570) 966-0106 Fax
herr@herrlibrary.org
http://www.herrlibrary.org/
Pennsylvania Room
Oral history of Mifflinburg

Huntingdon County Library
330 Penn Street
Huntingdon, PA 16652
(814) 643-0200
(814) 643-0132 Fax
http://www.youseemore.com/
    huntingdon/

Huntingdon Valley Library
625 Red Lion Road
Huntingdon Valley, PA 19006
(215) 947-5138
(215) 938-5894 Fax
director@huntingdonvalleylibrary.com
http://www.hvlibrary.org/

Intercourse Public Library
Pequea Valley Public Library
31 Center Street
Intercourse, PA 17534
(717) 768-3160
(717) 768-3888 Fax
director@pvpl.org
http://www.intercourse.lib.pa.us/
    pequeavalley/site/default.asp

James V. Brown Library
19 East 4th Street
Wiilliamsport, PA 117701
(570) 326-0536
http://www.jvbrown.edu/

Lancaster County Library
125 North Duke Street
Lancaster, PA 17602
(717) 394-2651
(717) 394-3083 Fax
http://www.lancaster.lib.pa.us/lcl/
    site/default.asp

**Library System of Lancaster
County**
1866 Colonial Village Lane, Suite 107
Lancaster, PA 17601
(717) 207-0500
(717) 207-0504 Fax
hauer@lancasterlibraries.org
http://www.lancasterlibraries.org/
    lslc/site/default.asp

**Memorial Library of Nazareth
and Vicinity**
295 East Center Street
Nazareth, PA 18064
(610) 759-4932
(610) 759-9513 Fax
nazlib1@nazarethlibrary.org
http://www.nazarethlibrary.org/
Digital Nazareth Area WWII
    Scrapbook
Digital historical newspapers

Middletown Public Library
20 North Catherine Street
Middletown, PA 17057
(717) 944-6412
Info@MiddletownPublicLib.org
http://www.middletownpubliclib.org/

Monessen Public Library and District Center
326 Donner Avenue
Monessen, PA 15062
(724) 684-4750
(724) 684-7077 Fax
reference@monpldc.org
http://www.monpldc.org/

Pottsville Free Public Library
215 West Market Street
Pottsville, PA 17901
(570) 622-8880
(570) 622-2157 Fax
potpublib@iu29.org
http://www.pottsvillelibrary.org/
Government information and
   publications

Public Library For Union County
255 Reitz Boulevard
Lewisburg, PA 17837
(570) 523-1172
http://www.publibuc.org/
Pennsylvania Collection

Quarryville Library
357 Buck Road
Quarryville, PA 17566
(717) 786-1336
library@quarryvillelibrary.org
http://www.quarryvillelibrary.org/
   quarryville/site/default.asp

Reading Public Library
100 South 5th Street
Reading, PA 19602
(610) 655-6350
(610) 478-9035 Fax
webmaster@reading.lib.pa.us
http://www.reading.lib.pa.us/#
Pennsylvania Room
Government documents
Reading Eagle archives 1989-Present

Scranton Public Library
Lackawanna County Library
System
Albright Memorial Library
500 Vine Street
Scranton, PA 18509
(570) 348-3000
(570) 348-3020 Fax
betty@albright.org
http://www.lclshome.org/albright/

State Library of Pennsylvania
333 Market Street
Harrisburg, PA 17126
(717) 787-4440
http://www.statelibrary.state.pa.us/
   libraries/site/default.asp
Pennsylvania Collection

Union County Library System
255 Reitz Boulevard
Lewisburg, PA 17837
(570) 523-1172
http://www.unioncountylibsys.org/
Pennsylvania Collection

Uniontown Public Library
24 Jefferson Street
Uniontown, OH 15401
(724) 437-1165
info@uniontownlib.org
http://www.uniontownlib.org/
Local history

Warren Library Association
205 Market Street
Warren, PA 16365
(814) 723-4650
(814) 723-4521 Fax
web@warrenlibrary.org
http://www.warrenlibrary.org/
Historic photographs and newspapers

West End Library
45 Ball Park Road
Laurelton, PA 17837
(570) 922-4773
http://www.westendlibrary.org/

**Whitehall Township
Public Library**
3700 Mechanicsville Road
Whitehall, PA 18052
(610) 432-4339
http://www.whitehall.lib.pa.us/
Local History Collection

Williamsburg Public Library
511 West 2nd Street
Williamsburg, PA 16693
(814) 832-3367
(814) 832-3845 Fax
wilpublib@yahoo.com
http://www.williamsburgpl.net/

Wissahickon Valley Public Library
650 Skippack Pike (Route 73)
Blue Bell, PA 19422
(215) 643-1320
questions@wvpl.org
http://www.wvpl.org/WVPLWeb/
    home_frame.htm

York County Libraries
159 East Market Street
York, PA 17401
(717) 846-5300
http://www.yorklibraries.org/

RHODE ISLAND

Ashaway Free Library
P. O. Box 70
Ashaway, RI 02804
(401) 377-2770 Phone/Fax
staff@ashfreelib.org
http://ashfreelib.org/

Barrington Public Library
281 County Road
Barrington, RI 02806
(401) 247-1920
(401) 247-3763 Fax
E-mail thru website
http://www.barringtonlibrary.org/

Clark Memorial Library
P. O. Box 190
Carolina, RI 02812
(401) 364-6100
(401) 364-7675 Fax
clacirc@gmail.com
http://www.clarklib.org/

Coventry Public Library
1672 Flat River Road
Coventry, RI 02816
(401) 822-9100
E-mail thru website
http://www.coventrylibrary.org/

Cross Mills Public Library
4417 Old Post Road
Charlestown, RI 02813
(401) 364-6211
ulla@crossmills.org
http://www.crossmills.org/

Cumberland Public Library
1464 Diamond Hill Road
Cumberland, RI 02864
(401) 333-2552
administration@cumberlandlibrary.org
http://www.cumberlandlibrary.org/
Cookbook collection

East Greenwich Free Library
82 Pierce Street
East Greenwich, RI 02818
(401) 884-9510
(401) 884-3790 Fax
karentr1@yahoo.com
http://www.eastgreenwichlibrary.org/

**East Providence Public
Library System**
41 Grove Avenue
East Providence, RI 02914
(401) 434-2453

George Hail Free Library
530 Main Street
Warren, RI 02885
(401) 245-7686
epatricrn@yahoo.com
http://www.georgehail.org/index.htm

Greene Public Library
179 Hopkins Hollow Road
Greene, RI 02827
(401) 397-3873
http://www.greenepubliclibrary.org/

Greenville Public Library
573 Putnam Pike
Greenville, RI 02828
(401) 949-3630
(401) 949-0530 Fax
info@greenvillelibrarymail.com
http://www.yourlibrary.ws/

Hope Library
374 North Road
Hope, RI 02831
(401) 821-7910
pdibiase@oslri.net
http://www.hopepubliclibrary.org/

Island Free Library
P. O. Box 1830
Block Island, RI 02807
(401) 466-3233
(401) 466-3236 Fax
circ@islandfreelibrary.org
http://www.islandfreelibrary.org/
Block Island Collection
Rhode Island Collection

Jamestown Philomenian Library
26 North Road
Jamestown, RI 02835
(401) 423-7280
(401) 423-7281 Fax
library@jamestownri.com
http://www.jamestownri.com/library/

Libraries of Foster
Foster Public Library
184 Howard Hill Road
Foster, RI 02825
(401) 397-4801
http://web.provlib.org/FosLib/

Lincoln Public Library
145 Old River Road
Lincoln, RI 02865
(401) 333-2422
(401) 333-4154 Fax
webmaster@lincolnlibrary.com
http://www.lincolnlibrary.com/

Middletown Public Library
700 West Main Road
Middletown, RI 02842
(401) 846-1573
(401) 846-3031 Fax
http://middletownpubliclibrary.org/

North Kingstown Free Library
100 Boone Street
North Kingstown, RI 02852
(401) 294-3306
(401) 294-1690 Fax
saylward@nklibrary.org
http://www.nklibrary.org/
Local history collection

North Scituate Public Library
606 West Greenville Road
North Scituate, RI 02857
(401) 647-5133
ivybe@scituatelibrary.org
http://www.scituatelibrary.org/
Local history collection

Pawtucket Public Library
13 Summer Street
Pawtucket, RI 02860
(401) 725-3714
sreed@pawtucketlibrary.org
http://www.pawtucketlibrary.org

Portsmouth Free Public Library
2658 East Main Road
Portsmouth, RI 02871
(401) 683-9457
(401) 683-5013 Fax
porlib@yahoo.com
http://web.provlib.org/porlib/
John T. Pierce Collection

Providence Public Library
150 Empire Street
Providence, RI 02903
(401) 455-8000
schausse@provlib.org
http://www.provlib.org/
Nicholson Whaling Collection
Images of Rhode Island Collection

Tiverton Library Services
238 Highland Road
Tiverton, RI 02878
(401) 625-6796
assistantdirector@tivertonlibrary.org
http://www.tivertonlibrary.org/

West Warwick Public Library
1043 Main Street
West Warwick, RI 02893
(401) 828-3750
ref@wwlibrary.org
http://wwlibrary.org/newsite/index.
    htm

SOUTH CAROLINA

ABBE Regional Library System
Aiken-Bamberg-Barnwell-Edge-
field Regional Library System
314 Chesterfield Street SW
Aiken, SC 29801
(803) 642-7575
http://www.abbe-lib.org/

Abbeville County Library System
201 South Main Street
Abbeville, SC 29620
(864) 459-4009
http://www.youseemore.com/
   Abbeville/

**Allendale-Hampton-Jasper Re-
gional library System**
P. O. Box 280
Allendale, SC 29810
(803) 584-3513
(803) 584-8134
oaharper@yahoo.com
http://www.ahjlibrary.org/

Anderson County Library
300 North McDuffie Street
Anderson, SC 29621
(864) 260-4500
administration@andersonlibrary.org
http://www.andersonlibrary.org/
South Carolina Room
Newspaper collections:
Anderson Intelligencer 1860-1900
Anderson Daily Mail 1900-1971
Anderson Independent 1929-1981
Anderson Independent-Mail
   1982-Present

Beaufort County Library
311 Scott Street
Beaufort, SC 29902
(843) 470-6500
(843) 470-6541 Fax
mcoleman@bcgov.net
http://www.beaufortcountylibrary.
   org/rooms/portal/page/Sirsi_
   HOME
The Donner [photographic] Collection

Berkeley County Library System
P. O. Box 1239
Moncks Corner, SC 29461
(843) 719-4223
bcls@berkeley.lib.sc.us
http://www.berkeley.lib.sc.us/

Calhoun County Library
208 Harry C. Raysor Drive N
St. Matthews, SC 29135
(803) 874-3389
http://www.calhoun.lib.sc.us/

Chapin Memorial Library
400 Fourteenth Avenue N
Myrtle Beach, SC 29577
(843) 918-1275
(843) 918-1288 Fax
cmldir@scgovdirect.com
http://www.chapinlibrary.org/

Charleston County Public Library
68 Calhoun Street
Charleston, SC 29401
(843) 805-6930
(843) 727-3741 Fax
E-mail thru website
http://www.ccpl.org/
Jerry and Anita Zucker Holocaust
    Collection
Shoah Visual History Collection
South Carolina history

Cherokee County Public Library
300 East Rutledge Avenue
Gaffney, SC 29340
(864) 487-2711
(864) 487-2752 Fax
cherokeelib@spiritcom.net
Cherokee County history
The Gaffney Ledger 1894-Present

Chester County Library System
100 Center Street
Chester, SC 29706
(803) 377-8145
(803) 377-8146 Fax
http://www.chesterlibsc.org/

**Chesterfield County
Library System**
119 West Main Street
Chesterfield, SC 29709
(843) 623-7489
(843) 623-3295 Fax
E-mail thru website
http://www.youseemore.com/chest
    erfield/

Colleton County Memorial Library
600 Hampton Street
Walterboro, SC 29488
(843) 549-5621
(843) 549-5122 Fax
srowland@colletoncounty.org
http://www.colletonlibrary.org/

Darlington County Library System
204 North Main Street
Darlington, SC 29532
(843) 398-4940
(843) 398-4942 Fax
E-mail thru website
http://www.darlington-lib.org/

Dillon County Library System
600 East Main Street
Dillon, SC 29536
(843) 774-0330
(843) 774-0733 Fax
dilloncountylibrary@yahoo.com
http://www.dillon.lib.sc.us/

Fairfield County Library
300 Washington Street
Winnsboro, SC 29180
(803) 635-4971
(803) 635-7715 Fax
http://www.fairfield.lib.sc.us/

Florence County Library System
509 South Dargan Street
Florence, SC 29506
(843) 662-8424
(843) 661-7544 Fax
reference@florencelibrary.org
http://www.florencelibrary.org/
Eugene N. "Nick" Zeigler South
    Carolina History Room

Greenville County Library
Hughes Library
25 Heritage Green Place
Greenville, SC 29601
(864) 242-5000
(864) 235-8375 Fax
maincirc@greenvillelibrary.org
http://www.greenvillelibrary.org/

Greenwood County Library
106 North Main Street
Greenwood, SC 29646
(864) 941-4650
(864) 941-4651 Fax
ptaylor@greenwoodcountylibrary.org
http://www.youseemore.com/
  Greenwood/default.asp

Harvin Clarendon County Library
215 North Brooks Street
Manning, SC 29102
(803) 435-8633
(803) 435-8101 Fax
hccl215@yahoo.com
http://www.hccl.lib.sc.us/

Horry County Library System
1008 Fifth Avenue
Conway, SC 29526
(843) 248-1544
http://www.horry.lib.sc.us/

Lancaster County Library
313 South White Street
Lancaster, SC 29720
(803) 285-1502
(803) 285-6004 Fax
lanclib@comporium.net
http://www.lanclib.org/
Caroliniana Collection
Historical manuscripts, maps,
newspapers, prints, photographs and
rare books

Laurens County Library
1017 West Main Street
Laurens, SC 29360
(864) 681-7323
(864) 681-0598 Fax
http://www.lcpl.org/
South Carolina Room

**Lexington County Public
Library System**
5440 Augusta Road
Lexington, SC 29072
(803) 785-2600
(803) 785-2683 Fax
http://www.lex.lib.sc.us/

Marion County Library
101 East Court Street
Marion, SC 29571
(843) 423-8300
(843) 423-8302 Fax
marionlibr@spiritcom.net
http://www.marioncountylibrary.org/
Historical photos

Newberry County Library
1100 Friend Street
Newberry, SC 29108
(803) 276-0854
(803) 276-7478 Fax
http://www.youseemore.com/
  Newberry/

Orangeburg County Library
510 Louis Street
Orangeburg, SC 29115
(803) 531-4636
OCLSNotify@orangeburgcounty.org
http://www.orangeburgcounty.org/
  library/

Pickens County Library System
Captain Kimberly Hampton Memorial Library
304 Biltmore Road
Easley, SC 29641
(864) 850-7077
reference@pickens.lib.sc.us
http://www.pickens.lib.sc.us/
Historical Photo Collection

Richland County public Library
1431 Assembly Street
Columbia, SC 29201
(803) 799-9084
E-mail thru website
http://www.richland.lib.sc.us/
Walker Local History Room

Saluda County Library
101 South Main Street
Saluda, SC 29138
(864) 445-2725
(864) 445-4500, Ext. 2264
saluda.library@saludacounty.sc.gov
http://www.youseemore.com/
  Saluda/default.asp
Local history

South Carolina State Library
P. O. Box 11469
Columbia, SC 29211
(803) 734-8026
(803) 734-8676 Fax
reference@statelibrary.sc.gov
http://www.statelibrary.sc.gov/
South Carolina Collection
Government publications
Out-of-print novels collection

**Spartanburg County
Public Libraries**
151 South Church Street
Spartanburg, SC 29306
(864) 596-3500
(864) 596-3518 Fax
patmb@infodepot.org
http://www.infodepot.org/
Kennedy Room of Local History
Historical photograph collections

Sumter County Library System
111 North Harvin Street
Sumter, SC 29150
(803) 773-7273
(803) 773-4875 Fax
sumtercolib@spiritcom.net
http://www.midnet.sc.edu/sumtercls/
South Carolina Room

Union County Carnegie Library
300 East South Street
Union, SC 29379
(864) 427-7140
(864) 427-5155 Fax
reference@unionlibrary.org
http://www.unionlibrary.org/

Williamsburg County Public Library
215 North Jackson
Kingstree, SC 29556
(843) 355-9486
(843) 355-9991 Fax
http://www.youseemore.com/
  williamsburgcounty/

York County Library
138 East Black Street
Rock Hill, SC 29730
(803) 981-5858
E-mail thru website
http://www.yclibrary.org/

SOUTH DAKOTA

Alexander Mitchell Public Library
519 South Kline Street
Aberdeen, SD 57401
(605) 626-7097
library@aberdeen.sd.us
http://ampl.sdln.net/

Beresford Public Library
115 South 3rd
Beresford, SD 57004
(605) 763-2782
books@bmtc.net
http://www.bmtc.net/~libone/

Big Stone City Library
655 Walnut Street
Big Stone City, SD 57216
(605) 862-8108
(605) 862-8640 Fax
Janelle.Kelly@k12.sd.us
http://www.bigstonecity.k12.sd.us/
   in_our_library.htm

Brookings Public Library
515 Third Street
Brookings, SD 57006
(605) 692-9407
elandau@sdln.net
http://www.brookingslibrary.org/

Centerville Community Library
419 Florida
Centerville, SD 57014
(605) 563-2540
http://lh066.k12.sd.us/

Custer County Library
447 Crook Street
Custer, SD 57730
(605) 673-4803
(605) 673-2385 Fax
cuslib@gwtc.net
http://www.custerlibrary.com/
South Dakota collection

Deadwood Public Library
435 Williams Street
Deadwood, SD 57732
(605) 578-2821
(605) 578-2170 Fax
dwd@sdln.net
http://dwdlib.sdln.net/
Local history collections

**Elk Point School-
Community Library**
402 South Douglas Street
Elk Point, SD 57025
(605) 356-5923 or 5941
http://www.epj.k12.sd.us/Library-
   Web/Default.htm

Grace Balloch Memorial Library
625 North 5th Street
Spearfish, SD 57783
(605) 642-1330
jcapp@sdln.net
http://spflib.sdln.net/

Grant County Public Library
207 East Park Avenue
Milbank, SD 57252
(605) 432-6543
gclibrary21@hotmail.com
http://grantcountylibrary.com/

Huron Public Library
521 Dakota Avenue S
Huron, SD 57350
(605) 353-8530
http://hpllib.sdln.net/

**Menno School and
Community Library**
414 Fifth Street
Scotland, SD 57059
(605) 387-5189
Barb.Sayler@k12.sd.us
http://www.menno.k12.sd.us/
   libraryrhome.htm

Mitchell Public Library
221 North Duff
Mitchell, SD 57301
(605) 995-8480
(605) 995-8482 Fax
mitchellib@sdln.net
http://mitlib.sdln.net/

Moody County Resource Center
610 West Community Drive
Flandreau, SD 57028
(605) 997-3326
http://www.flandreau.k12.
   sd.us/education/dept/dept.
   php?sectionid=177

Rapid City Public Library
610 Quincy Street
Rapid City, SD 57701
(605) 394-6139
E-mail thru website
http://www.rapidcitylibrary.org/

Rawlins Municipal Library
1000 East Church Street
Pierre, SD 57501
(605) 773-7421
(605) 773-7423 Fax
rawlinslibrary@yahoo.com
http://rpllib.sdln.net/

Redfield Carnegie Library
5 East 5th Avenue
Redfield, SD 57469
(605) 472-4556
http://www.redfield-sd.com/library.
   html

Siouxland Libraries
P. O. Box 7403
Sioux Falls, SD 57117
(605) 367-8720
(605) 367-4312 Fax
E-mail thru website
http://www.siouxlandlib.org/

South Dakota State Library
800 Governors Drive
Pierre, SD 57501
(605) 773-3131
(605) 773-6962 Fax
library@state.sd.us
http://library.sd.gov/

Sully Area Library
Sully County Library
500 Eighth Street
Onida, SD 57564
(605) 258-2133
http://www.sullybuttes.k12.sd.us/
   library.htm

Tripp County Library
425 West Monroe Street
Winner, SD 57580
(605) 842-0330 Phone/Fax
http://www.gwtc.net/~tclib/

Vermillion Public Library
18 Church Street
Vermillion, SD 57069
(605) 677-7060
(605) 677-7160 Fax
vpl@sdln.net
http://vpl.sdln.net/
SD history and culture collection

Watertown Regional Library
160 Sixth Street NE
Watertown, SD 57201
(605) 882-6220
(605) 882-6221 Fax
adminwat@sdln.net
http://watweb.sdln.net/
Dakota Room

White Lake Community Library
P. O. Box 185 – South Main Street
White Lake, SD 57383
(605) 249-2301
whitelakelibrary@midstatesd.net
http://www.midstatesd.net/~
   whitelakelibrary/

Yankton Community Library
515 Walnut Street
Yankton, SD 57078
(605) 668-5275
(605) 668-5277 Fax
ycllibrary@sdln.net

TENNESSEE

C. E. Weldon Public Library
100 Main Street
Martin, TN 38237
(731) 587-3148
(731) 587-4674 Fax
weldonlib@charter.net
http://www.ceweldonlibrary.org/
The Tennessee Room

Chattanooga-Hamilton County Bicentennial Library
1001 Broad Street
Chattanooga, TN 37402
(423) 757-5310
library@lib.chattanooga.gov
http://www.lib.chattanooga.gov/
Local history collection

Clarksville-Montgomery County Public Library
350 Pageant Lane
Clarksville, TN 37040
(931) 648-8826
(931) 648-8831 Fax
director@clarksville.org
http://cmc-websvr.clarksville.org/

Cleveland Bradley County Public Library
795 Church Street NE
Cleveland, TN 37311
(423) 472-2163
info@clevelandlibrary.org
http://www.clevelandlibrary.org/
  index.php
History branch and archives

Elmer Hinton Memorial Library
301 Portland Boulevard
Portland, TN 37148
(615) 325-2279
(615) 325-7061 Fax
portlandlibrary@bellsouth.net
http://www.youseemore.com/
  portland/

Greenback Public Library
6889 Morganton Road
Greenback, TN 37742
(865) 856-2841
cshammon@esper.com
http://www.discoveret.org/greenbkl/

Greeneville Greene County Public Library
210 North Main Street
Greeneville, TN 37745
(423) 638-5034
(423) 638-3841 Fax
grv@ggcpl.org
http://www.ggcpl.org/
T. Elmer Cox Historical Collection

Jacksboro Public Library
P. O. Box 460
Jacksboro, TN 37757
(423) 562-3675
(423) 562-9587 Fax
director@jacksboropubliclibrary.org
http://www.jacksboropubliclibrary.org/

Jellico Public Library
104 North Main Street, Suite 2
Jellico, TN 37762
(423) 784-7488
(423) 784-8745 Fax
jellico2@birch.net
http://www.jellico.tn.us/library/

Johnson City Public Library
100 West Millard Street
Johnson City, TN 37604
(423) 434-4450
info@jcpl.net
http://www.jcpl.net

Knox County Public Library System
500 West Church Avenue
Knoxville, TN 37902
(865) 215-8750
reference@knoxlib.org
http://www.knoxcounty.org/library/

Lebanon-Wilson County library
108 South Hatton Avenue
Lebanon, TN 37087
(615) 444-0632
(615) 444-0535 Fax
leblibrary@charter.net
http://www.lebanonlibrary.net/

Linebaugh Public Library
105 West Vine Street
Murfreesboro, TN 37130
(615) 893-4131
(615) 848-5038 Fax
linref@linebaugh.org
http://www.linebaugh.org/linebaugh/

Maynardville Public Library
296 Main Street
Maynardville, TN 37807
(865) 992-7106
(865) 992-0202 Fax
mayna2bk@comcast.net
http://www.maynardville.com/library/

Memphis Public Library
3030 Poplar Avenue
Memphis, TN 38111
(901) 415-2700
mccloyk@memphislibrary.org
http://www.memphislibrary.lib.tn.us/
History/Social Science collection
Civil War Collection

Nashville Public Library
615 Church Street
Nashville, TN 37219
(615) 862-5800
E-mail thru website
http://www.library.nashville.org/

Oak Ridge Public Library
1401 Oak Ridge Turnpike
Oak Ridge, TN 37830
(865) 425-3455
reference@cortn.org
http://www.ci.oak-ridge.tn.us/lib-
    html/orlib.htm
Oak Ridge Room

Overton County Public Library
107 East Main Street
Livingston, TN 38570
(931) 823-1888
(931) 403-0798
overtoncolib@comcast.net
http://www.overtoncolibrary.
    com/?page_id=9

Pigeon Forge Public Library
2449 Library Drive
Pigeon Forge, TN 37876
(865) 429-7490
help@pfpl.net
http://www.pfpl.net/
Tennessee Darling Collection of
   White House memorabilia
Thomas Kinkade "Painter of Light"
   Art Collection

Sequatchie County Public Library
8 Cherry Street W
Dunlap, TN 37327
(423) 949-2357
(423) 949-6619 Fax
bworley@mail.state.tn.us
http://www.sequatchie.com/library.
   htm

**Tennessee State Library and
Archives**
403 Seventh Avenue N
Nashville, TN 37243
(615) 741-2764
reference.tsla@state.tn.us
http://www.tennessee.gov/tsla/
19th century newspapers
Tennessee landmark documents

Watauga Regional Library
2700 South Roan Street, Suite 435
Johnson City, TN 37601
(423) 926-2951
(423) 926-2956 Fax
nrenfro@wrlibrary.org
http://www.wrlibrary.org/

Williamson County Public Library
1314 Columbia Avenue
Franklin, TN 37064
(615) 595-1250
(615) 595-1245 Fax
ref@williamson-tn.org
http://lib.williamson-tn.org/
Local history

TEXAS

Abilene Public Library
202 Cedar Street
Abilene, TX 79601
(325) 676-6025
(325) 738-8082 Fax
marie.noe@abilenetx.com
http://www.abilenetx.com/apl/

Alamo Public Library
416 North Tower Road
Alamo, TX 78516
(956) 787-6160
Alamostaff@yahoo.com
http://www.alamo.lib.tx.us/

Allen Public Library
300 North Allen Drive
Allen, TX 75013
(214) 509-4900
(469) 342-6672 Fax
jtimbs@cityofallen.org
http://www.cityofallen.org/depart
   ments/library/

Amarillo Public Library
413 East 4th
Amarillo, TX 79101
(806) 378-3054
E-mail thru website
http://www.amarillolibrary.org/
Texas history photo archive collection

Arlington Public Library
101 East Abram Street
Arlington, TX 76010
(817) 459-6900
libsuggestionbosdist@arlingtontx.gov
http://arlingtonlibrary.org/

Austin Public Library
Faulk Central library
800 Guadalupe Street
Austin, TX 78701
(512) 974-7400
nancy.byrd@ci.austin.tx.us
http://www.ci.austin.tx.us/library/

Bastrop Public Library
1100 Church Street
Bastrop, TX 78602
(512) 321-5441
http://www.bastroplibrary.org/

Bedford Public Library
1805 L. Don Dodson Drive
Bedford, TX 76021
(817) 952-2330
(817) 952-2396 Fax
E-mail thru website
http://lib.bedford.tx.us/

Benbrook Public Library
1065 Mercedes Street
Benbrook, TX 76126
(817) 249-6632
E-mail thru website
http://www.benbrooklibrary.org/

Bertha Voyer Memorial Library
P. O. Box 47
Honey Grove, TX 75446
(903) 378-2206
hallv@1starnet.com
http://www.honeygrove.org

Blanco Library
1118 Main
Blanco, TX 78606
(830) 833-4280
E-mail thru website
http://www.blancolib.org/

Boerne Public Library
210 North Main Street
Boerne, TX 78006
(830) 249-3053
(830) 249-8410 Fax
skovbjerg@boernelibrary.org
http://www.boerne.lib.tx.us/

Brazoria County Library System
451 North Velasco
Angleton, TX 77515
(979) 864-1505
(979) 864-1298 Fax
bcls@bcls.lib.tx.us
http://bcls.lib.tx.us/

Brownsville Public Library
2600 Central Boulevard
Brownsville, TX 78521
(956) 548-1055
(956) 548-0684 Fax
info@bpl.us
http://www.bpl.us/

Bryan-College Station Public Library System
201 East 26th Street
Bryan, TX 77803
(979) 209-5600
cmounce@bryantx.gov
http://www.bcslibrary.org/

Buda Public Library
P. O. Box 608
Buda, TX 78610
(512) 295-5899
(512) 295-6525 Fax
librarian@budalibrary.org
http://www.buda.lib.tx.us/

Burleson Public Library
248 SW Johnson Avenue
Burleson, TX 76028
(817) 295-6131
kcunningham@burlesontx.com
http://www.burlesonlibrary.com/

Butt-Holdsworth Memorial Library
505 Water Street
Kerrville, TX 78028
(830) 257-8422
(830) 792-5552 Fax
Library.Webmaster@kerrvilletx.gov
http://kerrville.org/index.aspx?NID=92

Central Texas Library System
1005 West 41st Street, Suite 100
Austin, TX 78756
1-800-262-4431
(512) 583-0709 Fax
pat.tuohy@ctls.net
http://www.ctls.net/

Comfort Public Library
P. O. Box 536
Comfort, TX 78013
(830) 995-2398
(830) 995-5574 Fax
library@comfort.txed.net
http://www.comfort-library.txed.net/

Corpus Christi Public Libraries
805 Comanche
Corpus Christi, TX 78401
(361) 826-7070
(361) 826-7046 Fax
library@cclibraries.com
http://www.cclibraries.com/
Digitized archival collection

Dallas Public Library
1515 Young Street
Dallas, TX 75201
(214) 670-1400
director@dallaslibrary.org
http://dallaslibrary.org/

Denton Public Library
3020 North Locust Street
Denton, TX 76209
(940) 349-8752
library@cityofdenton.com
http://www.cityofdenton.com/
  pages/library.cfm
Local history
Texana Collection

DeSoto Public Library
211 East Pleasant Run Road
DeSoto, TX 75115
(972) 230-9656
E-mail thru website
http://www.ci.desoto.tx.us/index.
  aspx?NID=110

Donna Public Library
301 South Main
Donna, TX 78537
(956) 464-2221
library@donna.lib.tx.us
http://www.donna.lib.tx.us/

**Dripping Springs Community
Library**
501 Sportsplex Drive
Dripping Springs, TX 78620
(512) 858-7825
cara@dscl.org
http://www.dscl.org/

Ector County Library
321 West 5th Street
Odessa, TX 79761
(432) 332-0633
(432) 337-6502 Fax
webmaster@ector.lib.tx.us
http://www.ector.lib.tx.us/
Southwestern history

Edinburg Public Library
Dustin Michael Sekula Memorial
Library
1906 South Closner
Edinburg, TX 78539
(956) 383-6246
reference@edinburg.lib.tx.us
http://www.edinburg.lib.tx.us/

El Paso Public Library
501 North Oregon Street
El Paso, TX 79901
(915) 543-5401
reference@elpasotexas.gov
http://www.elpasotexas.gov/library/
The Southwest Collection
Otis A. Aultman Photo Collection
Raza: The Mexican-American Collection
Historical documents

Elsa Public Library
711 North Hidalgo Street
Elsa, TX 78543
(956) 262-3061
(956) 262-3066
hilda@elsa.lib.tx.us
http://www.elsa.lib.tx.us/

Farmers Branch Manske Library
13613 Webb Chapel
Farmers Branch, TX 75234
(972) 247-2511
(972) 247-9606 Fax
marci.chen@farmersbranch.info
http://www.farmersbranch.info/
   play/manske-library

**Fayette Library/Heritage
Museum/Archives**
855 South Jefferson Street
La Grange, TX 78945
(979) 968-3765 Library
(979) 968-6418 Museum/Archives
(979) 968-5357 Fax
library@cityoflg.com
http://www.cityoflg.com/
   librarybody.htm

Fort Bend County Libraries
1001 Golfview Road
Richmond, TX 77469
(281) 342-4455
crussell@fortbend.lib.tx.us
http://www.fortbend.lib.tx.us/

Fort Stockton Public Library
500 North Water
Fort Stockton, TX 79735
(432) 336-3374
(432) 336-6648 Fax
E-mail thru website
http://www.fort-stockton.lib.tx.us/

Fort Worth Public Library
500 West 3rd Street
Fort Worth, TX 76102
(817) 871-7705
LibraryWebMail@FortWorthGov.org
http://www.fortworthgov.org/
   library/
Local History Collections
Archives Collections

Friendswood Public Library
416 South Friendswood Drive
Friendswood, TX 77546
(281) 482-7135
maryp@friendswood.lib.tx.us
http://www.friendswood.lib.tx.us/

Frisco Public Library
6101 Frisco Square Boulevard,
Suite 3000
Frisco, TX 75034
(972) 292-5669
(972) 292-5699 Fax
E-mail thru website
http://www.friscolibrary.com/

Gatesville Public Library
111 North 8th Street
Gatesville, TX 76528
(254) 865-5367
(254) 248-0986 Fax
faye.nichols@ci.gatesville.tx.us
http://www.ci.gatesville.
   tx.us/index.asp?Type=B_
   BASIC&SEC={4CD91B06-88AC-
   432D-B8CD-5D9DBD09959A}

Georgetown Public Library
402 West 8th Street
Georgetown, TX 78626
(512) 930-3551
(512) 930-3764 Fax
library@georgetowntx.org
http://www.georgetowntex.org/

Gibbs Memorial Library
305 East Rusk Street
Mexia, TX 76667
(254) 562-3231
http://www.gibbslibrary.com/

Harris County Public Library
8080 El Rio
Houston, TX 77054
(713) 749-9000
rgoldber@hcpl.net
http://www.hcpl.net/index.htm

Helen Hall Library
100 West Walker
League City, TX 77573
(281) 554-1111
E-mail thru website
http://www.leaguecitylibrary.org/

Highland Park Library
4700 Drexel Drive
Highland Park, TX 75205
(214) 559-9400
hplibrary@hptx.org
http://www.youseemore.com/
   highland/default.asp

Houston Area Library System
500 McKinney Street, Suite 400
Houston, TX 77002
(832) 393-1397
(832) 393-1474 Fax
dwaynea.brown@cityofhouston.net
http://www.hals.lib.tx.us/

Houston Public Library
500 McKinney Street
Houston, TX 77002
(832) 393-1313
E-mail thru website
http://www.houstonlibrary.org/
   index.html
Local history
Government documents
African-American Collection
Greenburg Collection (the arts)

Howard County Library
500 Main Street
Big Spring, TX 79720
(432) 264-2260
(432) 264-2263 Fax
hclref@hotmail.com
http://www.howard-county.lib.
   tx.us:8080/bgs

Huntsville Public Library
1216 Fourteenth Street
Huntsville, TX 77340
(936) 291-5472
linda.dodson@ci.huntsville.tx.us
http://www.huntsville.lib.tx.us/

Hurst Public Library
901 Precinct Line Road
Hurst, TX 76053
(817) 788-7300
E-mail thru website
http://www.ci.hurst.tx.us/lib/index.htm

Irving Public Library
825 West Irving Boulevard
Irving, TX 75060
(972) 721-2600
http://www.cityofirving.org/library/

Jacksonville Public Library
502 South Jackson Street
Jacksonville, TX 75766
(903) 586-7664
webmaster@jacksonvillelibrary.com
http://www.jacksonvillelibrary.com/

Jenny Trent Dew Library
1101 Hutchings
Goldthwaite, TX 76844
(325) 648-2447
librarian@jtdlibrary.net
http://jtdlibrary.net/

Joe Barnhart Bee County Library
110 West Corpus Christi Street
Beeville, TX 78102
(361) 362-4901
(361) 358-8694 Fax
E-mail thru website
http://www.bclib.org/

Kaufman County Library
3790 South Houston Street
Kaufman, TX 75142
(972) 932-6222
(972) 932-0681 Fax
http://www.kaufmancountylibrary.
  org/

Keller Public Library
1100 Bear Creek Parkway
Keller, TX 76248
(817) 743-4822
(817) 743-4890 Fax
jprock@cityofkeller.com
http://www.cityofkeller.com/index.
  aspx?page=35

Lampasas Public Library
201 South Main Street
Lampasas, TX 76550
(512) 556-3251
(512) 556-4065 Fax
E-mail thru website
http://www.cityoflampasas.com/bins/
  site/templates/splash.asp?area_2
  =departments/library/main

**Lancaster Veterans
Memorial Library**
1600 Veterans Memorial Parkway
Lancaster, TX 75134
(972) 227-1080
cloucksl@lancaster-tx.com
http://www.lancastertxlib.org/
Lancaster history

Laredo Public Library
1120 East Calton Road
Laredo, TX 78041
(956) 795-2400
(956) 795-2403 Fax
mgsoliz@laredolibrary.org
http://www.laredolibrary.org/
Luciano Guajardo Historical
  Collection

Leon Valley Public Library
6425 Evers
Leon Valley, TX 78238
(210) 684-0720
librarian@leonvalley.lib.tx.us
http://www.leonvalley.lib.tx.us/

Library of Graham
910 Cherry Street
Graham, TX 76450
(940) 549-0600
library@grahamtexas.net
http://biz.grahamtexas.net/library/

Longview Public Library
222 West Cotton
Longview, TX 75601
(903) 237-1350
manager@longview.lib.tx.us
http://www.longview.lib.tx.us/New
   web/library_templates/front.html
Local history
Government documents

Lubbock Public Library
Mahon Library
1306 Ninth Street
Lubbock, TX 79401
(806) 775-2834 or 2835
jclausen@mylubbock.us
http://library.ci.lubbock.tx.us/

Lucy Hill Patterson Memorial Library
201 Ackerman Street
Rockdale, TX 76567
(512) 446-3410
(512) 446-5597 Fax
pattersonlib@rockdalecityhall.com
http://www.main.org/patlib/library.
   htm

Mansfield Public Library
104 South Wisteria
Mansfield, TX 76063
(817) 473-4391
mpl@mansfield-tx.gov
http://www.mansfield-tx.gov/
   departments/library/

Mesquite Public Library
300 West Grubb Drive
Mesquite, TX 75149
(972) 216-6220
mainbr@library.mesquite.tx.us
http://www.cityofmesquite.com/
   library/

Midland County Public Library
301 West Missouri Avenue
Midland, TX 79701
(432) 688-4320
(432) 688-4939 Fax
E-mail thru website
http://www.youseemore.com/
   midland/

Montgomery County Memorial Library System
104 I-45 North
Conroe, TX 77301
(936) 539-7814
webmaster@countylibrary.org
http://www.countylibrary.org/

Moore Memorial Public Library
1701 Ninth Avenue N
Texas City, TX 77590
(409) 643-5979
(409) 948-1106 Fax
esteiner@texas-city-tx.org
http://www.texascity-library.org/

Mount Pleasant Public Library
213 North Madison
Mount Pleasant, TX 75455
(903) 575-4180
(903) 577-8000 Fax
lrigney@mpcity.org
http://www.mpcity.net/library_
   public.htm
Local history collection

Nacogdoches Public Library
1112 North Street
Nacogdoches, TX 75961
(936) 559-2970
askalibrarian@ci.nacogdoches.tx.us
http://npl.sfasu.edu/

New Braunfels Public Library
700 East Common Street
New Braunfels, TX 78130
(830) 221-4300
gpruett@nbpl.lib.tx.us
http://www.nbtexas.org/index.
   aspx?nid=114

**Nicholson Memorial
Library System**
625 Austin Street
Garland, TX 75040
(972) 205-2500
http://www.nmls.lib.tx.us/Home/
   Departments/Recreation+and+Cu
   ltural+Services/Nicholson+Memor
   ial+Library+System/Default

**North Richland Hills
Public Library**
9015 Grand Avenue
North Richland Hills, TX 76180
(817) 427-6800
(817) 427-6808 Fax
reference@nrhtx.com
http://www.library.nrhtx.com/

**North Texas Regional
Library System**
6320 Southwest Boulevard,
Suite 101
Fort Worth, TX 76109
1-800-856-3050
cdavidson@ntrls.org
http://www.ntrls2.org/default.asp

Palestine Public Library
101 North Cedar Street
Palestine, TX 75801
(903) 729-4121
http://www.youseemore.com/
   palestine/default.asp

Pioneer Memorial Library
115 West Main Street
Fredericksburg, TX 78624
(830) 997-6613
(830) 997-6514 Fax
http://www.fredericksburg.lib.tx.us/

Plano Public Library System
[no address given]
(972) 769-4208
E-mail thru website
http://www.plano.gov/Departments/
   Libraries/Pages/default.aspx

Port Arthur Public Library
4615 Ninth Avenue
Port Arthur, TX 77642
(409) 985-8838
(409) 985-5969 Fax
jmartine@pap.lib.tx.us
http://www.pap.lib.tx.us/
Port Arthur History Collection

Richardson Public Library
900 Civic Center Drive
Richardson, TX 75080
(972) 744-4350
E-mail thru website
http://www.cor.net/library/
Richardson History Collection

**Rita and Truett Smith
Public Library**
800 Thomas Street
Wylie, TX 75098
(972) 442-7566
(972) 442-4075 Fax
libinfo@wylietexas.gov
http://www.ci.wylie.tx.us/library/

Rosenberg Library
2310 Sealy Avenue
Galveston, TX 77550
(409) 763-8854
(409) 763-0275 Fax
admin@rosenberg-library.org
http://www.rosenberg-library.org/
Galveston and Texas History Collections

Rowlett Public Library
3900 Main Street
Rowlett, TX 75088
(972) 412-6161
kcockcroft@rowlett.com
http://www.rowlett.lib.tx.us/
   Rowlett/Departments/Library/

Rusk County Library System
106 East Main Street
Henderson, TX 75652
(903) 657-8557
(903) 657-7637 Fax
pipkinp@rclib.org
http://www.youseemore.com/Rusk/
Texas Collection

San Antonio Public Library
600 Soledad
San Antonio, TX 78205
(210) 207-2644
LibraryDirector@sanantonio.gov
http://www.mysapl.org/

San Marcos Public Library
625 East Hopkins Street
San Marcos, TX 78666
(512) 393-8200
(512) 754-8131 Fax
SMPL@sanmarcostx.gov
http://www.ci.san-marcos.tx.us/
departments/library/
Historical San Marcos Collection

**Seguin-Guadalupe County
Public Library**
707 East College Street
Seguin, TX 78155
(830) 401-2422
(830) 401-2477 Fax
seguinlibrary@seguin.lib.tx.us
http://www.seguin.lib.tx.us/

Speer Memorial Library
801 East 12th Street
Mission, TX 78572
(956) 580-8750
(956) 580-8756 Fax
library@mission.lib.tx.us
http://www.mission.lib.tx.us

Sterling Municipal Library
Mary Elizabeth Wilbanks Avenue
Baytown, TX 77520
(281) 427-7331
(281) 420-5347 Fax
ask@baytownlibrary.org
http://baytownlibrary.org/

Taylor Public Library
801 Vance Street
Taylor, TX 76574
(512) 352-3434
(512) 352-8080 Fax
karen.ellis@ci.taylor.tx.us
http://www.ci.taylor.tx.us/index.
  aspx?nid=25

Texarkana Public Library
600 West 3rd Street
Texarkana, TX 75501
(903) 794-2149
(903) 794-2139 Fax
txarkpublib@txar-publib.org
http://www.txar-publib.org/

**Texas State Library &
Archives Commission**
P. O. Box 12927
Austin, TX 78711
(512) 463-5455
info@tsl.state.tx.us
http://www.tsl.state.ts.us/

Tyler Public Library
201 South College Avenue
Tyler, TX 75702
(903) 593-7323
(903) 531-1329 Fax
E-mail thru website
http://cityoftyler.org/Library/Library
  /tabid/542/Default.aspx

Unger Memorial Library
825 Austin Street
Plainview, TX 79072
(806) 296-1149
johnsigwald@texasonline.net
http://unger.myplainview.com/

Victoria Public Library
302 North Main Street
Victoria, TX 77901
(361) 485-3302
(361) 485-3295 Fax
refmail@victoria.lib.tx.us
http://victoriapubliclibrary.org/
Local history collection

Waco-McLennan County Library
1717 Austin Avenue
Waco, TX 76701
(254) 750-5941
referencewaco@ci.waco.tx.us
http://www.waco-texas.com/
  city_depts/libraryservices/
  libraryservices.htm

Weatherford Public Library
1014 Charles Street
Weatherford, TX 76086
(817) 598-4150
(817) 598-4161 Fax
dfleeger@ci.weatherford.tx.us
http://ci.weatherford.tx.us/index.
  aspx?nid=142

Wells Branch Community Library
15001 Wells Port Drive
Austin, TX 78728
(512) 989-3188
director@wblibrary.org
http://wblibrary.org/

Weslaco Public Library
525 South Kansas
Weslaco, TX 78596
(956) 968-4533
(956) 968-8922 Fax
http://www.weslaco.lib.tx.us/
Texas history collection

Westbank Community Library
1309 Westbank Drive
Austin, TX 78746
1-888-896-0671
(512) 327-3074 Fax
askus@westbank.lib.tx.us
http://www.westbank.lib.tx.us/

Whitewright Public Library
P. O. Box 984
Whitewright, TX 75491
(903) 364-2955
E-mail thru website
http://pecan.tsl.state.tx.us:8080/
   netls/whitewright

Wichita Falls Public Library
600 Eleventh Street
Wichita Falls, TX 76301
(940) 767-0868
E-mail thru website
http://www.wfpl.net/

William T. Cozby Public Library
P. O. Box 9478
Coppell, TX 75019
(972) 304-3655
Library@ci.coppell.tx.us
http://www.ci.coppell.tx.us/

Wimberley Village Library
P. O. Box 1240
Wimberley, TX 78676
(512) 847-2188
wimberleylibrary@austin.rr.com
http://www.wimberleylibrary.org/

UTAH

Brigham City Library
26 E. Forest Street
Brigham City, UH 84302
(435) 723-5850
brighamlibrary@gmail.com
http://bcpl.lib.ut.us/

[President Millard] Fillmore Library
25 South 100 West
Fillmore, UT 84631
(435) 743-5314
(435) 754-6710 Fax
info@fillmorelibrary.org
http://www.fillmorelibrary.org/

Orem Public Library
58 North State Street
Orem, UT 84057
(801) 229-7050
E-mail thru website
http://lib.orem.org/

Park City Library
P. O. Box 668
Park City, UT 84060
(435) 615-5600
ltillson@parkcity.org
http://www.youseemore.com/
   parkcity/default.asp

Provo City Library
550 N. University Avenue
Provo, UT 84601
(801) 852-6650
webadultref@provo.lib.ut.us
http://www.provo.lib.ut.us/

Salt Lake City Public Library
210 East 400 South
Salt Lake City, UT 84111
(801) 524-8200
E-mail thru website
http://www.slcpl.lib.ut.us/index.jsp
Alternative Press Collection

Salt Lake County Library System
2530 South 500 East
South Salt Lake City, UT 84106
(801) 943-4636
(801) 942-6323 Fax

Summit County Library System
6505 N. Landmark Dr.
Park City, Utah 84098
(435) 615-3900
dskousen@co.summit.ut.us
http://www.youseemore.com/
   SummitCounty/default.asp

Uintah County Library
155 East Main
Vernal, UT 84078
(435) 789-0091
(435) 789-6822 Fax
passey@co.uintah.ut.us
http://uintah.lib.ut.us/

Washington County Library
88 West 100 South
St. George, UT 84770
(435) 634-5737
help@washco.lib.ut.us
http://library.washco.utah.gov/

Weber County Library
2464 Jefferson Avenue
Ogden, UT 84401
(801) 337-2632
(801) 337-2615 Fax
E-mail thru website
http://www.weberpl.lib.ut.us/

VERMONT

Ainsworth Public Library
2338 Vt. Route 14
Williamstown, VT 05679
(802) 433-5887
(802) 433-2161 Fax
ainsworthpl@yahoo.com
http://www.williamstown.lib.vt.us/

Aldrich Public Library
6 Washington Street
Barre, VT 05641
(802) 476-7550
AldrichLibrary@charter.net
http://www.aldrich.lib.vt.us/

Arvin A. Brown Public Library
88 Main Street
Richford, VT 05476
(802) 848-3313
arvinabrown@gmail.com
http://arvinabrown.wordpress.com/
Vermont collection

Bennington Free Library
101 Silver Street
Bennington, VT 05201
(802) 442-9051
webmaster@bfli.org
http://www.benningtonfreelibrary.org/
Vermont History Room

Bixby Memorial Library
258 Main Street
Vergennes, VT 05491
(802) 877-2211
Bixby_Verg@vals.state.vt.us
http://www.bixbylibrary.org/
Vermont Collection

Bradford Library
P. O. Box 619
Bradford, VT 05033
(802) 222-4536
http://www.bradford.lib.vt.us/

Brooks Memorial Library
224 Main Street
Brattleboro, VT 05301
(802) 254-5290
(802) 257-2309 Fax
brattlib@brooks.lib.vt.us
http://www.brooks.lib.vt.us/
Local history collection

Brown Public Library
93 South Main Street
Northfield, VT 05663
(802) 485-4621
http://www.brownpubliclibrary.org/

Brownell Library
6 Lincoln Street
Essex Junction, VT 05452
(802) 878-6955
brownell_library@yahoo.com
http://www.brownelllibrary.org/

Burnham Memorial Library
898 Main Street (Route 2A)
Colchester, VT 05446
(802) 879-7576
(802) 879-5079 Fax
info@burnham.lib.vt.us
http://www.burnham.lib.vt.us/

Calef Memorial Library
P. O. Box 141
Washington, VT 05675
(802) 883-2343
washington@vals.state.vt.us
http://www.librarian.net/calef/

Carpenter-Carse Library
P. O. Box 127
Hinesburg, VT 05461
(802) 482-2878
carpentercarselibrary@gmavt.net
http://www.carpentercarse.org/

Charlotte Library
P. O. Box 120
Charlotte, VT 05445
(802) 425-3864
adultservices@charlottepublic
    library.org
http://www.charlottepubliclibrary.org/

Cobleigh Public Library
14 Depot Street
Lyndonville, VT 05851
(802) 626-5475
http://cobleighlibrary.org/main/

Dorothy Alling Memorial Library
21 Library Lane
Williston, VT 05495
(802) 878-4918
E-mail thru website
http://www.williston.lib.vt.us/
Local history

Fairlee Public Library
221 US Route 5N
Fairlee, VT 05045
(802) 333-4716
fairlee_pub@vals.state.vt.us
http://fairleelibrary.org/

Fletcher Free Library
235 College Street
Burlington, VT 05401
(802) 863-3403
(802) 865-7227 Fax
reference@ci.burlington.vt.us
http://www.fletcherfree.org/

Georgia Public Library
1697 Ethan Ellen Highway
Fairfax, VT 05454
(802) 524-4643
gplvt@yahoo.com
http://www.georgia.lib.vt.us/

Goodrich Memorial Library
202 Main Street
Newport, VT 05855
(802) 334-7902
(802) 334-3890 Fax
info@goodrichlibrary.org
http://www.goodrichlibrary.org/

Guilford Free Library
4024 Guilford Center Road
Guilford, VT 05301
(802) 257-4603
guilford_pl@vals.state.vt.us
http://www.sover.net/~wilken/
    guilfordlibrary/
Vermont collection

Hartland Public Library
P. O. Box 137
Hartland, VT 05048
(802) 436-2473
hartlandvtlib@vermontel.net
http://www.hartlandlibraryvt.org/
Writers group

Haskell Free Library & Opera House
P. O. Box 337
Derby Line, VT 05830
(802) 873-3022
(802) 873-3634 Fax
info@haskellopera.org
http://www.haskellopera.org/

Ilsley Public Library
75 Main Street
Middlebury, VT 05753
(802) 388-4095
david.clark@ilsleypubliclibrary.org
http://www.ilsleypubliclibrary.org/

Jaquith Public Library
122 School Street
Marshfield, VT 05658
(802) 426-3581
jaquitpubliclibrary@hotmail.com
http://www.marshfield.lib.vt.us/

John G. McCullough Free Library
P. O. Box 339
North Bennington, VT 05257
(802) 447-7121
mflibrary@comcast.net
http://www.mccullough.lib.vt.us/

Joslin Memorial Library
P. O. Box 359
Waitsfield, VT 05673
(802) 496-4205
waitsfield@vals.state.vt.us
http://www.joslinmemoriallibrary.com/

Kellogg-Hubbard Library
135 Main Street
Montpelier, VT 05602
(802) 223-3338 Phone/Fax
info@kellogghubbard.org
http://www.kellogghubbard.org/

Kimball Public Library
67 Main Street
Randolph, VT 05060
(802) 728-5073
randolph@vals.state.vt.us
http://www.kimballlibrary.org/

Lincoln Library
222 River Road
Bristol, VT 05443
(802) 435-2665
http://www.lincoln.lib.vt.us/

Mark Skinner Library
P. O. Box 438
Manchester Village, VT 05254
(802) 362-2607
info@MarkSkinnerLibrary.org
http://www.markskinnerlibrary.org/

Norwich Public Library
P. O. Box 290
Norwich, VT 05055
(802) 649-1184
(802) 649-3470 Fax
lucinda.walker@norwichlibrary.org
http://www.norwichlibrary.org/

Peacham Library
P. O. Box 253
Peacham, VT 05862
(802) 592-3216
peachamlib@fairpoint.net
http://sites.google.com/site/
   peachamlibrary/

Pettee Memorial Library
Box 896
Wilmington, VT 05363
(802) 464-8557
petteelibrary@yahoo.com
http://www.petteelibrary.org/

Pierson Library
5376 Shelburne Road
Shelburne, VT 05482
(802) 985-5124
(802) 985-5129 Fax
pierson@vals.state.vt.us
http://www.shelburnevt.org/
    departments/63.html

Richmond Free Library
201 Library Street
Richmond, VT 05477
(802) 434-3036
(802) 434-3223 Fax
richmond@dol.state.vt.us
http://www.richmond.lib.vt.us/

Rockingham Free Public Library
65 Westminster Street
Bellows Falls, VT 05101
(802) 463-4270
(802) 463-1566 Fax
rocklib@sover.net
http://rfpl.kohalibrary.com/

Roxbury Free Library
P. O. Box 95
Roxbury, VT 05669
(802) 485-6860
roxbury_free@vals.state.vt.us
http://www.librarian.net/roxbury/

Rutland Free Library
10 Court Street
Rutland, VT 05701
(802) 773-1860
paulajb@rutlandfree.org
http://www.rutlandfree.org/

Solomon Wright Public Library
P. O. Box 400
Pownal, VT 05261
(802) 823-5400
pownal_pub@vals.state.vt.us
http://www.solomonwrightlibrary.org/

**South Burlington
Community Library**
550 Dorset Street
South Burlington, VT 05403
(802) 652-7080
LMurphy@sbschools.net
http://sbcl.sbschools.net/

South Londonderry Free Library
P. O. Box 95
South Londonderry, VT 05155
(802) 824-3371
http://www.londonderryvt.org/
    library.html
Vaile [photography] Collection

St. Albans Free Library
11 Maiden Lane
St. Albans, VT 05478
(802) 524-1507
stalbans@vals.state.vt.us
http://www.stalbans.lib.vt.us/

St. Johnsbury Athenaeum
1171 Main Street
St. Johnsbury, VT 05819
(802) 748-8291
E-mail thru website
http://www.stjathenaeum.org/
    library.htm

Stowe Free Library
90 Pond Street
Stowe, VT 05672
(802) 253-6145
(802) 253-4808 Fax
E-mail thru website
http://www.stowelibrary.org/
Vermont and Stowe collections

Wardsboro Public Library
P. O. Box 157
Wardsboro, VT 05355
(802) 896-6988
wardsboro@vals.state.vt.us
http://www.wardsboropubliclibrary.
  org/

Warren Public Library
P. O. Box 287
Warren, VT 05674
(802) 496-3913
warren@vals.state.vt.us
http://www.warrenlibrary.com/

Waterbury Public Library
28 North Main Street
Waterbury, VT 05671
(802) 244-7036
http://www.waterburyvt.com/
  community/libraries.htm

Westford Public Library
P. O. Box 86
Westford, VT 05494
(802) 878-5639
http://www.westford.lib.vt.us/
Vermont Collection

Whiting Library
117 Main Street
Whiting, VT 05778
(802) 875-2277
http://chester.govoffice.
  com/index.asp?Type=B_
  BASIC&SEC={1280FA0D-E7DD-
  4CD1-BA69-20F6758C00FB}

Windsor Public Library
43 State Street
Windsor, VT 05089
(802) 674-2556
windsordirector@comcast.net
http://www.windsorlibrary.org/

Winooski Memorial Library
19 East Spring Street
Winooski, VT 05404
(802) 655-6424
winooski@dol.state.vt.us
http://www.winooski.lib.vt.us/

VIRGINIA

Alexandria Library
Charles E. Beatley, Jr. Central
Library
5005 Duke Street
Alexandria, VA 22304
(703) 519-5900
(703) 519-5915 Fax
E-mail thru website
http://www.alexandria.lib.va.us/
Local history collections
Civil War collection
Collections of photographs from
    Civil War to present
Manuscript collection

Amherst County Library
P. O. Box 370
Amherst, VA 24521
(434) 946-9488
(434) 946-9348 Fax
spreston@acpl.us
http://209.43.125.189/
    department/?fDD=27-0

**Appomattox Regional
Library System**
Maude Langhorne Nelson Library
209 East Cawson Street
Hopewell, VA 23860
(804) 458-6329 or 861-0322
(804) 458-4349 Fax
E-mail thru website
http://www.arls.org/

**Arlington County
Department of Libraries**
1015 North Quincy Street
Arlington, VA 22201
(703) 228-5990
E-mail thru website
http://www.arlingtonva.us/
    Departments/Libraries/
    LibrariesMain.aspx
The Virginia Room

Augusta County Library
1759 Jefferson Highway
Fishersville, VA 22939
(540) 949-6354 or 885-3961
ask@augustacountylibrary.org
http://www.augustacountylibrary.org/

Blue Ridge Regional Library
P. O. Box 5264
Martinsville, VA 24115
(276) 403-5430
(276) 632-1660 Fax
martinsville@brrl.lib.va.us
http://www.brrl.lib.va.us/

Bristol Public Library
701 Goode Street
Bristol, VA 24201
(276) 645-8780
(276) 669-5593 Fax
judbarry@bristol-library.org
http://www.bristol-library.org/

Buchanan County Public Library
1185 Poe Town Street
Grundy, VA 24614
(276) 935-5721
(276) 935-6292 Fax
sherry@bcplnet.org
http://www.bcplnet.org

**Central Rappahannock
Regional Library**
1201 Caroline Street
Fredericksburg, VA 22401
(540) 372-1144
(540) 899-9867 Fax
webmaster@crrl.org
http://www.librarypoint.org/

Charlotte County Library
P. O. Box 788
Charlotte Courthouse, VA 23923
(434) 542-5247
cclibrary@hovac.com
http://www.cclibrary.net/

Chesapeake Public Library System
298 Cedar Road
Chesapeake, VA 23322
(757) 410-7100
jblanton@chesapeake.lib.va.us
http://www.chesapeake.lib.va.us/#

**Chesterfield County
Public Library**
9501 Lori Road
Chesterfield, VA 23832
(804) 751-4955
http://library.co.chesterfield.va.us/

Colonial Heights Public Library
1000 Yacht Basin Drive
Colonial Heights, VA 23834
(804) 520-9384
(804) 524-8740 Fax
http://www.colonial-heights.com/
   Library.htm

Culpeper County Library
271 Southgate Shopping Center
Culpeper, VA 22701
(540) 825-8691
(540) 825-7486 Fax
cclva@cclva.org
http://tlc.library.net/culpeper/
   default.asp
Civil War collection
Local history collection

Danville Public Library
511 Patton Street
Danville, VA 24541
(434) 799-5195
E-mail thru website
http://danvillelibrary.org/

Eastern Shore Public Library
P. O. Box 360
Accomac, VA 23301
(757) 787-3400 or 678-7800
http://www.espl.org/
Eastern Shore collection (stories,
   drawings and photos)

Fairfax County Public Library
12000 Government Center Parkway, Suite 324
Fairfax, VA 22035
(703) 324-3100
E-mail thru website
http://www.fairfaxcounty.gov/library/

Falls Church Public Library
120 North Virginia Avenue
Falls Church, VA 22046
(703) 248-5031
mcmahon@falls-church.lib.va.us
http://www.falls-church.lib.va.us/

Fauquier County Public Library
11 Winchester Street
Warrenton, VA 20186
(540) 347-8750
(540) 349-3278 Fax
E-mail thru website
http://www.fauquiercounty.gov/
    government/departments/library/
Local history collection

Fluvanna County Public Library
214 Commons Boulevard
Palmyra, VA 22963
(434) 589-1400
E-mail thru website
http://www.youseemore.com/
    fluvanna/default.asp

Galax-Carroll Regional Library
101 Beaver Dam Road
Hillsville, VA 24343
(276) 728-2228
http://galaxcarroll.lib.va.us/

Gloucester Public Library
6920 Main Street
Gloucester, VA 23061
(804) 693-2998
(804) 693-1477 Fax
mmalcolm@gloucesterva.info
http://www.co.gloucester.va.us/lib/
    home.html
The Virginia Room

**Halifax County-South Boston
Regional Library System**
P. O. Box 1729
Halifax, VA 24558
(434) 476-3357
(434) 476-3359 Fax
webmaster@halifaxlibrary.org
http://www.halifaxlibrary.org/

Hampton Public Library
4207 Victoria Boulevard
Hampton, VA 23669
(757) 727-1154
E-mail thru website
http://www.hamptonpubliclibrary.org/
Virginia Collection
Historic photographs
Historic newspapers

Handley Regional Library
100 Piccadilli Street
Winchester, VA 22601
(540) 662-9041
(540) 722-4769 Fax
hlref@hrl.lib.state.va.us
http://www.hrl.lib.state.va.us/
    handley/default.asp

Henrico County Public Library
1001 North Laburnum Avenue
Henrico, VA 23223
(804) 652-3200
(804) 222-5566 Fax
library@henrico.lib.va.us
http://www.henricolibrary.org/

Highland County Public Library
P. O. Box 519
Monterey, VA 24465
(540) 468-2373
(540) 468-2085 Fax
mail@highlandlibrary.com
http://highlandlibrary.homestead.com/

**Jefferson-Madison
Regional Library**
201 East Market Street
Charlottesville, VA 22902
(434) 979-7151
halliday@jmrl.org
http://jmrl.org/
Historical collection
African-American collection

Jones Memorial Library
2311 Memorial Avenue
Lynchburg, VA 24501
(434) 846-0501
(434) 846-1572 Fax
refdesk@jmlibrary.org
http://www.jmlibrary.org/
Numerous 17th and 18th century
  newspapers
Historic photographs
Architectural Archives

L. E. Smoot Memorial Library
9533 Kings Highway
King George, VA 22485
(540) 775-7951
(540) 775-5292 Fax
rschepmoes@smoot.org
http://www.smoot.org/

Lancaster Community Library
P. O. Box 850
Kilmarnock, VA 22482
(804) 435-1729
(804) 435-0255 Fax
lgardner@lancasterlibrary.org
http://www.lancasterlibrary.org/

**Library Information
Network of Chesterfield**
Chesterfield County Public Library
9501 Lori Road
Chesterfield, VA 23832
(804) 751-4955
http://library.co.chesterfield.va.us/

Lonesome Pine Regional Library
124 Library Road SW
Wise, VA 24293
(276) 328-4806
(276) 328-1739 Fax
reglib@lprlibrary.org
http://www.youseemore.com/LPRL/

Loudoun County Public Library
908-A Trailview Boulevard SE
Leesburg, VA 20175
(703) 777-0368
E-mail thru website
http://library.loudoun.gov/Default.
  aspx?tabid=36

Lovettsville Library
P. O. Box 189
Lovettsville, VA 20180
(540) 822-5824
(540) 822-5998 Fax
Chuck.Wood@loudoun.gov
http://library.loudoun.gov/Default.
  aspx?tabid=198

Lynchburg Public Library
2315 Memorial Avenue
Lynchburg, VA 24501
(434) 455-6300
lynn.dodge@lynchburgva.gov
http://www.lynchburgva.gov/Index.
   aspx?page=4287

Massanutten Regional Library
174 South Main Street
Harrisonburg, VA 22801
(540) 434-4475
(540) 434-4382 Fax
maryg@mrlib.org
http://www.mrlib.org/
Local history collection

Mathews Memorial Library
P. O. Box 980
Mathews, VA 23109
(804) 725-5747
(804) 725-7668 Fax
bettedillehay@mathewslibrary.org
http://www.mathewslibrary.org/

**Montgomery-Floyd
Regional Library**
125 Sheltman Street
Christiansburg, VA 24073
(540) 382-6965
palston@mfrl.org
http://www.mfrl.org/

Newport News Library System
700 Town Center Drive, Suite 300
Newport News, VA 23606
(757) 926-1350
nnlibrary@nngov.com
http://www.newport-news.va.us/
   library/
Virginiana Room – scrapbooks,
   photographs, etc.

Norfolk Public Library
1155 Pineridge Road
Norfolk, VA 23502
(757) 664-7328
debby.folkama@norfolk.gov
http://www.npl.lib.va.us/
Norfolk history collection

Northumberland Public Library
7204 Northumberland Highway
Heathsville, VA 22473
(804) 580-5051
(804) 580-5202 Fax
library@nplva.org
http://www.nplva.org/

Nottoway County Library
414 Tyler Street
Crewe, VA 23930
(434) 645-9310
(434) 645-8513 Fax
npierce@nottlib.org
http://www.nottlib.org/nottoway/
   default.asp

Pamunkey Regional Library
P. O. Box 119
Hanover, VA 23069
(804) 365-6211
(804) 537-6389 Fax
ask@pamunkeylibrary.org
http://www.pamunkeylibrary.org/

Pearisburg Public Library
209 Fort Branch Road
Pearisburg, VA 24134
(540) 921-2556
http://pearisburg.org/library.htm

Petersburg Public Library System
William R. McKenney Library
137 South Sycamore Street
Petersburg, VA 23803
(804) 733-2387
wcrocker@ppls.org
http://www.ppls.org/

**Pittsylvania County
Public Library**
24 Military Drive
Chatham, VA 24531
(434) 432-3271
(434) 432-1405 Fax
http://www.pcplib.org/

Poquoson Public Library
500 City Hall Avenue
Poquoson, VA 23662
(757) 868-3060
(757) 868-3106 Fax
library@poquoson-va.gov
http://library.poquoson-va.gov:8088
   /rooms/portal/media-type/html/
   language/en/country/US/user/
   anon/page/Sirsi_HOME.psml
Digital archives of historic photos

Powhatan County Public Library
2270 Mann Road
Powhatan, VA 23139
(804) 598-5670
http://powhatanlibrary.org/

**Prince William Public
Library System**
13083 Chinn Park Drive
Prince William, VA 22192
(703) 792-6100
(703) 792-4875 Fax
E-mail thru website
http://www.co.prince-william.va.us/
   default.aspx?topic=040010

Pulaski County Library System
60 West 3rd Street
Pulaski, VA 24301
(540) 980-7770
(540) 980-7775 Fax
swarburton@pclibs.org
http://www.pclibs.org/

Radford Public Library
30 West Main Street
Radford, VA 24141
(540) 731-3621
(540) 731-4857 Fax
afisher@radford.va.us
http://www.radford.va.us/library/

Richmond Public Library
101 East Franklin Street
Richmond, VA 23219
(804) 646-7223
harriet.henderson@richmondgov.com
http://www.richmondpubliclibrary.
   org/

Roanoke County Public Libraries
3131 Electric Road, SW
Roanoke, VA 24018
(540) 772-7507
(540) 989-3129 Fax
drosapepe@roanokecountyva.gov
http://www.roanokecountyva.gov/
   Departments/Library/

Roanoke Public Libraries
706 South Jefferson Street
Roanoke, VA 24016
(540) 853-2473
Main.Library@roanokeva.gov
http://www.roanokeva.gov/
   WebMgmt/ywbase61b.nsf/
   DocName/$library
Historic photograph collections

Rockbridge Regional Library
138 South Main
Lexington, VA 24450
(540) 463-4324
(540) 464-4824 Fax
abobowski@rrlib.net
http://www.youseemore.com/
  rockbridge/

Russell County Public Library
P. O. Box 247
Lebanon, VA 24266
(276) 889-8044
(276) 889-8045 Fax
kbritt@russell.lib.va.us
http://www.russell.lib.va.us/

Salem Public Library
28 East Main Street
Salem, VA 24153
(540) 375-3089
(540) 389-7054 Fax
library@salemva.gov
http://www.salemlibrary.info/

Samuels Public Library
330 East Criser Road
Front Royal, VA 22630
(540) 635-3153
reference@samuelslibrary.net
http://www.samuelslibrary.net/
  index_js.shtml

Shenandoah County Library
514 Stoney Creek Boulevard
Edinburg, VA 22824
(540) 984-8200, Ext. 206
(540) 984-8207 Fax
rlp_scl@shentel.net
http://www.shenandoah.co.lib.va.us/
Shenandoah Room with digital
  archives

Smyth-Bland Regional Library
118 South Sheffey Street
Marion, VA 24354
(276) 783-2323
(276) 783-5279 Fax
path@sbrl.org
http://www.sbrl.org/
Sherwood Anderson collections,
  including 1929 newspapers

Southside Regional Library
P. O. Box 10
Boydton, VA 23917
(434) 738-6580
(434) 738-6070 Fax
E-mail thru website
http://www.youseemore.com/
  southside/default.asp

Staunton Public Library
1 Churchville Avenue
Staunton, VA 24401
1-800-995-6215
(540) 332-3906 Fax
library@ci.staunton.va.us
http://www.staunton.va.us/default.
  asp?pageID=48BD7E6B-787C-
  49EE-A7C1-8DD714653A32

Suffolk Public Library
443 West Washington Street
Suffolk, VA 23434
(757) 514-7323
http://www.suffolk.lib.va.us/

Tazewell County Public Library
P. O. Box 929
Tazewell, VA 24651
(276) 988-2541
(276) 988-5980 Fax
http://www.tcplweb.org/
Virginia collection

Virginia Beach Public Library
2416 Courthouse Drive
Municipal Center, Building 19
Virginia Beach, VA 23456
(757) 385-8244
msims@vbgov.com
http://www.vbgov.com/vgn.
    aspx?dept_list=0b81fd67f3ad901
    0VgnVCM100000870b640aRCRD
    &x=8&y=9

Virginia State Library
The Library of Virginia
800 East Broad Street
Richmond, VA 23219
(804) 692-3500
E-mail thru website
http://www.lva.virginia.gov/
Architectural records
Manuscripts
Rare books, prints and photographs

Washington County Public Library
205 Oak Hill Street
Abingdon, VA 24210
(276) 676-6222
(276) 676-6235 Fax
RefDesk@wcpl.net
http://www.wcpl.net/

Williamsburg Regional Library
7770 Croaker Road
Williamsburg, VA 23188
(757) 259-4040
(757) 259-7798 Fax
E-mail thru website
http://www.wrl.org/

Wythe-Grayson Regional Library
147 South Independence Avenue
Independence, VA 24348
(276) 773-2761
(276) 773-3289 Fax
awebb@wythegrayson.lib.va.us
http://wythegrayson.lib.va.us/

York County Public Library
Tabb Library
100 Long Green Boulevard
Yorktown, VA 23693
(757) 890-5105
library_services@yorkcounty.gov
http://www.yorkcounty.gov/library/

WASHINGTON

Anacortes Public Library
1220 10th Street
Anacortes, WA 98221
(360) 293-1910
E-mail thru website
http://library.cityofanacortes.org

Asotin County Library
417 Sycamore Street
Clarkston, WA 99403
(509) 758-5454
admin.acl@valnet.org
http://www.aclib.org

Bleyhl Community Library
311 Division St.
Grandview, WA 98930
(509) 882-9217
library@grandview.wa.us
http://www.grandview.wa.us/
    library.htm

Burlington Public Library
820 E. Washington Ave.
Burlington, WA 98233
(360) 755-0760
(360) 755-0717 Fax
blibrary@ci.burlington.wa.us
http://www.ci.burlington.wa.us/
    page.asp_Q_navigationid_E_70

Camas Public Library
625 NE 4th Avenue
Camas, WA 98607
(360) 834-4692
info@ci.camas.wa.us
http://www.ci.camas.wa.us/library

Ellensburg Public Library
209 N. Ruby
Ellensburg, WA 98926
(509) 962-7250
library@ci.ellensburg.wa.us
http://www.ellensburglibrary.org

Enumclaw Public Library
1700 First Street
Enumclaw, WA 98022
(360) 825-2938
(360) 825-0825 Fax
library@ci.enumclaw.wa.us
http://www.enumclaw.lib.wa.us

Everett Public Library
2702 Hoyt Avenue
Everett, WA 98201
(425) 257-8000
libref@ci.everett.wa.us
http://www.epls.org

Ft. Vancouver Regional Library
1007 E. Mill Plain Blvd.
Vancouver, WA 98663
(360) 695-1561
contact@fvrl.org
http://www.fvrl.org

Jefferson County Library
620 Cedar Avenue
Port Hadlock, WA 98339
(360) 385-6544
(360) 385-7921 Fax
rserebrin@jclibrary.info
http://www.jcl.lib.wa.us

Kelso Public Library
314 Academy Street
Kelso, WA 98626
(360) 423-8110
E-mail thru website
http://www.kelso.gov/library

Kitsap Regional Library
1301 Sylvan Way
Bremerton, WA 98310
Toll-free 1-877-883-9900
E-mail thru website
http://www.krl.org

La Conner Regional Library
Box 370 - 614 Morris Street
La Conner, WA 98257
(360)466-3352
(360) 466-9178 Fax
library@lclib.lib.wa.us
http://www.lclib.lib.wa.us

Longview Public Library
1600 Louisiana Street
Longview, WA 98632
(360) 442-5300
chris.skaugset@ci.longview.wa.us
http://www.longviewlibrary.org

Lopez Island Library
P. O. Box 770
Lopez Island, WA 98261
(360) 468-2265
(360) 468-3850 Fax
http://wlo.statelib.wa.gov/detail.
   cfm?LibraryID=195

Mercer Island Library
4400 88th Avenue SE
Mercer Island, WA 98040
(360) 236-3537
http://www.kcls.org/mercerisland

Neill Public Library
210 North Grand Ave.
Pullman, WA 99163
(509) 334-3595
E-mail thru website
http://www.neil-lib.org

Ocean Shores Library
P.O. Box 669
Ocean Shores, WA 98569
(360) 289-3919
oslibrary@osgov.com
http://www.osgov.com/library.html

Orcas Island Library
500 Rose Street
Eastsound, WA 98245
(360) 376-4985
(360) 376-5750 Fax
pheikkinen@orcaslibrary.org
http://www.orcaslibrary.org

Pierce County Library
3005 112th Street E
Tacoma, WA 98446
(253) 536-6500
(253) 537-4600 Fax
director@piercecountylibrary.org
http://www.piercecountylibrary.org

Port Townsend Public Library
1220 Lawrence Street
Port Townsend, WA 98368
(360) 385-3181
(360) 385-5805 Fax
ptlibrary@cityofpt.us
http://www.cityofpt.us/library

Puyallup Public Library
324 S Meridian
Puyallup, WA 98371
(253) 841-5454
(253) 841-5483
puylib@ci.puyallup.wa.us
http://www.cityofpuyallup.org/
   page.php?id=334

Renton Public Library
100 Mill Avenue South
Renton, WA 98057
(425) 430-6610
E-mail thru website
http://rentonwa.gov/living/default.
   aspx?id=842

Richland Public Library
1270 Lee Boulevard
Richland WA 99352
(509) 942-7454
(509) 942-7447 Fax
emokler@richland.lib.wa.us
http://www.richland.lib.wa.us

Ritzville Public Library
302 W. Main Street
Ritzville, WA 99169
(509) 659-1222
ritzlib@ritzcom.net
http://www.ritzcom.net/ritzlib
Regional art & photographs

Roslyn Public Library
P. O. Box 451
Roslyn, WA 98941
(509) 649-3420
rpl@inlandnet.com
http://server1.inlandnet.com/~rpl/

Seattle Public Library
1000 Fourth Avenue
Seattle, WA 98104
(206) 386-4636
E-mail thru website
http://www.spl.org

Spokane Public Library
906 West Main Street
Spokane, WA 99201
(509) 444-5300
E-mail thru website
http://www.spokanelibrary.org

Tacoma Public Library
1102 Tacoma Avenue S
Tacoma, WA 98402
(253) 591-5666
ddomkoski@tacomapubliclibrary.org
http://www.tacomapubliclibrary.org

Whitman County Library
102 South Main Street
Colfax, WA 99111
Toll free 1-877-733-3375
info@whitco.lib.wa.us
http://www.whitco.lib.wa.us

Washington State Library
P. O. Box 42460
Olympia WA 98504-2460
(360) 704-5200
jwalsh@secstate.wa.gov
http://www.secstate.wa.gov/library

WEST VIRGINIA

Boliver-Harpers Ferry Public Library
600 Polk Street
Harpers Ferry, WV 25424
(304) 535-2301 Phone/Fax
bhflib@martin.lib.wv.us
http://www.youseemore.com/bhf/

Brideport Public Library
1200 Johnson Avenue
Bridgeport, WV 26330
(304) 842-8248
saye@bridgeportwv.com
http://www.bridgeportwv.com/
 library.cfm
West Virginia Collection

Brooke County Public Library
945 Main Street
Wellsburg, WV 26070
(304) 737-1551
http://wellsburg.lib.wv.us/

Cabell County Public Library
455 Ninth Street Plaza
Huntington, WV 25701
(304) 528-5700
(304) 528-5701 Fax
cabelllibrary@cabell.lib.wv.us
http://cabell.lib.wv.us/
Local history room

Calhoun County Public Library
P. O. Box 918
Grantsville, WV 26147
(304) 354-6300
amyallen@mail.min.lib.wv.us
http://calhoun.lib.wv.us/

Clarksburg-Harrison Public Library
404 West Pike Street
Clarksburg, WV 26301
(304) 627-2236
(304) 627-2239 Fax
chplref@clark.lib.wv.us
http://clarksburglibrary.info/

Craft Memorial Library
600 Commerce Street
Bluefield, WV 24701
(304) 325-3943
(304) 325-3702 Fax
http://craftmemorial.lib.wv.us/

Dora B. Woodyard Memorial Library
P. O. Box 340
St. Elizabeth, WV 26143
(304) 275-4295 Phone/Fax
watsonb@mail.mln.lib.wv.us
http://dorabwoodyard.lib.wv.us/
Local history

Fayetteville Public Library
200 West Maple Avenue
Fayetteville, WV 25840
(304) 574- 0070
http://fayetteville.lib.wv.us/

Gassaway Public Library
536 Elk Street
Gassaway, WV 26624
(304) 364-8292 Phone/Fax
hickmanb@clark.lib.wv.us
http://gassaway.lib.wv.us/

Greenbrier County Public Library
152 Robert W. McCormick Drive
Lewisburg, WV 24901
(304) 647-7568
(304) 657-7569 Fax
greenbrier.library@mail.mln.wv.us
http://greenbrier.lib.wv.us/
Local history room

Hampshire County Public Library
153 West Main Street
Romney, WV 26757
(304) 822-3185
(304) 822-3955 Fax
amanda.snyder@martin.lib.wv.us
http://www.hampshirecopubliclib.
  com/
Local history room

Hardy County Public Library
102 North Main Street
Moorefield, WV 26836
(304) 538-6560
(304) 538-2639 Fax
hardycpl@martin.lib.wv.us
http://hardycounty.martin.lib.wv.us/

Jackson County Public Library
208 North Church Street
Ripley, WV 25271
(304) 372-5343
(304) 372-7935 Fax
lowesuz@mail.mln.lib.wv.us
http://jackson.park.lib.wv.us/

Kanawha County Public Library
123 Capitol Street
Charleston, WV 25301
(304) 343-4646
webmaster@kanawha.lib.wv.us
http://kanawha.lib.wv.us/

Keyser-Mineral County Public Library
105 North Main Street
Keyser, WV 26726
(304) 788-3222 Phone/Fax
http://keyser.lib.wv.us/

Kingswood Public Library
205 West Main Street
Kingswood, WV 26537
(304) 329-1499 Phone/Fax
beanejo@clark.lib.wv.us
http://kingwood.lib.wv.us/
West Virginia history

Louis Bennett Public Library
148 Court Avenue
Weston, WV 26452
(304) 269-5151
(304) 269-7332 Fax
http://louisbennett.lib.wv.us/

Mannington Public Library
109 Clarksburg Street
Mannington, WV 26582
(304) 986-2803
(304) 986-3425 Fax
http://marioncountypubliclibrary.
  org/index.php?option=com_cont
  ent&task=view&id=28&Itemid=13

Marion County Public Libraries
321 Monroe Street
Fairmont, WV 26554
(304) 366-1210
(304) 366-4831 Fax
http://www.
  marioncountypubliclibrary.org

**Martinsburg-Berkeley County
Public Library**
101 West King Street
Martinsburg, WV 25401
(304) 267-8933
E-mail thru website
http://www.youseemore.com/
    martinsburg/berkeley

Mary H. Weir Public Library
3442 Main Street
Weirton, WV 26062
(304) 797-8510
http://weirton.lib.wv.us/

McDowell Public Library
90 Howard Street
Welch, WV 24801
(304) 436-3070
(304) 436-8079 Fax
http://mcdowell.lib.wv.us/
West Virginia history collection

Mineral County Library Association
Keyser-Mineral County Public
Library
105 North Main Street
Keyser, WV 26726
(304) 788-3222 Phone/Fax
http://keyser.lib.wv.us/

Monroe County Public Library
103 South Street
Union, WV 24983
(304) 772-3038
(304) 772-4052 Fax
mccurdy@mail.mln.lib.wv.us
http://monroe.lib.wv.us/

**Morgantown Public
Library System**
373 Spruce Street
Morgantown, WV 26505
(304) 291-7425
hathaway@clark.lib.wv.us
http://morgantown.lib.wv.us/

Ohio County Public Library
52 Sixteenth Street
Wheeling, WV 26003
(304) 232-0244
ocplweb@weirton.lib.wv.us
http://wheeling.weirton.lib.wv.us/

Old Charles Town Library
200 East Washington Street
Charles Town, WV 25414
(304) 725-2208
http://www.ctlibrary.org/

**Parkersburg and Wood County
Public Library**
3100 Emerson Avenue
Parkersburg, WV 26104
(304) 420-4587
(304) 420-4589 Fax
http://parkersburg.lib.wv.us/

Paw Paw Public Library
P. O. Box 9
Paw Paw, WV 25434
(304) 947-7013 Phone/Fax
nellie@pawpawpubliclibrary.com
http://www.pawpawpubliclibrary.
    com/

Pocahontas County Free Libraries
500 Eighth Street
Marlinton, WV 24954
(304) 799-6000
(304) 799-3988 Fax
director@pocahontaslibrary.org
http://www.pocahontaslibrary.org/
Railroad and Logging Collection
West Virginia Appalachian
   Collection
Pearl S. Buck E Pluribus Unum
   Collection

Princeton Public Library
205 Center Street
Princeton, WV 24740
(304) 487-5045
(304) 487-5046 Fax
http://princeton.lib.wv.us/

Putnam County Public Library
4219 State Route 34
Hurricane, WV 25526
(304) 757-7308
(304) 757-7384 Fax
putnam@cabell.lib.wv.us
http://putnam.lib.wv.us/

Raleigh County Public Library
221 North Kanawha Street
Beckley, WV 25801
(304) 255-0511
mcmillid@raleigh.lib.wv.us
http://rcpl.lib.wv.us/

Richwood Public Library
9 White Avenue
Richwood, WV 26261
(304) 846-6099
(304) 846-9290 Fax
bartlettr@mail.mln.lib.wv.us
http://richwood.lib.wv.us/

Ritchie County Public Library
130 North Court Street
Harrisville, WV 26362
(304) 643-2717 Phone/Fax
seesee@mail.mln.lib.wv.us
http://ritchie.lib.wv.us/

Roane County Library
110 Parking Plaza
Spencer, WV 25276
(304) 927-1130
(304) 927-1196 Fax
karen.leisch@mail.mln.lib.wv.us
http://roanecountylibrary.org/

Shepherdstown Public Library
P. O. Box 278
Shepherdestown, WV 25443
(304) 876-2783
(304) 876-6213 Fax
taylor_h@martin.lib.wv.us
http://www.lib.shepherdstown.wv.us/

South Charleston Public Library
312 Fourth Avenue
South Charleston, WV 25303
(304) 744-6561
(304) 744-8808 Fax
E-mail thru website
http://www.infospot.org/

South Jefferson Public Library
P. O. Box 17
Summit Point, WV 25446
(304) 725-6227
(304) 728-2586 Fax
jenkinsd@martin.lib.wv.us
http://www.youseemore.com/
   southjefferson/

Summers County Public Library
201 Temple Street
Hinton, WV 25951
(304) 466-4490
(304) 466-5260 Fax
zieglerm@mail.mln.lib.wv.us
http://summers.lib.wv.us/

Summersville Public Library
6201 Webster Road
Summersville, WV 26651
(304) 872-0844
(304) 872-0845 Fax
spl@mail.mln.lib.wv.us
http://summersville.lib.wv.us/

Taylor County Public Library
200 Beech Street
Grafton, WV 26354
(304) 265-6121
(304) 265-6122 Fax
Taylib@clark.lib.wv.us
http://taylor.clark.lib.wv.us/

Upshur County Public Library
RR 6, Box 480 – Tennerton Road
Buckhannon, WV 26201
(304) 473-4219
(304) 473-4222 Fax
upshur@clark.lib.wv.us
http://upshurcounty.lib.wv.us/

Vienna Public Library
2300 River Road
Vienna, WV 26105
(304) 295-7771
(304) 295-7776 Fax
info@viennapubliclibrary.org
http://vienna.park.lib.wv.us/

Wayne County Public Library
Ceredo-Kenova Memorial
Public Library
1200 Oak Street
Kenova, WV 25530
(304) 453-2462 Phone/Fax
wcpl@cabell.lib.wv.us
http://wcpl.lib.wv.us/

**White Sulphur Springs
Public Library**
203 West Main Street
White Sulphur Springs, WV 24986
(304) 536-1171
(304) 536-3801 Fax
heather.bladen@mail.mln.lib.wv.us
http://whitesulphursprings.lib.wv.us/

Williamson Public Library
101 Logan Street
Williamson, WV 25661
(304) 235-6029
william@wvlc.lib.wv.us
http://williamsonlibrary.lib.wv.us/

Wyoming County Public Library
P. O. Box 130
Pineville, WV 24874
(304) 732-6899
gaddisc@mail.mln.lib.wv.us
http://wyoming.lib.wv.us/

WISCONSIN

Abbotsford Public Library
203 First Street
Abbotsford, WI 54405
(715) 223-3920
http://wvls.lib.wi.us/AbbotsfordPL/

Adams County Public Library
569 North Cedar Street, Suite 1
Adams, WI 53910
(608) 339-4250
(608) 339-4575 Fax
calef@scls.lib.wi.us
http://www.scls.lib.wi.us/acl/

Algoma Public Library
406 Fremont Street
Algoma, WI 54201
(920) 487-2295
ALG@mail.nfls.lib.wi.us
http://www.nfls.lib.wi.us/alg/

Alice Baker Library
820 E. Main Street
Eagle, WI 53119
(262) 594-2800
chase@eagle.lib.wi.us
http://www.alicebaker.lib.wi.us/

Angie W. Cox Public Library
P. O. Box 370
Pardeeville, WI 53954
(608) 429-2354
(608) 429-4308 Fax
parstaff@scls.lib.wi.us
http://www.scls.lib.wi.us/par/

Appleton Public Library
225 North Oneida Street
Appleton, WI 54911
(920) 832-6177
(920) 832-6182 Fax
tdawson@apl.org
http://www.apl.org/

Arrowhead Library System
210 Dodge Street
Janesville, WI 53548
(608) 758-6690
(608) 758-6689 Fax
montgomery.ruthann@als.lib.wi.us
http://als.lib.wi.us

Balsam Lake Public Library
P. O. Box 340
Balsam Lake, WI 54810
(715) 485-3215
balsamlakepl@ifls.lib.wi.us
http://www.balsamlakepubliclibrary.
  org/

Baraboo Public Library
230 Fourth Avenue
Baraboo, WI 53913
(608) 356-6166
http://www.scls.lib.wi.us/bar/

Berlin Public Library
121 West Park Avenue
Berlin, WI 54923
(920) 361-5420
(920) 361-5424 Fax
director@berlinlibrary.org
http://www.berlnlibrary.org

Boyceville Public Library
P. O. Box 129
Boyceville, WI 54725
(715) 643-2106
boycevillepl@ifls.lib.wi.us
http://www.boycevillelibrary.org/

Brandon Public Library
117 East Main Street
Brandon, WI 53919
(920) 346-2350
(920) 346-5895 Fax
director@brandonlibrary.net
http://www.brandonlibrary.net/

Brodhead Memorial Public Library
1207 25th Street
Brodhead, WI 53520
(608) 897-4070
E-mail thru website
http://www.brodheadlibrary.org/
    Home.cfm?DepartmentID=3&CFI
    D=1533205&CFTOKEN=35003401

Brookfield Public Library
1900 North Calhoun Road
Brookfield, WI 53005
(262) 782-4140
Brookfieldpubliclibrary@
    ci.brookfield.wi.us
http://www.ci.brookfield.wi.us/
    index.aspx?NID=38

Burlington Public Library
166 East Jefferson
Burlington, WI 53105
(262) 342-1130
director@burlington.lib.wi.us
http://www.burlingtonlibrary.com/

Caestecker Public Library
518 Hill Street
Green Lake, WI 54941
(920) 294-3572
denell@greenlakelibrary.org
http://www.greenlakelibrary.org/

Cedar Grove Public Library
131 Van Altena Avenue
Cedar Grove, WI 53013
(920) 668-6834
(920) 668-8744 Fax
cgref@esls.lib.wi.us
http://www.cedargrove.lib.wi.us/

Chippewa Falls Public Library
105 West Central Street
Chippewa Falls, WI 54729
(715) 723-1146
cflib@ifls.lib.wi.us
http://www.chippewafallslibrary.org/

Clinton Public Library
P. O. Box 487
Clinton, WI 53525
(608) 676-5569
(608) 676-5984 Fax
dennis.michelle@als.lib.wi.us
http://als.lib.wi.us/CPL/

Coloma Public Library
155 Front Street
Coloma, WI 54930
(715) 228-2530
(715) 228-2532 Fax
zuehlke@colomalibrary.org
http://www.colomalibrary.org/

Columbus Public Library
223 West James Street
Columbus, WI 53925
(920) 623-5910
http://www.scls.lib.wi.us/col/index.
  html

Deerfield Public Library
12 West Nelson Street
Deerfield, WI 53531
(608) 764-8102
dplstf@scls.lib.wi.us
http://www.scls.lib.wi.us/deerfield/

Dwight Foster Public Library
102 East Milwaukee Avenue
Fort Atkinson, WI 53538
(920) 563-7790
(920) 563-7774 Fax
connect@fortlibrary.org
http://www.fortlibrary.org/

Eager Free Public Library
39 West Main Street
Evansville, WI 53536
(608) 882-2260
eagerfree@als.lib.wi.us
http://als.lib.wi.us/EFPL/
Local history collection

Fond du Lack Public Library
32 Sheboygan Street
Fond du Lac, WI 54935
(920) 929-7080
(920) 929-7082 Fax
hall@fdlpl.org
http://www.fdlpl.org/

Frances L. Simek Memorial Library
400 North Main Street
Medford, WI 54451
(715) 748-2505
medref@wvls.lib.wi.us
http://www.sws-wis.com/
  medfordpubliclibrary/

Grafton Public Library
USS Library Memorial Public
Library
1620 Eleventh Avenue
Grafton, WI 53024
(262) 375-5315
(262) 375-5317 Fax
grafton@esls.lib.wi.us
http://www.grafton.lib.wi.us/

Kenosha Public Library
P. O. Box 1414
Kenosha, WI 53141
(262) 564-6324
(262) 564-6370 Fax
E-mail thru website
http://www.kenosha.lib.wi.us/

**L. E. Phillips Memorial
Public Library**
400 Eau Claire Street
Eau Claire, WI 54701
(715) 833-5318
admstaff@eauclaire.lib.wi.us
http://www.ecpubliclibrary.info/

La Crosse County Library
103 State Street
Holmen, WI 54636
(608) 526-9600
mcardle-rojo.chris@lacrossecounty.org
http://www.lacrossecountylibrary.org/

Lake Geneva Public Library
918 West Main Street
Lake Geneva, WI 53147
(262) 249-5299
(262) 249-5284 Fax
lakegene@lakegeneva.lib.wi.us
http://www.lakegeneva.lib.wi.us/

Lakes Country Public Library
P. O. Box 220
Lakewood, WI 54138
(715) 276-9020
pellings@mail.nfls.lib.wi.us
http://www.nfls.lib.wi.us/lak/

Madison Public Library
201 West Mifflin Street
Madison, WI 53703
(608) 266-6300
madcirc@scls.lib.wi.us
http://www.madisonpubliclibrary.org/
Regional collection

Manitowoc Public Library
707 Quay Street
Manitowoc, WI 54220
(920) 683-4863
(920) 683-4873 Fax
E-mail thru website
http://www.manitowoc.lib.wi.us/

Marathon County Public Library
300 North 1st Street
Wausau, WI 54403
(715) 261-7200
E-mail thru website
http://www.mcpl.us/

McMillan Memorial Library
490 East Grand Avenue
Wisconsin Rapids, WI 54494
(715) 423-1040
(715) 423-2665 Fax
askmcm@scls.lib.wi.us
http://www.mcmillanlibrary.org/
index.shtml

Mead Public Library
710 North 8 Street
Sheboygan, WI 53081
(920) 459-3400
swinkle@esls.lib.wi.us
http://www.meadpubliclibrary.org/

**Mid-Wisconsin Federated
Library System**
112 Clinton Street
Horicon, WI 53032
1-800-660-6899
(920) 485-0899 Fax
wburkh@mwfls.org
http://www.mwfls.org/

**Wilwaukee County Federated
Library System**
814 West Wisconsin Avenue
Milwaukee, WI 53233
(414) 286-5934
steve.heser@mcfls.org
http://www.mcfls.org/

Milwaukee Public Library
814 West Wisconsin Avenue
Milwaukee, WI 53233
(414) 286-3000
E-mail thru website
http://www.mpl.org/
Richard E. and Lucile Krug Rare
Books Room

Monona Public Library
1000 Nichols Road
Monona, WI 53716
(608) 222-6127
(608) 222-8590 Fax
dgerber@scls.lib.wi.us
http://www.scls.lib.wi.us/monona/

Neenah Public Library
P. O. Box 569
Neenah, WI 54957
(920) 886-6315
library@neenahlibrary.org
http://www.neenahlibrary.org/

Nicolet Federal Library System
515 Pine Street
Green Bay, WI 54301
(920) 448-4410
(920) 448-4420 Fax
nmerrifi@mail.nfls.lib.wi.us
http://www.nfls.lib.wi.us/

Omro Public Library
405 East Huron Street
Omro, WI 54963
(920) 685-7016
director@omrolibrary.org
http://www.omrolibrary.org/

Oshkosh Public Library
106 Washington Avenue
Oshkosh, WI 54901
(920) 236-5205
E-mail thru website
http://www.oshkoshpubliclibrary.org/

Park Falls Public Library
121 North 4th Avenue
Park Falls, WI 54552
(715) 762-3121
(715) 762-2286 Fax
pfpl@ifls.lib.wi.us
http://www.parkfallslibrary.org/
Historic photo collection
History Room

Pine River Public Library
Leon-Saxeville Township Library
P. O. Box 247
Pine River, WI 54965
(920) 987-5110
director@pineriverlibrary.org
http://www.pineriverlibrary.org/

Portage County Public Library
1001 Main Street
Stevens Point, WI 54481
(715) 346-1548
(715) 346-1239 Fax
E-mail thru website
http://library.uwsp.edu/pcl/

Racine Public Library
75 Seventh Street
Racine, WI 53403
(262) 636-9241
director@racinelibrary.info
http://www.racinelib.lib.wi.us/

South Central Library System
5250 East Terrace Drive
Madison, WI 53718
(608) 246-7970
(608) 246-7958 Fax
cbecker@scls.lib.wi.us
http://www.scls.info/

**Southwest Wisconsin
Library System**
1775 Fourth Street
Fennimore, WI 53809
1-866-866-3393
kross@swls.org
http://www.swls.org/
Local history

Sparta Free Library
P. O. Box 347
Sparta, WI 54656
(608) 269-2010
(608) 269-1542 Fax
spartalibrary@wrlsweb.org
http://www.spartalibrary.org/

Viola Public Library
137 South Main
Viola, WI 54664
(608) 627-1850
lowens@swls.org
http://www.swls.org/member.vi.html

W.J. Niederkorn Library
316 West Grand Avenue
Port Washington, WI 53074
(262) 284-5031
(262) 284-7680 Fax
dnimmer@esls.lib.wi.us
http://www.portwashington.lib.
   wi.us/WJN/
Welcome/Welcome.html

Watertown Public Library
100 South Water Street
Watertown, WI 53094
(920) 262-4090
(920) 261-8943 Fax
dmalosh@mwfls.org
http://www.watertown.lib.wi.us

Waukesha Public Library
321 Wisconsin Avenue
Waukesha, WI 53186
(262) 524-3680
E-mail thru website
http://www.waukesha.lib.wi.us/

Waupun Public Library
123 South Forest Street
Waupun, WI 53963
(920) 324-7925
wpl@mwfls.org
http://www.waupunpubliclibrary.
   org/index.php

Wauwatosa Public Library
7635 West North Avenue
Wauwatosa, WI 53213
(414) 471-8487
shawn.duffy@mcfls.org
http://tpublib.fp.execpc.com/
Wauwatosa History Collection

West Allis Public Library
7421 West National Avenue
West Allis, WI 53214
(414) 302-8503
E-mail thru website
http://www.ci.west-allis.wi.us/
   library/library_services.htm

Frank L. Weyenberg Library of Mequon-Thiensville
11345 North Cedarburg Road
Mequon, WI 53092
(262) 242-2593
(262) 478-3200 Fax
admin@flwlib.org
http://www.flwlib.org/

Winnefox Library System
106 Washington Avenue
Oshkosh, WI 54901
(920) 236-5220
(920) 236-5228 Fax
wallace@winnefox.org
http://www.winnefox.org/

WYOMING

Big Horn County Library
P. O. Box 231
Basin, WY 82410
(307) 568-2388
(307) 568-2011 Fax
bhawkins@will.state.wy.us
http://www-wsl.state.wy.us/
   bighorn/index.html

Campbell County Public Library
2101 South 4J Road
Gillette, WY 82718
(307) 687-0009
pmyers@will.state.wy.us
http://www.ccpls.org/

Converse County Library
300 Walnut Street
Douglas, WY 82633
(307) 358-3644
(307) 358-6743 Fax
khopkins@will.state.wy.us
http://www.conversecounty
   library.org/

**Crook County Public
Library System**
P. O. Box 910
Sundance, WY 82729
(307) 283-1008
(307) 283-1006 Phone/Fax
crookcountylib@rangeweb.net
http://www-wsl.state.wy.us/crook/
Hosts writers' groups

Fremont County Libraries
451 North 2nd Street
Lander, Wyoming 82520
(307) 332-5194
(307) 332-3909 Fax
boakleaf@fclsonline.org
http://www.fremontcountylibraries.
   org/

Goshen County Library
2001 East A Street
Torrington, WY 82240
(307) 532-3411
ihoy@will.state.wy.us
http://will.state.wy.us/goshen/

Johnson County Library
171 North Adams Avenue
Buffalo, WY 82834
1-800-661-7071
(307) 684-7888 Fax
ctwing@will.state.wy.us
http://www-wsl.state.wy.us/johnson/
Johnson County history collection

Laramie County Library System
2200 Pioneer Avenue
Cheyenne, WY 82001
(307) 773-7220
losborn@lclsonline.org
http://www.lclsonline.org/

Lincoln County Library
519 Emerald Street
Kemmerer, WY 83101
(307) 877-6961
(307) 877-4147 Fax
lincill@linclib.org
http://linclib.org/

Natrona County Public Library
307 East 2nd Street
Casper, WY 82601
(307) 237-4935
(307) 266-3734 Fax
natrref@will.state.wy.us
http://www.natronacountylibrary.org/

Niobrara County library
P. O. Box 510
Lusk, WY 82225
(307) 334-3490
dsturman@niobraracountylibrary.org
http://www.niobraracountylibrary.org/
Historical archives of Niobrara County

Park County Library System
1500 Heart Mountain Street
Cody, WY 82414
(307) 527-1880
(307) 527-8823 Fax
parkill@will.state.wy.us
http://parkcountylibrary.org/

Platte County Public Library
904 Ninth Street
Wheatland, WY 82201
1-888-841-0964
(307) 322-3540 Fax
platcircmgr@will.state.wy.us
http://www-wsl.state.wy.us/platte/

Sheridan County Library System
335 West Alger Street
Sheridan, WY 82801
(307) 674-8585
(307) 674-7374 Fax
http://www.sheridanwyolibrary.org/

Sublette County Library
P. O. Box 489
Pinedale, WY 82941
(307) 367-4114
(307) 367-6722 Fax
info@sublettecountylibrary.org
http://sublettecountylibrary.org/

**Sweetwater County
Library System**
300-N First E
Green River, WY 82935
(307) 872-3200
(307) 872-3249 Fax
info@sweetwaterlibraries.com
http://www.sweetwaterlibraries.com/

Teton County Library
P. O. Box 1629
Jackson, WY 83001
(307) 733-2164
(307) 733-4568 Fax
tetnref@tclib.org
http://tclib.org/

Washakie County Library
1019 Coburn Avenue
Worland, WY 82401
(307) 347-2231
dkoch@will.state.wy.us
http://will.state.wy.us/washakie/

Weston County Library System
23 West Main Street
Newcastle, WY 82701
(307) 746-2206
jbramwell@will.state.wy.us
http://will.state.wy.us/weston/

Wyoming State Library
2800 Central Avenue
Cheyenne, WY 82002
(307) 777-6333
(307) 777-6289 Fax
E-mail thru website
http://will.state.wy.us/

LaVergne, TN USA
18 March 2010
176499LV00003B/44/P